ASP: Active Server Pages

ASP: Active Server Pages

Andrew M. Fedorchek
and David K. Rensin

IDG Books Worldwide, Inc.
An International Data Group Company

Foster City, CA ◆ Chicago, IL ◆ Indianapolis, IN ◆ Southlake, TX

ASP: Active Server Pages

Published by
IDG Books Worldwide, Inc.
An International Data Group Company
919 E. Hillsdale Blvd.
Suite 400
Foster City, CA 94404
http://www.idgbooks.com (IDG Books Worldwide Web site)

Library of Congress Catalog Card No.: 97-73223

ISBN: 0-7645-8042-6

Printed in the United States of America

10 9 8 7 6 5 4 3 2 1

1E/RY/QW/ZX/FC

Distributed in the United States by IDG Books Worldwide, Inc.

Distributed by Macmillan Canada for Canada; by Transworld Publishers Limited in the United Kingdom; by IDG Norge Books for Norway; by IDG Sweden Books for Sweden; by Woodslane Pty. Ltd. for Australia; by Woodslane Enterprises Ltd. for New Zealand; by Longman Singapore Publishers Ltd. for Singapore, Malaysia, Thailand, and Indonesia; by Simron Pty. Ltd. for South Africa; by Toppan Company Ltd. for Japan; by Distribuidora Cuspide for Argentina; by Livraria Cultura for Brazil; by Ediciencia S.A. for Ecuador; by Addison-Wesley Publishing Company for Korea; by Ediciones ZETA S.C.R. Ltda. for Peru; by WS Computer Publishing Corporation, Inc., for the Philippines; by Unalis Corporation for Taiwan; by Contemporanea de Ediciones for Venezuela; by Computer Book & Magazine Store for Puerto Rico; by Express Computer Distributors for the Caribbean and West Indies. Authorized Sales Agent: Anthony Rudkin Associates for the Middle East and North Africa.

For general information on IDG Books Worldwide's books in the U.S., please call our Consumer Customer Service department at 800-762-2974. For reseller information, including discounts and premium sales, please call our Reseller Customer Service department at 800-434-3422.

For information on where to purchase IDG Books Worldwide's books outside the U.S., please contact our International Sales department at 415-655-3200 or fax 415-655-3295.

For information on foreign language translations, please contact our Foreign & Subsidiary Rights department at 415-655-3021 or fax 415-655-3281.

For sales inquiries and special prices for bulk quantities, please contact our Sales department at 415-655-3200 or write to the address above.

For information on using IDG Books Worldwide's books in the classroom or for ordering examination copies, please contact our Educational Sales department at 800-434-2086 or fax 817-251-8174.

For press review copies, author interviews, or other publicity information, please contact our Public Relations department at 415-655-3000 or fax 415-655-3299.

For authorization to photocopy items for corporate, personal, or educational use, please contact Copyright Clearance Center, 222 Rosewood Drive, Danvers, MA 01923, or fax 508-750-4470.

is a trademark under exclusive
license to IDG Books Worldwide, Inc.,
from International Data Group, Inc.

Credits

ACQUISITIONS EDITOR
John Osborn

DEVELOPMENT EDITOR
Barbra Guerra

TECHNICAL EDITOR
Jeff Bankston

COPY EDITOR
Nate Holdread

PRODUCTION COORDINATOR
Katy German

BOOK DESIGNERS
Jim Donohue
Kurt Krames

GRAPHICS AND PRODUCTION SPECIALIST
Andreas F. Schueller

QUALITY CONTROL SPECIALIST
Mick Arellano

PROOFREADER
Davis Wise

INDEXER
David Heiret

To my wife Andrea, the light of my life.
  Andrew

To my wife Lia, whose patience and love shepherds me through my darkest hours.
  Dave

Preface

The year 1996 was an interesting year in the computer industry. For some reason, everyone decided that the Web was the "next big thing." (We don't exactly know how something gets to be the "big thing," but we are pretty sure that we will become rich if we ever find out.) Consequently, vendors decided that the old ways of writing Web applications were no good. New and better ways had to be invented. During much of 1996 and 1997, a pitched battle has been raging between competing architectures and standards to figure out which is better.

Most modern software development tools are a compromise between two important features: ease of use and raw power. As developers, we spend a lot of time trying to figure out which tool (or set thereof) has the optimal mix of each, all the while hoping that the perfect programming implement will come along and bring us closer to Nerdvana. (For those of you not in the know, *Nerdvana* is a state of complete bliss for computer geeks and is a term invented by Scott Adams, the creator of Dilbert.)

We are by no stretch saying that Active Server Pages is the perfect Web development tool. It is, however, as close to one as we have ever seen. Consider the following:

◆ First, ASP imposes no restrictions on the client machine and requires no mass distribution of runtime files.

◆ Second, you can code ASP from a simple text editor. No fancy IDE is required.

◆ Third, ASP completely integrates into the native operating systems on which it runs.

◆ Finally, ASP lets you reuse the capabilities of hundreds of tested and proven commercial applications.

Sure, as a Microsoft product, ASP has some instant limitations – the most notable of which are that it only runs on Windows NT and Windows 95, and it requires a Microsoft Web server such as Internet Information Server or Personal Web server. Also, ASP applications need extra logic to scale across multiple machines. The first platform and Web server restrictions are non-negotiable. You either live with them or find something else. However, because NT is rapidly becoming an operating system quite capable of running a production Web server, the first of these restrictions is not usually a big deal. The second restriction, although a little annoying, is pretty easy to work around.

All of this brings us to the next point – why we wrote this book.

Why We Wrote This Book

We don't know why other people write computer books, but we do it because we love computers. To us, programming is less of a job and more of an act of creative indulgence for which we happen to get paid. More than that, though, we love to show other people how to use their computers in unexpected and better ways. We write for the sense of self-gratification we get whenever we get e-mail from a reader who figured a way out of a problem because of something we said. In short, we do it for the ego.

So, why should you care? Put simply, our pride is your assurance of quality. We both hold full-time jobs as computer consultants and write only in our "free" time (translation: time we should be sleeping). Because of this, we don't write nearly enough material in any given month to make the venture financially rewarding. Instead, we choose to write because of the sense of accomplishment we get when people tell us that our book has helped them in some way. As a result, we are insanely meticulous about our text. We work extremely hard to make sure that what you read is both technically correct and easy to understand. If the text fails in either case, then we have failed with it.

Who We Are

Our publisher tells us that every good introduction talks a little about the qualifications of the authors. Apparently, they think you actually read this stuff! The problem, of course, is that it is difficult to write glowing things about yourself in the third person. After all, it's not like either of us has cured a major disease or won a Nobel prize. Nonetheless, our publisher insists that we do this, so here goes. First, Dave is going to introduce you to Andrew. Then Andrew will introduce you to Dave. To us, this seems like the best way to handle this awkward moment.

What Dave Has to Say about Andrew

Do you ever wonder what happened to that guy you knew in school who was so smart it boggled your mind? You know, the one who learned French in a weekend because he thought it would be "neat." He grew up to be Andrew.

Andrew Mark Fedorchek is, without question, the smartest person I have met. (Remember, I'm a professional computer geek, so I know a lot of very smart people!) In this regard, I speak not only of the keenness of his intellect but also of the litheness at which it moves. Never have I met anyone so adept at quickly mastering the finer points of a completely foreign subject.

Here's a perfect example. I spent four years in college as a UNIX system administrator, during which time I used a language called Perl. I watched, over the course of one week, Andrew master things in Perl that took me four full years to figure out! Of course, what would you expect from someone who graduated at the top of his class from both West Point and Stanford, the latter at which he earned a graduate degree in Mathematics. Frankly, if Andrew weren't such a nice guy, I would have to resent him.

Sure, having a friend this bright can really come in handy when you encounter a problem in Quantum Mechanics that you just can't solve. Other than that, though, it mostly reminds you of just how ordinary you truly are.

In fact, it was Andrew, while in Boston working for a client, who first introduced me to ASP. Since then, he has proven himself both a capable teacher and a stellar practitioner. In fact, the site he built in Boston is often extolled by Microsoft as an ASP success story. In short, Andrew is qualified to write this text because he is a true wizard with the tool. On the other hand, I . . . Well, I'm a different story.

What Andrew Has to Say about Dave

When I was first getting to know Dave, I heard someone call him a geek and rushed to his defense, saying that perhaps something like "engineer" might be more polite. Dave replied that "engineer" was probably the base class and "geek" inherits from that. Okay, I fold. David Kallet Rensin's motto must be something like "Code to eat, eat to live, live to code." Dave was staying up late at night writing Java applications when the first alpha release was available from Sun, while the rest of us were just starting to hear about what Java was. Dave's a geek, but a geek from whom I have learned a lot, and I think you will, too, when you read this book.

However, Dave's technical abilities are only the tip of the iceberg. I read his lies, er, comments, about me, and I'm here to tell you that he has plenty of his own intellectual might, including the following.

Dave is gifted when it comes to computers. Society has for centuries recognized gifted artists, gifted mathematicians, and gifted scientists, but we are novices at finding the gifted programmers. Dave is a gifted programmer, by which I mean he can learn computer languages faster than the rest of us, extend them to perform new things that no one ever thought of, and elevate programming to an art. Furthermore, like many gifted people, Dave further possesses the ability to explain his craft to the rest of us clearly and concisely.

Dave seeks out and maintains mastery on all developing technologies in our profession. Typically, this requires Dave to figure out how something works before there's any documentation of any kind. Hence, he stays up late, trying out this and that on his wireless home LAN of both UNIX and NT machines. (I told you he was a geek.) Don't forget that Dave uses all these technologies by day, too, as a consultant. All this knowledge and experience make him uniquely suited to write books. He understands your perspective no matter which computer field you hail from, and he has no end of personal experience with what really works.

Finally, Dave is well rounded, including a great sense of humor. You will find his wit setting you at ease as you digest meaty technical material.

Who You Are (Or Ought to Be)

Unlike other tools, ASP doesn't require that you bring much to the table. All we ask is that you have a little familiarity with HTML and have done some programming before. Other than that, your qualifications and history are wholly irrelevant. Sure, there are some sections of this book that a seasoned C++ programmer will find more useful. For example, in Chapter 11 we talk about how to build a custom ASP component in Visual C++. Generally speaking, though, this is anomalous. You should find the vast majority of this text approachable, no matter what your level of expertise. Don't get us wrong. This book isn't simply an introduction to the tool. In fact, we take great pains to cover every aspect of ASP that we could think of. It's just that you don't need a great deal of experience to get started.

What You Can Expect from Us

Brutal honesty and an obsessive attention to detail. We never lie to you or hide any fact from you. If, for example, ASP has a bug (and it has one or two), you can be sure that we highlight it for you. After all, why should you spend hours banging your head against a problem that isn't your fault? In addition, we also provide you with sensible workarounds for the bugs we discuss. We never point out a problem without also suggesting a solution or two.

What We Expect from You

Feedback. Please feel free to send any comments, questions, or suggestions you may have. We are both quite religious about reading our e-mail and even more so about answering it. That having been said, our e-mail addresses are

Andrew Fedorchek: afedorchek@noblestar.com

Dave Rensin: drensin@noblestar.com

If, for some reason, you feel strange about sending mail directly to us, we encourage you either to send mail to IDG Books Worldwide directly (their address is somewhere in the front of this book) or to fill out the reader survey card in the back of this book. In the past, we have used both to make subsequent texts better.

Writing a computer book is a lot of hard work. Mostly, it's a task that makes your relatives wonder why they are still related to you and your friends wonder what it is they that have done to drive you away. In fact, the act of writing isn't much fun at all. The true joy comes when the book is published and people begin to use it. If we have done an inadequate job, then this will have been for naught. We do truly hope that you enjoy reading this book and that it helps you in your tasks ahead. ASP is a powerful and elegant environment. It is our sincere hope that this text helps you wield ASP's power - both more creatively and productively. In fact, we hope that you refer to this book many times over the course of your work as both an introduction and a constant reference.

And now, into the fray!

Acknowledgements

Thank you. Next to "I love you," a heartfelt expression of thanks is about the nicest thing any person can say to another. It's no wonder people have such a hard time with it. Every year at the Academy Awards, millions of people watch some of the most articulate and well-rehearsed people on earth stand dumbfounded on a stage and stumble to express a few simple words of thanks to those who made them what they are. As lowly computer book authors, what chance have we to fare any better? It is with this understanding that we stand here (in a virtual sense) and stumble to humbly express our thanks to those who have helped make this book what it is.

John Osborn has been our Acquisitions Editor for the last two books and two years. His ever present admonition that a "well-written book that sells no copies is as useless as a book never written," reminds us daily that the key to a good book is not only to be right, but to be interesting. His is the litmus test that all of our ideas must first pass. He gave us our start at IDG and continually raises the standards of excellence to which we must adhere. For his diligence, patience, good humor, and trust, we thank him.

Barbra Guerra is the Development Editor for this book. Her job is to see that all the schedules are met and that the text is rigorously reviewed for both technical accuracy and conceptual clarity. Barb likes to practice a style of management we like to call *optimal restraint*. Barb lets us go off in whatever direction we choose, so long as we don't stray to far afoul of our objectives. She applies enough rigor that we remain on course, but not so much that we are stifled. She has been very supportive and has remained patient with us as Life has occasionally superceded our schedule. Thank you for everything, Barb.

Nate Holdread is the Copy Editor for this text. His job is to make sure that the things that make sense to us also make sense to you. To this end, he is exceptional. Nate's suggestions and edits have, no doubt, made this book much easier to read. He is outstanding at what he does and has been a joy to work with. Thanks Nate. You're the man!

There are, of course, a whole host of other people who make this effort possible. Artists, proofreaders, marketers - they all contribute to the success of this work. Although we have never spoken to most of them, we are grateful for their efforts. We especially want to thank Jeff Bankston for reviewing this material for technical accuracy and Garrett Culhane for his wonderful suggestions for the front and back covers of the book.

Lastly, we want to thank our friends, families, and colleagues who have allowed us to virtually ignore them for the last few months.

Dave Rensin:

When Andrew and I finished our last book, I thought I would never write another book again. We wrote 850 pages in a little over four and a half months. On top of that, I started a new job, moved into a new house, and was in my first year of marriage. Boy, was I stupid! Through it all, my wife, Lia, stood patiently by and allowed me to pursue my sadomasochistic dream of being an author. When Andrew and I got the "itch" to do this book, I thought she was going to beat the heck out of me! Instead, she made me promise that I would try to spend at least a little time with her and let me go on my merry way. Why my wife loves me is a complete mystery to me. I work entirely too many hours and stay up too late working on the computer. Lia, you have to be the most patient and forgiving person on the planet. Thank you, and I love you!

Quality springs forth from pride. It's the truest adage I know and is affirmed daily at work. My colleagues at Noblestar Systems are a true joy to work with. They are an army of 300 people hell-bent on being the best there ever was at whatever they happen to be doing and provide me with daily inspiration and humor. It is a real pleasure to work at a place where individual skill is celebrated and hard work rewarded. Other companies would do well to follow the example.

Finally, I want to express with deepest thanks to my best friend and co-author, Andrew Fedorchek. For the majority of this book, Andrew was on five-day-a-week travel to Boston. (The work he did there with ASP eventually earned Noblestar a spot as a finalist for Microsoft's Solution Provider of the Year award.) This left him with only the weekends to write. On top of that, he and his wife, Andrea, moved into a new house! I have absolutely no idea where he found the time to write half this book. Andrew, I bow in awe of your ability to accomplish so much in so little time.

Andrew Fedorchek:

Frequently you read acknowledgments in books thanking spouses for their tolerance and support. It's so common that it barely catches your attention. I owe it to my wife Andrea to do better.

Writing books is not my day job. I work as a software developer, often much more than 40 hours a week. I write for a number of reasons, one of which is my sincere hope that reading about my experiences will enable you to limit yourself to 40 hours a week. An hour or two each night and the weekends are all Andrea and I have. When I write a book we lose that. She's asleep right now, so I can't ask her why she puts up with this, but I suspect that it is true love; she wants me to have whatever makes me happy, and writing makes me happy. So I gratefully acknowledge her patience, her support, and her love. She is, and always shall be, the light of my life. Andrea, I thank you from the bottom of my heart.

Next, I want to acknowledge the help and inspiration of my best friend, Dave Rensin. Working with you is a true privilege. You are all at once a brilliant programmer, a clear and creative writer, and a caring friend. I wouldn't have gotten past the first page without you.

Finally, I have had the distinct privilege of working with many outstanding developers, who have contributed, directly or indirectly, to my knowledge of ASP. I want to thank Eric Kemp and Vivian Young of the Family Education Network and Craig Maccubbin and Wayne Jackson of Noblestar Systems for their support.

Contents at a Glance

Contents

Part 1

Up and Running with ASP

Chapter 1

ASP Architecture Overview

IN THIS CHAPTER

Somewhere, we are sure, there must be a law that mandates that all computer books have a chapter on how to install the product mentioned in the title. Being law-abiding citizen-authors, we decided to include one of these chapters, too. So . . . welcome to our ubiquitous installation and getting-to-know-your-product chapter. Sure, right about now you are probably chomping at the bit to blow right past this and move on to the "cool" stuff, but don't. We value your sanity (and hate to write boring material), so we've put some items in here that are sure to make reading this chapter worth your while. Specifically, we cover the following:

- ◆ What is Active Server Pages and how it relates to other Web technologies

- ◆ What makes ASP tick

- ◆ What the basic ASP pieces are and why you should care

- ◆ What ASP does when it installs

- ◆ What the interesting things are that ASP does to your registry and how to change them

Now, aren't you glad you aren't skipping past this?

What Is Active Server Pages (ASP) ?

Good question.

Active Server Pages is a technology that allows a Web developer to combine any number of server-side programming languages within an HTML file in order to create dynamic Web content.

Granted, that's not the clearest possible definition, but it's hard to come up with one sentence that describes something so interesting. Perhaps a more protracted explanation is needed.

Where Did These Guys Learn to Speak English, Anyway?

Some of you nit-picky types out there may have balked at the construction "Active Server Pages is." We checked our grammar books, and this is correct. Active Server Pages is a technology and is therefore singular. We know that this seems a little odd because the last word is plural, but trust us, it's right. You really shouldn't worry too much anyway, since we refer to it as ASP for the rest of the book. We just thought we'd mention it here so that you didn't think that we were somehow grammatically challenged.

A Ridiculously Quick History of Web Technologies

In order to understand what ASP is, you really need to understand how it came about. Just to make sure that everybody is reading from the same page (so to speak), the next section presents a ridiculously quick history of Web technologies so that you have a better notion of where ASP fits in.

STATIC HTML

While working at the European Particle Physics Laboratory (CERN), a man named Tim Berners-Lee invented a little thing people like to call the World Wide Web. He designed the Web as "an Internet-based hypermedia initiative for global information sharing." (This phrase is taken straight from Tim Berners-Lee's biography. For the complete text, go to `http://www.w3.org/pub/WWW/People/Berners-Lee/`.)

In a nutshell, his idea was to ceate a way for people to share media-rich information in a common fashion. In order to accomplish this, however, Tim had to create a standard language to describe each page of content. Eventually, this language – which he based on Standard Generalized Markup Language (SGML) – became the HyperText Markup Language (HTML).

Many people get confused about what HTML is and is not. HTML is a presentation description language. It is *not* a programming language. In other words, HTML is intended to describe how a Web page should look, not how it should behave. This basic understanding describes the biggest problem with HTML – it's static.

Pretty soon after developers started using HTML, they became tired of its limitations and began looking for ways to make the information on their Web sites more dynamic in nature. They wanted to create pages that would update themselves automatically, and thereby minimize the need for human maintenance. They didn't know it, but what they needed was the Common Gateway Interface (CGI).

COMMON GATEWAY INTERFACE (CGI) APPLICATIONS

The famous French philosopher, Francois Rabelais, once wrote that "[n]ature abhors a vacuum." Human beings are certainly no different. Just as people began to complain seriously about the shortcomings of HTML, the kind folks at the National

Center for Supercomputing Applications (NCSA) at the University of Illinois at Urbana-Champaign came up with a solution. They called it the Common Gateway Interface (CGI), and it changed the Web forever.

CGI is really nothing more than a set of standards describing how a Web server program can communicate with an external application. It's really very simple.

Despite its basic nature, CGI opened up a whole new level of Web development. Users could create pages that called external programs, which, in turn, returned dynamic HTML. It was a real breakthrough. Soon Web sites everywhere were displaying information in real time, from databases and collecting information to HTML forms. Life was good.

IN-PROCESS APPLICATIONS

Actually, life was only pretty good. CGI applications suffer from some problems. The most important of these problems is that each time a user loads a Web page that calls the CGI application, a new process is created on the Web server machine. For sites with many simultaneous users, this could lead to slow performance due to intensive memory and CPU needs. As sites grew bigger and CGI applications grew more complex, the problem became more acute. Pretty soon, Web server vendors starting looking for ways to speed up CGI applications. They focused on two areas:

1. The transfer of data between the Web server and the CGI application

2. The consolidation of needed processes to run a CGI application

The vendors wound up creating a set of Application Programming Interfaces (APIs) to their Web server software. Using these interfaces, developers can access internal data structures and other information directly without having to pass it through the operating system first.

The second thing these APIs allow a developer to do is to create an application that runs in the same memory space as the Web server program. This means that each call to the CGI application only starts a new thread in the operating system instead of starting a whole new process.

These two major advantages make applications written with these APIs much more efficient and faster than standard CGI applications. The only drawback to these programs is that they are proprietary to the Web server being used. In other words, an application written for Microsoft's Internet Information Server using its Internet Server API (ISAPI) cannot run on Netscape's Enterprise Server, or vice versa.

ASP = OLE + STEROIDS

Now that you have an idea about the general state of Web applications, it's a good time to talk about where ASP fits into the picture.

The majority of ASP functionality is controlled by a single 364K file named *asp.dll*. This file is, in fact, an OLE component that the Microsoft family of Web servers calls to perform some specialized processing.

All Is Not Quite As It Seems

The truth of the matter is that a fair bit of processing is also performed in the component and language .DLLs. The point we are trying to make here is that the basic ASP functionality is accomplished in one file. We cover these other factors later in the book when we discuss how to use other languages in ASP.

How do we know this? Easy. Simply search the registry for the text *asp.dll.* You find that it is referenced under a tree named **CLSID**. This special tree is where Microsoft keeps the critical information about all OLE components registered with the system.

The ASP process is actually straightforward. The first time a call is made to a page that is to be handled by ASP, the Web server creates an instance of the ASP OLE component in memory and passes it the request. From then on, that same component handles all user requests. This means that every call to ASP after the first will be extremely fast.

Why ASP ?

Now that you know what ASP is, you are probably wondering why you should use it. In this section, we compare ASP with some of your other development options.

ASP VERSUS CGI

ASP enables you to embed program code in the middle of HTML to create dynamic Web pages. You can accomplish the same thing, however, by writing your own CGI applications. What's important to remember here is *how* these things are accomplished.

As an in-process component, ASP runs in the same memory space as the Web server application. Unlike a CGI program, ASP does not require the operating system to start a new process for each user request. This makes ASP much faster than even a well-optimized CGI application. Also, ASP exposes certain internal structures of the Web server to the developer. This means that you can have more control over the flow of information in your code.

ASP VERSUS IN-PROCESS APPLICATIONS

Fine, you say. Using ASP is better than writing a CGI program. What about in-process applications using the Web server's native API? Won't that accomplish the same thing?

The answer is yes. Writing an application using the native API makes it comparably fast to ASP. The thing to remember, however, is that you have to compile the application each time you want to change it. That can be a big waste of time! This is especially true for more complicated programs.

It is therefore true that you *can* perform the same things using the native API. The question is why you would *want* to.

ASP Requirements

As you have probably guessed by now, ASP must meet a few requirements before it can run. Specifically, ASP will run using either Microsoft's Internet Information Server for Windows NT or Microsoft's Personal Web Server for Windows 95.

Windows NT

ASP runs on any of the three major platforms for Windows NT: Alpha, PowerPC, or Intel. In addition, it runs on either NT 3.51 or NT 4.0. However, if you want to run ASP on NT 3.51, then you have to apply the service packs and make sure that you are running the appropriately patched IIS version.

If you want our advice — and, after all, that is why you bought the book, right? — then run NT 4.0 and IIS 3.0. NT 4.0 has a far more robust set of networking capabilities than NT 3.51, and it uses less memory.

Windows 95

Microsoft, recognizing that not all Web developers are running NT on their desktops, has also made it possible to run ASP on Windows 95. All you need to do is install the Microsoft Personal Web Server. That installation process updates any Windows 95 files that need to be patched and configures your machine appropriately. After you install the Personal Web Server, simply run the same ASP install program that you ran for your Windows NT machine.

Where to Get All This Stuff

At the time of this writing, both IIS 3.0 and the Personal Web Server are available free from the Microsoft Web site. You can get IIS 3.0 (including ASP) from `http://www.microsoft.com/iis/GetIIS/DownloadIIS3/` and the Personal Web Server from `http://www.microsoft.com/msdownload/ieplatform/iewin95/10000.htm`.

The Basic ASP Pieces

Now that you know what ASP is and where to get it, it's time to talk about its basic architecture.

Where ASP Runs

You first need to understand that ASP usually performs its work *server-side*. This means that the program code you embed in your ASP pages usually runs on the server. (We say *usually* here because you can embed code in an ASP page that runs on the client browser. That's just not how it's usually done.)

This is different than the embedded JavaScript or VBScript that you may already have seen in some Web pages. That code is run by *your* browser on *your* machine. It is executed *client-side*.

The ASP Model

With that out of the way, we can talk about the three basic pieces of the ASP Model: *objects, components,* and *languages.*

OBJECTS

In order to make your life a little easier, ASP exposes some of its internal structures to you. These items provide the foundation for most of your work. They are:

◆ **The Application object.** The object used to share information with other users accessing the same ASP application.

◆ **The Request object.** The object used to retrieve values the client browser passed to the Web server during a request.

◆ **The Response object.** The object used to send output to client browsers.

◆ **The Server object.** The object used to access some of the internal properties of the Web server.

◆ **The Session object.** The object used to track information specific to a given user's session. This is especially helpful for applications that allow users to purchase items online.

Each of these objects is covered in greater detail later in the book. We thought that we would introduce the terms to you now so that they seem familiar when you encounter them later.

COMPONENTS

If ASP only provided you with the objects we have discussed already, it would still be useful. As it turns out, ASP also provides you a way to add in your own objects. These add-ins are called *components*. In this section, we briefly cover the five components that ship with ASP. Later in the book, we show you how to build and use your own components.

ASP ships with the following components:

- ◆ **The Ad Rotator component.** This component automatically rotates advertisements displayed on a page.

- ◆ **The Browser Capabilities component.** This component determines the capabilities of the client browser connected to the server. This is useful for determining whether or not to send a special HTML command to the client machine.

- ◆ **The Database Access component.** This component allows you to interact with any ODBC-compliant database.

- ◆ **The Content Linking component.** This component creates a table of contents for your Web pages so that you can treat your site like pages in a book. This is useful for organizing your site's information.

- ◆ **The File Access component.** This component allows you to create and read text files from the local disk. This will be helpful to you as you get into some more advanced ASP programming.

Again, we cover each of these items in greater detail later in the book.

SUPPORTED LANGUAGES

The last major piece of the ASP architecture is its support for multiple scripting languages. In fact, ASP can support *any* language for which a proper component has been written. All you need is a special OLE control that supports certain ASP interfaces. This support is especially nice because it allows you to take advantage of the features of some very robust tools. It may also reduce your maintenance and conversion times.

For example, say you already have a site that is run with a bunch of CGI programs written in Perl. You can get a PerlScript component (which already exists), install it, and move the majority of your code into ASP without rewriting it.

In its most basic configuration, ASP supports two languages – *VBScript* and *JScript.* VBScript is a subset of Microsoft's Visual Basic programming language. It is one of the simpler languages you will ever encounter and is a favorite among many Web developers.

The other language that comes built in, JScript, is Microsoft's implementation of Netscape's JavaScript language. This language is also quite popular among Web developers and offers a few more networking features that VBScript lacks.

What is truly nice, though, is that you don't have to commit to any particular language. ASP allows you to mix and match your languages within the same page. It supports this by allowing you to call a function written in one language from code written in another. This is really nice when you need to leverage the special capabilities of one tool without committing completely to it.

Don't worry now about understanding the ins and outs of how ASP manages its languages. We cover these topics in great depth a little later.

ASP and the Registry

ASP, like every other 32-bit program these days, makes some critical entries in your registry. In this section, we discuss what they are, where they are, and how to change them to suit your needs.

Where to Find ASP Registry Keys

The ASP registry keys can be found in the following registry path:

```
HKEY_LOCAL_MACHINE
\SYSTEM
\CurrentControlSet
\Services
\W3SVC
\ASP
\Parameters
```

You can edit these entries by using **regedit.exe** (if you are using Windows 95) or **regedt32.exe** (if you are using Windows NT). Actually, you can also use **regedit.exe** in Windows NT, as well. In fact, you may want to because it allows you to search for keys.

The ASP Registry Entries

The following sections provide detailed information about each registry entry used and installed by ASP. You find the name of each entry, what the legal value for it is, what the entry means, and what the default value is. Please be careful, though. Changing these entries may result in your ASP installation not functioning properly or at all.

ALLOWOUTOFPROCCMPTS
Type: REG_DWORD   **Range:** 0,1   **Default:** 0
This key controls whether ASP allows you to invoke OLE processes *off-site* using the **Server.Create()** method. The default value is 0 because using such components may jeopardize the stability of your Web server software. We cover this much more in Chapter 4.

ALLOWSESSIONSTATE
Type: REG_DWORD   **Range:** 0,1   **Default:** 1
This flag controls whether ASP can track session states for each connected user. A session state enables ASP to keep track of what selections a user makes, where they go in the site, and just about anything else you can think of to tie to a session. Use of these states is often a critical component of an interactive Web site.

Each session is tracked by sending an ASPSessionID cookie to the user's browser when he or she accesses the Web site. This enables ASP to track which session a user is in when he or she enters a given page.

A value of 1 enables this option, and a value of 0 disables it. If you choose to disable this preference, then any attempt in your program code to store information in ASP's **Session** object will generate an error.

BUFFERINGON

Type: REG_DWORD **Range:** 0,1 **Default:** 0

This entry controls whether ASP buffers output before sending it to the client browser. *Buffered output* means that all information to be sent to the client is first collected before being sent. *Non-buffered output,* however, means that information is sent as soon as it is prepared. Non-buffered output can make pages draw faster on the client machine, but buffered output allows you to send HTTP headers from anywhere within your script. In either case, you can use the **Response.Buffer()** method to change the buffering state on the fly.

A value of 0 means that all output is non-buffered, while a value of 1 means that all output is buffered.

CHECKFORNESTEDVROOTS

Type: REG_DWORD **Range:** 0,1 **Default:** 1

Say that you map the physical path c:\temp to the virtual path /temp. If there exists a directory named c:\temp\foo, then you can access it via the virtual path /temp/foo. It is also possible, however, to explicitly map the virtual path /foo to the physical path c:\temp\foo. In this case, you have nested virtual roots (vroots). By leaving this setting at 1, ASP performs the proper checking to see that the virtual roots are handled correctly.

DEFAULTSCRIPTLANGUAGE

Type: REG_SZ **Range:** Any string **Default:** VBScript

This key determines the script language that is used as the primary scripting language for all ASP applications. The primary scripting language can be used inside the ASP scripting delimiters <% and %>. If you want to override the default language from within your program code, you can issue the following command at the beginning of your script:

```
<%@ LANGUAGE = ScriptingLanguage %>
```

If you elect to change this item using this registry setting, you have to stop and restart the Web server for the change to take effect.

ENABLEPARENTPATHS

Type: REG_DWORD **Range:** 0,1 **Default:** 1

This flag controls whether ASP allows paths relative to the current directory. In other words, it controls whether ASP will allow references to ".." from within generated HTML. The default setting of 1 allows such operations but constitutes a minor security risk. This is because an include path could access a file outside the server's virtual root space. If you are particularly security conscious and want to restrict these operations, you can set this value to 0. Like many of the other options discussed so far, changing this value requires you to stop and restart the server.

LOGERRORREQUESTS
Type: REG_DWORD   Range: 0,1   Default: 1

This flag controls whether the Web server writes unsuccessful client requests to the Windows NT event log file. The value 1 turns error logging on, and 0 turns it off. If you change this setting, you do not have to stop and restart the Web server for the change to take effect.

MEMFREEFACTOR
Type: REG_DWORD   Range: 50 - 150   Default: 50

This value indicates the maximum length of the free memory list as a percentage of the used memory list. For example, a value of 50 means that ASP does not allow the length of the free memory list to be more than 50 percent as long as the used memory list. If you change this setting, then you must stop and restart the Web server for the change to take effect.

MINUSEDBLOCKS
Type: REG_DWORD   Range: 5 - 20   Default: 10

This value indicates the minimum length of the used memory list before elements can be freed. This setting has implications on how much information is held in cache. The lower this setting, the more information will be held in cache before memory is freed. If you change this setting, you must stop and restart the Web server for the change to take effect.

NUMINITIALTHREADS
Type: REG_DWORD   Range: 1 - 10   Default: 2

This value indicates the number of worker threads that ASP creates when it is started. If this value exceeds the maximum number of threads possible as indicated by **ProcessorThreadMax** attribute, then ASP honors the **ProcessorThreadMax** value over the **NuminitialThreads** value. If you change this item, then you must stop and restart the Web server for the change to take effect.

PROCESSORTHREADMAX
Type: REG_DWORD   Range: 1 - 0x000000C8   Default: 10

This value specifies the maximum number of worker threads to create per processor. As a rule, you don't want to create more than 20 threads per processor. If you change this value, then you must stop and restart the Web server for the change to take effect.

REQUESTQUEUEMAX
Type: REG_DWORD   Range: 1 - 0xFFFFFFFF   Default: 500

This value specifies the maximum number of .ASP file requests to maintain in the request queue available for each thread. When the limit is reached, clients are sent the value from the registry value **ServerTooBusy**. In other words, this value controls how many requests will be accepted before the server appears too busy to the client. Five hundred is a good number with which to start. If you change this value, then you must stop and restart the Web server for the change to take effect.

SCRIPTENGINECACHEMAX
Type: REG_DWORD   Range: 0 - 0xFFFFFFFF   Default: 30

This value indicates the maximum number of ActiveX language engines that ASP will keep cached in memory. Since it is not likely that you will use more than two or three languages throughout your entire site, the default value of 30 should be more than enough. If you change this value, then you must stop and restart the Web server for the change to take effect.

SCRIPTERRORMESSAGE
Type: REG_SZ   Range: Any String   Default: "An error occurred on the server when processing the URL. Please contact the system administrator."

This message appears on a browser if an error occurs and ASP has been instructed *not* to display the error to the client browser (for example, **ScriptErrorsSentToBrowser** is set to 0). If you change this setting, you do not have to stop and restart the Web server for the change to take effect.

SCRIPTERRORSSENTTOBROWSER
Type: REG_DWORD   Range: 0,1   Default: 1

This flag controls whether the Web server writes debugging specifics (filename, error and line numbers, description) to the browser in addition to the log. If this value is set to 0, then the text stored in the **ScriptErrorMessage** key is sent to the browser. If you change this setting, you do not have to stop and restart the Web server for the change to take effect.

SCRIPTFILECACHESIZE
Type: REG_DWORD   Range: 0 - 0xFFFFFFFF   Default: -1

This value specifies the amount of memory in bytes to allocate for the caching of precompiled script files, which improves the performance of ASP. What happens is that ASP compiles each script before executing. If a second request is made for the script and it is still in memory, then the server won't recompile the script before executing it. This helps performance. A special value of 0 indicates that no script files will be cached, and a special value of -1 indicates that all script files requested will be cached. As you might guess, performance may be low if caching is not used.

If you change this value, then you must stop and restart the Web server for the change to take effect.

SCRIPTFILECACHETTL

Type: REG_DWORD   **Range:** 0 - 0x7FFFFFFF   **Default:** 300

This value specifies the amount of time (in seconds) that script files remain in the Memory Cache before being phased out if there have been no references to those scripts. If the number of data files is limited or clients access only a small portion of files, then increasing this value can be beneficial as it keeps scripts in memory for a longer period of time. A value of 0xFFFFFFFF means that files will be cached indefinitely. If you change this value, then you must stop and restart the Web server for the change to take effect.

SCRIPTTIMEOUT

Type: REG_DWORD   **Range:** 0 - 0xFFFFFFFF   **Default:** 90

This value indicates the length of time (in seconds) that ASP allows a script to run to completion. If the script fails to complete within this time period, then the server terminates the script and writes an event to the event log. This is especially helpful in restricting the amount of resources a poorly written script can take. You can override this parameter in your program code by using the **Server.ScriptTimeout()** method call.

A special value of -1 allows scripts to run for an indefinite amount of time. For what it's worth, we don't think it's ever a good idea to set this entry to -1.

Changing this setting does not require you to stop and restart the Web server for the change to take effect.

SESSIONTIMEOUT

Type: REG_DWORD   **Range:** 1 - 0xFFFFFFFF   **Default:** 20

This value specifies the default amount of time (in minutes) that a **Session** object should be maintained after the last request associated with the object is made. This can be overridden in a script using the **Session.Timeout()** method call. In general, there's not much call for increasing this value as it is unlikely that any user will linger on a particular page for more than 20 minutes. Changing this setting does not require you to stop and restart the Web server for the change to take effect.

STARTCONNECTIONPOOL

Type: REG_DWORD   **Range:** 0,1   **Default:** 1

This flag controls whether ODBC connection pooling is turned *on* or *off*. We can't think of any reason why you would want to keep this value set to anything other than 1 (True). If you change this setting, then you must stop and restart the Web server for the change to take effect. Beware, though, that setting connection pooling to *on* causes serious problems with ODBC data sources that are from MS Access.

THREADCREATIONTHRESHOLD
Type: REG_DWORD   **Range:** 1 - 0xFFFFFFFF   **Default:** 5

This value indicates the number of requests that can be maintained in the common queue (that is, requests which have not yet been assigned a specific thread on which to run) for ASP. If requests in the common queue exceed this number, then a new thread is created in the thread pool (that is, the total number of threads that ASP creates to service incoming requests), but only if the number of threads in the thread pool is less than the configured maximum of **ProcessorThreadMax**. Increasing this value reduces the number of resources needed by ASP but may slow down performance. If you change this value, then you must stop and restart the Web server for the change to take effect.

Summary

In this chapter, we have given you a flavor of the history behind ASP and where it fits in the grand scheme of things. We have also tried to help you through some of the more difficult configuration issues that you may face. By now, you should be ready to install and configure ASP to run to suit your particular needs. In the next chapter, we show you how to start using ASP for your Web programming tasks.

Chapter 2

Building Your First ASP Pages with VBScript

IN THIS CHAPTER

In the previous chapter, we discussed where ASP fits into the world of Internet programming and how to install the product. Now we want to dive right in and create some interactive Web pages with ASP. This chapter discusses the basics that you need to make sense out of the rest of the book.

In this chapter, we cover the following:

- ◆ Creating a basic ASP application

- ◆ Features of ASP that you need to read the rest of the book

- ◆ The tools for writing and debugging ASP scripts

- ◆ How to include multiple files and languages in your scripts

A word of warning before we start. In order to present a complete discussion of how ASP works, we have to use features that we have not yet fully explained. The complete details come in subsequent chapters; this is merely an overview.

Hello World

The traditional way to start a discussion of any programming language is to output the text "Hello World." This is appropriate, because the output of your program is frequently the only way you can see if your program is doing what you want it to do. Therefore, you must learn how to get feedback from your program before you can test your knowledge of anything else. Here is the "Hello World" of ASP:

```
<!DOCTYPE HTML PUBLIC "-//W3C//DTD HTML 3.2 Final//EN">
<TITLE>Hello World ASP</TITLE>
<%Response.write( "<H1>Hello World!</H1>" ) 'Our first Script %>
```

Now we'll dissect this to figure out what's going on.

HTML 3.2

Throughout this book, we use HTML 3.2, which at the time of writing has been endorsed as a W3C Recommendation (http://www.w3.org/pub/WWW/TR/REC-html32.html).

One of the first changes you notice in HTML 3.2 is that the <HTML>, <HEAD>, and <BODY> tags are optional. The minimal HTML 3.2 document looks like this:

```
<!DOCTYPE HTML PUBLIC "-//W3C//DTD HTML 3.2 Final//EN">
<TITLE>The minimal HTML 3.2 document</TITLE>
```

The first two lines of our Hello World script are therefore simply standard HTML 3.2 commands.

Delimiters

You are already familiar with the fact that HTML commands are enclosed in the angle brackets — (<) and (>). These tokens, which separate commands from text, are called *delimiters*. The delimiters for ASP scripting commands are the angle brackets with percent signs — (<%) and (%>). ASP interprets any text enclosed in a pair of these symbols as scripting commands. It considers everything else either HTML tags or plain text.

A few finer points on the behavior of delimiters:

◆ The scripting commands enclosed in the delimiters can be of arbitrary length and can span multiple lines.

◆ You can't have any white space between the angle brackets (<,>) and the percent (%) characters. This code doesn't work:

```
< %Response.write( "<H1>Hello World!</H1>" )% >
```

When you execute this code, the angle brackets, the percent sign, and the "Response.write" all appear as text on the HTML page.

◆ It doesn't matter how much white space, if any, is between the delimiters and the scripting commands. This code is legal:

```
<%
Response.write( "<H1>Hello World!" )
%>
```

◆ Every beginning delimiter (<%) must have a closing mate (%>), and delimiters don't nest. Therefore, this code gives you a scripting error:

```
<% <%Response.write( "<H1>Hello World!</H1>" )%> %>
```

◆ The closing delimiter (%>) functions as a new line character for terminating scripting commands.

To return to our Hello World example, the first ASP delimiter begins on line three. Therefore, the browser should interpret the first two lines as ordinary HTML.

Script Resolution

Knowing that <% . . . %> denotes ASP scripts, you can view an ASP file and see what is script and what isn't. However, the client browser doesn't see the scripts. All it sees is HTML. What happens?

When a browser requests an ASP file, ASP passes the file to the appropriate scripting engine for processing. A scripting engine is a DLL that evaluates the scripting commands and inserts their output, if any, inside the HTML of the file.

If you're having trouble picturing this, here is a conceptual model of what's happening under the covers. Imagine taking all the non-script text and loading it into an array of strings. Then create a program that consists of the scripts and the commands to print the text. For example, if your ASP file looks like this:

```
Some stuff
<% Some scripts %>
Some more stuff
<% Some more scripts %>
```

then the scripting engine executes a program like this:

```
print array_of_strings[0]
some scripts
print array_of_strings[1]
some more scripts
```

This model of understanding execution becomes critical when we discuss how control of flow commands affects ASP output.

Script Language

The individual scripting engines parse the ASP file into script commands and non-script commands. When you don't tell ASP which scripting language you are going to use, it uses the default scripting language found in the Registry. This is initially VBScript. When you want to use another language, the first scripting command must be

```
<%@ LANGUAGE = ScriptingLanguage %>
```

ScriptingLanguage is the language that you intend to use. This must be the first scripting command, but it need not be the first line in the file – you can put as much HTML as you want before the command.

Throughout this book, if we do not specify the scripting language, we are using VBScript. ASP also ships with JScript, which is Microsoft's implementation of Netscape's JavaScript language. To specify JScript, you simply include this line:

```
<%@ LANGUAGE = JScript %>
```

Notice that you do not put the scripting language in quotes.

The only other scripting language that we use in this book is PerlScript, which is an ASP implementation of Perl. Perl – short for Practical Extraction and Reporting Language – was invented by Larry Wall and is used primarily for text processing and system administration. Perl has become popular as a CGI programming language because it can manipulate text so efficiently.

You may use the @language command only once in a given page. Therefore, it is not possible to switch directly between languages in one ASP file. However, you can define subroutines in other languages. There is no restriction on switching languages from one page to the next. Each page may specify its own language with @language.

Comments

Where would any language be without the facility to comment your code? You want to be able to comment all your scripts from the get-go, so let's review how comments work in ASP.

With ASP you are using some scripting language, and hopefully that scripting language supports comments (VBScript, JScript, and PerlScript all do). These comments behave the way comments should behave: the scripting engine ignores them, and they have no effect whatsoever on the execution of the script.

The tricky part is that ASP is outputting HTML, and HTML can include comments, too. Any HTML comments (<!– . . . –>) are sent to the client browser, but not the ASP comments. You can use this feature to include comments in your normal HTML that you don't want the world to see.

VBScript comments start with either an apostrophe (') or the keyword REM. Therefore, the text "Our first Script," from our example, is a comment. The new line character ends a comment. Remember that the end of script tag (%>) allows functions as a new line, so you can write code like this:

```
<% a = "Hello World!" 'Comments here %><% Response.write( a ) %>
```

ASP Objects

Much of the power and flexibility of ASP comes from the objects that it provides. If you are not already familiar with object-oriented programming, think of an object this way: "An object is a combination of programming and data that can be treated as a unit." (Active Server Pages Scripting Guide, http://LocalServer/IASDocs/Guide/asgobj.htm)

The syntax for calling objects varies with the scripting language. In both VBScript and JScript, the period operator (.) separates an object name from an object method. Therefore, you address the write method of the response object as "Response.Write" in both VBScript and JScript. However, in PerlScript, object names and methods are separated by a dash and greater than sign (->), and scalar variables (an object is addressed though a scalar reference) are preceded by a dollar sign ($). Therefore, the correct PerlScript syntax is "$Response->Write."

There are also differences in calling functions between scripting languages. In both VBScript and PerlScript, parentheses are optional in function calls when the meaning is clear without them. Therefore, you can write

```
<% Response.Write "<H1>Hello World!</H1>" %>
```

We do not use this method in this book. Always using the parentheses adds clarity and makes our examples more portable to JScript writers.

Writing Output

At this point, we know that our "Hello World" script contains two lines of HTML that are copied directly to the output, and one section of scripting commands that are to be sent to the VBScript engine. This command is simply

```
<%Response.write( "<H1>Hello World!</H1>" ) 'Our first Script %>
```

We know that this calls the write method of the response object. Therefore, it prints "Hello World!"

Writing data to the current HTTP output is something so fundamental to ASP that Microsoft has provided a shortcut for it. If you use an equal sign (=) on a scripting command all on it's own, then ASP treats it as a response write. Therefore, we could have written our example as

```
<% = "<H1>Hello World!</H1>" %><% 'Our first Script %>
```

In this case, the equal sign is just shorthand for the Response.write method. Notice that we had to put our command into its own set of delimiter tags. When you use the equal sign shorthand, it must be the only command in the script block.

Writing and Debugging ASP Scripts

We hope that you actually typed the three lines of text from our Hello World program into an editor and ran them. You could also have copied them from the CD-ROM. Either way, you should have seen "Hello World!" in your browser. Let's talk about what to do if this didn't work, or if other examples don't work for you.

Writing ASP Code

There is no shame in using the Windows Notepad (NOTEPAD.EXE) application to write scripts. If you do choose Notepad, keep these few points in mind:

- Notepad wants to save everything as text files. If you create the Hello World file above and save it as "hello.asp," Notepad creates a file named "hello.asp.txt." This isn't what you want. The solution is either to type the filename with quotes around it or to change the type to *All Files*.

- Notepad can store files in Unicode format. This shouldn't be the default, but if you do accidentally save a file as Unicode, ASP won't be able to read it.

- Notepad doesn't give you line numbers. You will long for an editor that provides this, because the error messages you get from ASP reference the row number of the text.

The tool that we use to write scripts is the InterDev Studio. This looks and feels much like the Microsoft Visual C++ Development environment. InterDev provides many highly sophisticated features for code development, but it uses more memory and doesn't come free with the operating system the way that Notepad does.

No matter what editor you use, just be sure to save your document as an ASCII text file. As you would expect, ASP only works with text files; it can't read .rtf or .doc files.

Getting an ASP Script to Run

You've written your script and it doesn't work. Here are few things to try to save debugging time:

1. Make sure that the problem is ASP. Create a simple HTML document in the same directory as your ASP file and try to open it. If you can't see the HTML file, you know that the problem isn't ASP. (You have to allow Read privileges on the directory to do this. Remember to turn them off for production work.)

2. Ensure that the ASP file is stored in a directory in which IIS allows Execute Access. If the ASP file is stored in a read-only directory, such as wwwroot, IIS treats the script as pure HTML.

3. Use HTTP to access the file. A simple trap to fall into is to load a file using the File⇨Open command on the browser and load a file directly without using HTTP. Make sure that your location starts with "http://."

4. See if any other DLLs work. If you have PerlIS installed on your machine, you might try to load a .pl file. If nothing executes, then ASP isn't the issue.

Debugging an ASP Script

The first hurdle is getting the ASP script file successfully shipped off to the scripting engine. The second is debugging your script. How the scripting engine reacts to bugs is language-dependent. VBScript is a true interpreted language. If you write a dozen lines of code and the first 10 are valid and executable by themselves, VBScript runs those 10 lines for you and then prints an error message when you get to line 11.

One special feature in VBScript to be aware of is the On Error Resume Next statement. When you include this command in your VBScript file:

```
<% On Error Resume Next %>
```

you are telling VBScript to ignore errors and continue processing the remaining valid commands in a procedure.

PerlScript, like Perl, behaves more like a compiled language in some respects. Your entire script must be syntactically correct if you want even the first line to run. If there are any syntax errors, PerlScript prints the first syntax error it finds to an HTML document and stops right there. JScript performs the same way.

Case Sensitivity

Whether or not your ASP commands are case-sensitive depends on the scripting language that you use. VBScript is not case-sensitive. These commands are equivalent:

```
<% Response.Write( "<H1>Hello World!</H1>" ) %>
<% response.write( "<H1>Hello World!</H1>" ) %>
<% RESPONSE.WRITE( "<H1>Hello World!</H1>" ) %>
```

In JScript, however, only the first line is correct. The **Response** object is named *Response*. There are no objects named *response* or *RESPONSE*. PerlScript is also case-sensitive.

More ASP Features

Before we get into ASP objects in Chapter 3, we want to cover a few more basic scripting concepts. These concepts include how to handle server-side includes, how control of flow language behaves in ASP, and how to mix scripting languages.

Including Files

A common practice in C programming is to use the *#include* preprocessor directive to include other files in a program. This is functionally equivalent to inserting the file itself into your program.

Most Web servers, to include IIS, support including files in this manner, but Web servers call this feature a *server-side include*. When you want to include another file in your script, you may simply write

```
<!— #include file="Your file name here.ASP" —>
```

Notice that this is not an ASP command. The Web server executes these directives *before* the scripting engine runs. This means that you can't dynamically decide which files to include.

In Chapter 7, we discuss how to retrieve information from a database and display it on your Web page. There you have the opposite problem. The scripting engine parses the scripting commands *before* it runs any database queries. Therefore, any attempt to put scripting commands in the database will fail unless you explicitly evaluate the commands as script with a language that offers such a feature, as PerlScript does with the eval function.

Control of Flow Language

Every language includes commands to control the flow of execution, such as for loops, if then statements, and while loops. How this interacts with ASP isn't necessarily obvious until you get used to it. For example, what should the following code mean to the scripting engine?

```
<% if something = something_else then %>
<H1>Do this</H1>
<% else %>
<H1>Do the<BR>
<I>other</I> thing</H1>
<% end if %>
```

The key is to remember that ASP writes the plain HTML text as a block with the Response.Writeblock function that we discuss in Chapter 5. Therefore, the previous code is equivalent to this code:

```
<% if something = something_else then
response.writeblock(1)
else
response.writeblock(2)
end if %>
```

In this case, writeblock(1) and writeblock(2) return the HTML of the actual ASP file.

In effect, you can write conditional HTML with ASP, which opens whole new vistas of page creation. You can change the contents of a page based on all sorts of decision criteria, such as the date, URL parameters, cookies, and so forth.

Using Multiple Scripting Languages

Each scripting language has its strengths and weaknesses. Sometimes you wish you could use one language part of the time and another language elsewhere. ASP makes this possible. Before we tell you how this works, let's state up front what you can't do. You can't switch languages at will with the @language command. For example, this code will fail:

```
<%@language = VBScript %>
<% Response.write( "VBScript says hello" ) %>
<%@language = JScript %>
<% Response.write( "JScript says hello" ) %>
```

The way to use multiple languages is with the HTML SCRIPT TAG. The format for the Script tag is:

```
<SCRIPT LANGUAGE=ScriptingLanguage RUNAT=Server>
Procedure definition here
</SCRIPT>
```

This is the same HTML tag that you use to send JavaScript or VBScript to the client browser. The difference is the RUNAT=Server attribute. As an example, you may want to use a JScript function within your VBScript code:

```
<%@ language = VBScript %>
<!DOCTYPE HTML PUBLIC "-//W3C//DTD HTML 3.2 Final//EN">
<TITLE>Hello World ASP</TITLE>
<SCRIPT LANGUAGE=JScript RUNAT=Server>
function JscriptTest() {
  Response.write( "This is JScript" )
}
</SCRIPT>
<% call JscriptTest %>
```

Summary

ASP provides a simple, easy way to mix scripting commands with HTML text. The <% and %> delimiters tell ASP where your scripting commands are. The scripting language you use is up to you, but you need to tell ASP if you aren't going to use the default language. You can include multiple files and scripting languages in your ASP code. ASP uses object syntax to encapsulate such actions as writing information to the current HTTP output. Control of flow language gives you opportunity to construct Web pages with conditional HTML.

Part II

The ASP Internal Object Model

Chapter 3

The Request Object

IN THIS CHAPTER

If ASP is your first introduction to dynamic HTML, you are lucky. If you are a CGI programmer, you have found that one of the ugliest parts of CGI programming is retrieving information from a client browser. All data gets stuffed into the HTTP header, and then the Web server writes pieces of this header to environment variables. You read these variables and typically perform some complex string manipulation to get the information you want. The ASP **Request** object cleans up this mess and gives a developer a logical, easy-to-use model for retrieving information from the client. The **Request** object provides a consistent interface to all information you could possibly want to retrieve for use in your application. Whether you want parameters from the URL, Form data, or environment variables, the **Request** object provides it. In this chapter, we discuss retrieving information from the following:

◆ Query Strings

◆ HTML Forms

◆ Browser Cookies

◆ HTTP header variables

Request Collections

The **Request** object itself has no methods or properties. It is simply an umbrella for five collection objects. The objects contained by the **Request** object are as follows:

◆ QueryString

◆ Form

◆ Cookie

◆ ClientCertificate

◆ ServerVariables

We discuss each of these objects in turn. As collection objects, they function similarly. We can't quite say that if you know one you know them all, but it's pretty close. That's the beauty of a good design.

The **Request** object does provide one other critical function in addition to these five collections. As you see below, most information is retrieved from the **Request** object as

```
Request.collection("variable")
```

where *collection* is one of the five collection objects listed previously. However, you can simply write

```
Request("variable")
```

and leave it to the **Request** object to search each collection in turn for the variable that you have requested. The **Request** object searches the collections in the order in which we present them – QueryString, Form, Cookies, ClientCertificate, ServerVariables – and it stops as soon as it finds the parameter.

QueryString

One way to pass information back to a server is to put it right in the Uniform Resource Locator (URL). When a URL is of this form:

```
http://virtual_directory/path/executable_file?v1=x&v2=y&v3=z
```

the question mark (?) after the executable file tells the server that what follows are parameters to be passed to the application. The entire string after the ? is called the QueryString. It is sent in the HTTP header in name-value pair format:

```
variable_name=value
```

Each pair is separated with an ampersand (&). In the CGI programming model, the Web server puts the QueryString into an environment variable, named QUERY_STRING. Then the executable file must retrieve this string from the environment variable and parse it into its component pieces. ASP does all this parsing for you and puts information in the **QueryString** object. Let's look at where query strings come from and then how to break them apart.

Generating QueryStrings

Query strings come from a number of programming constructs:

♦ **HTML forms.** The block level HTML body elements <FORM> ... </FORM> collect data from the user. When you set the METHOD attribute to GET, the input fields from the form are posted to the query string.

- ◆ **The Anchor <A> text level HTML element.** Using HREF, you can specify a complete URL as a link in order to include a QueryString.

- ◆ **The <ISINDEX> element of the HTML HEAD.** Unlike the <FORM> element, <ISINDEX> produces one big string – not named value pairs.

- ◆ **Query strings typed explicitly in the URL.** Any user can type the QueryString that they want directly into their browser, and this string is passed in the HTTP request exactly as if it had come from one of the methods above.

Breaking this QueryString back into its component pieces is something you do over and over and again, so ASP gives you the **QueryString** collection to handle the job.

Using the QueryString Collection

The syntax for the using the QueryString collection is

```
Request.QueryString(variable)[(index)|.Count]
```

where *variable* is the name of the querystring variable whose value you want to retrieve. If multiple values were passed for this parameter, then you need *index,* which specifies *which* value you want, starting at one. (Yet almost all other objects start counting from zero. Go figure.) *Count* tells you how many values were passed for a parameter.

The catch, of course, is that you have to know what variable you are looking for. Presuming that you are expecting a parameter named "foo," you can write:

```
<%= Request.QueryString("foo") %>
```

The interesting question is: What happens when "foo" is not passed in the URL? It would be nice if Request.QueryString("foo") returned NULL, so that you could differentiate between the case when foo is not passed and the case when foo is passed as "...&foo=&...", intentionally set to the empty string. Unfortunately, Request.QueryString doesn't return NULL; it returns the empty string. Therefore, to test for the existence of a parameter, you must write:

```
<% if Request.QueryString("foo") = "" then %>
```

Remember that Request.QueryString does indeed return a string. If you are expecting foo to be a number, you might write this kind of test:

```
<% if Request.QueryString("foo") = 0 then 'WRONG! %>
```

If and only if Request.QueryString("foo") exists, then VBScript converts it to a number for comparison purposes. If it doesn't exist, then VBScript won't set it to zero for you. These are the kinds of limitations you face in VBScript, because there is only one comparison operator for equality test. (In PerlScript, there are two tests: "==" for numbers and "eq" for strings.) The correct way to write the previous query is to convert the querystring parameter to an integer explicitly:

```
<% if Cint(Request.QueryString("foo")) = 0 then 'OKAY %>
```

Manipulating Collections

The key to manipulating collections is the VBScript *for each* construct. If you aren't already familiar with the for each construct, it is a generalization of a *for next* loop. In a basic for next loop, your loop variable (often *i*, dating back to the days of FORTRAN code) assumes each of a range of numeric values. You specify the start, end, and increments of this numeric range. With for each, the loop variable iterates over whatever set you want – typically, a set of strings. The Request.QueryString collection is such a set, so you may iterate over it. The basic loop looks like this:

```
<%
for each x in request.querystring
'do whatever you need to do with each x
next
%>
```

If your code in the middle is to simply print x, you get a list of all the URL parameters. For example, you can create a complete ASP script that is simply:

```
<%
for each x in request.querystring
    response.write( x & "<BR>" & request.querystring( x ) & "<P>" )
next
%>
```

If you name this file *rq.asp* and call it as **Error! Reference source not found.**, you see this output:

```
BAR
2, 3

FOO
1
```

This may be all that you need, but it might be nice to split the multiple values of the parameter bar. This is where index and count come into play. You revise your script this way:

```
<%
for each x in request.querystring
  y = request.querystring( x ).count
  if y = 1 then
    response.write( x & "<BR>" & request.querystring( x ) & "<P>" )
  else
    for z = 1 to y
      response.write( x & "(" & z & ") = " & request.querystring( x
  )( z ) & "<BR>" )
    next
    response.write( "<P>" )
  end if
next
%>
```

Dictionary Objects

Microsoft has added a new object to the VB domain just for the sake of ASP: the scripting dictionary, called the **Dictionary** object. In Perl, this is called a hash. In JScript, there is no explicit equivalent, although you can certainly create such an object for your own use. Because name-value pairs are natural Dictionary objects, the **Request** object uses Dictionary objects extensively. If you are already familiar with how an associative array works, you may want to skip the next few paragraphs. Otherwise, we want to share a few thoughts with you.

A VBScript Dictionary object is an *associate array,* an array whose index is a string rather than a number. This string is called the *key,* and the value is called the *item.* Unlike arrays, dictionary objects are intrinsically unordered. If you want to iterate through the values, you must choose the order in which to do so. The syntax for creating a Dictionary object in VBScript is

```
Set my_hash = CreateObject("Scripting.Dictionary")
```

VBScript provides such methods as Add, Exists, Items, Keys, Remove, and RemoveAll. Because our goal here is just to familiarize you with hashes, we'll only give you an overview of what these methods do, without getting bogged down in the Syntax (refer to the VBScript Language Reference for that). Following is a list of the methods that VBScript provides:

- ◆ **Add.** Enters another element into the dictionary.

- ◆ **Exists.** Test to see if a particular key is part of the dictionary. Because you don't have an explicit range for the index as you do with a normal array, you need this function to see if a key is in the array.

- ◆ **Items.** Returns a *normal* array (one indexed by integers) consisting of all the items in the dictionary.

- ◆ **Keys.** Does the same as Items, but for the Keys.

- ◆ **Remove.** One of the joys of a Dictionary is that you can delete items at will. Deleting items out of the middle of a normal array would force you to move all other elements down, but a Dictionary has no "middle."

- ◆ **RemoveAll.** This is a shortcut for emptying the entire dictionary.

There are also four properties to a VBScript Dictionary:

- ◆ **CompareMode.** Controls how strings are compared. We won't be using this property.

- ◆ **Count.** A count of the number of items in the Dictionary. This is a helpful number to have after you have exported the keys or items of a Dictionary object into an array.

- ◆ **Item.** Retrieves the item for a specific key. The keyword *Item* is optional in VBScript.

- ◆ **Key.** Sets or retrieves a key value.

Retrieving the Entire QueryString

You can retrieve the entire QueryString through the ServerVariables, which we discuss later in this chapter, or you can simply access it via Request.QueryString with no parameters. For example:

```
Your complete QueryString is <%= Request.QueryString %>
```

Therefore, you can define your QueryString Dictionary object this way:

```
<% set QueryString = Server.CreateObject("Scripting.Dictionary") %>
<% t1 = split( Request.QueryString, "&" ) %>
<% for each x in t1
  t2 = split( x, "=" )
  QueryString.Add t2(0), t2(1)
  next %>
```

This definition has many advantages, because you get to use all the Dictionary methods, such as Exists, Items, and Keys. Therefore, this solves our problem about detecting whether or not a particular parameter was passed.

Retrieving Multiple Items with the Same Name

The syntax for the QueryString HTTP header element allows the same name to be used in more than one name-value pair, so you can have a URL like this:

```
http://server_name?foo=bar&foo=glarch
```

Now what? Does Request.QueryString("foo") return *bar* or *glarch?* To compensate for this, the QueryString collection supports Index and Count. You can see all the instances of a variable with this script:

```
<% For I = 1 To Request.QueryString("foo").Count
   Response.Write Request.QueryString("foo")(I) & "<BR>"
   Next %>
```

Form

The HTML tags <FORM> and </FORM> allow you to request information from the user. The ACTION parameter of the <FORM> tag can be GET, which produces a query string. However, ACTION is more commonly set to POST, which puts the HTML Form data (the user's responses) elsewhere in the HTTP header. In the CGI programming model, you then retrieve this data from environment variables.

One of the wonderful features of ASP is that the **Request** object makes HTML Form and query string data look the same. Everything we said previously about QueryString data applies to HTML Form data. It is accessed with the exact same syntax:

```
Request.Form(parameter)[(index)|.Count]
```

You can see the entire Form as one string with:

```
Request.Form
```

You can write some elegant and simple code by simply referencing everything as:

```
Request(parameter)
```

Let ASP figure out whether the data came from a Form or the QueryString.

Cookies

A *cookie* is information that your browser stores for the server on your workstation. The browser and the server exchange these cookies through the HTTP headers, so they are typically not too large. The virtue of the cookies lies in personalizing a Web site to your specific needs. For example, servers that are hosting online stores typically use cookies to record the items that you are considering buying.

With CGI programs, you have to dig into the HTTP header to get the cookies. This isn't too difficult, but there is no reason for it. With the Cookies collection, ASP takes care of getting the cookies for you. In Chapter 5, we discuss how to write to cookies. For now, our task is simply to read them.

As with most information passed via HTTP, cookies are name-value pairs. The Request.Cookies collection takes this one step farther – the value of the cookie may itself be a name-value pair, so that you have nested pairs. The nesting goes only one level deep, however.

The syntax for the Cookies collection is

```
Request.Cookies(cookie)[(key)|.attribute]
```

where *cookie* is the name of the cookie you want to retrieve and *key* is the name part of the name-value pair, if you created a cookie that has keys. Finally, *attribute* can be only *haskeys,* and it returns a Boolean telling you whether the cookies has keys.

If you are looking for a cookie named "foo," you simply write

```
Request.cookies("foo")
```

If such a cookie exists, the **Request** object returns it. If it does not exist, you get an empty string.

Cookies with keys are just as simple. If you have a cookie named "statistics" and a key of "age" within that, you would write

```
Request.cookies("statistics")("age")
```

Finally, because Request.cookies is a collection, you may find all the cookies with a *for each* construct, as in this example:

```
<%
for each x in request.cookies
  response.write( x & "<BR>" & request.cookies( x ) & "<P>" )
next
%>
```

The only problem with this script is that if you have a cookie with keys, it prints like this:

```
STATISTICS
AGE=29&HEIGHT=6%27
```

This is perhaps not what you wanted, so you might modify the script above to print cookies with keys differently, like so:

```
<%
for each x in request.cookies
  if not request.cookies( x ).haskeys then
    response.write( x & "<BR>" & request.cookies( x ) & "<P>" )
  else
    response.write( x & "<P>" )
    for each y in request.cookies( x )
```

```
      response.write( y & "=" & request.cookies(x)(y) & "<BR>" )
    next
    response.write( "<P>" )
  end if
next
%>
```

Server Variables

There is no end to information contained in the HTTP header, and there is also a wealth of information in the environment variables. ASP provides all this data to you in the ServerVariables collection. By now, you are familiar with the usual idiom for handling collections. You can get a list of all the items in the ServerVariables collection this way:

```
<%
for each x in request.servervariables
  response.write( x & "<BR>" & _
    request.servervariables( x ) & "<P>" )
next
%>
```

This script produces quite a list of variables. On our browser, we get the following:

```
AUTH_TYPE
CONTENT_LENGTH
CONTENT_TYPE
GATEWAY_INTERFACE
LOGON_USER
PATH_INFO
PATH_TRANSLATED
QUERY_STRING
REMOTE_ADDR
REMOTE_HOST
REQUEST_METHOD
SCRIPT_MAP
SCRIPT_NAME
SERVER_NAME
SERVER_PORT
SERVER_PORT_SECURE
SERVER_PROTOCOL
SERVER_SOFTWARE
URL
HTTP_ACCEPT
HTTP_ACCEPT_LANGUAGE
HTTP_CONNECTION
HTTP_HOST
HTTP_PRAGMA
HTTP_UA_PIXELS
```

```
HTTP_UA_COLOR
HTTP_UA_OS
HTTP_UA_CPU
HTTP_USER_AGENT
HTTP_COOKIE
```

We want to highlight a couple of these variables that we find especially useful.

SCRIPT_NAME, PATH_INFO, and QUERY_STRING

All these server variables are important when you want your script to reference itself, or when you want to pass a return URL to another ASP file. In order to get the follow-on ASP to return the user to exactly where he or she started, remember to include the QUERY_STRING parameter. For example:

```
<A HREF="<%= Request.ServerVariables("PATH_INFO") &
  Request.ServerVariables("SCRIPT_NAME") & "?" &
  Request.ServerVariables("QUERY_STRING") %>">Go Back</A>
```

REMOTE_ADDR

This server variable lets you perform your own custom IP restrictions. To limit a given page to subnet 206.138.153, for example, you would write:

```
<% if left(request.servervariables("REMOTE_ADDR"),11) =
  "206.138.153" then
'Do whatever the purpose of this ASP is.
Else %>
<H1>Sorry, access to this page is restricted to the company
  subnet</H1>
<% end if %>
```

Reasons Not to Use ServerVariables

Although the ASP ServerVariables collection is quite useful, ASP provides better ways to access much of this information, so make sure that you explore your alternatives. Specifically, you should be careful about using these ServerVariables items:

◆ QUERY_STRING. As you know from this chapter, the request.QueryString collection provides easier access to this information.

◆ HTTP_USER_AGENT. Please check out the browser capabilities component first.

◆ HTTP_COOKIE. As we discussed in this chapter, there is a request.cookies collection that parses the cookie string for you.

Summary

All the information that you may reasonably want, such as parameters from the URL, data from a Form, Cookies, or environment variables, is contained in the **Request** object. The **Request** object eliminates the need for complex string parsing to get this information, and it allows you to search multiple sources for a particular name-value pair. The **Request** object allows for multiple instances of querystring and form parameters, and it can read cookies that are themselves name-value pairs.

Chapter 4

The Server Object

IN THIS CHAPTER
In the previous chapter, you learned about the **Request** object. As you have seen, that particular piece of the ASP puzzle is critical because it is the mechanism by which you communicate with your users.

In this chapter, you learn about another critical part of ASP – the **Server** object. This object lets you extend ASP's native capabilities. Specifically, we discuss the following:

◆ Using OLE automation servers in your program code to extend the capabilities of your programs

◆ Discovering what really happens when you use an OLE object in your ASP pages

◆ Using the **Server** object to ensure that the content you create does not wreak havoc with your browser

◆ Keeping runaway processes from eating up all your resources

◆ Constructing useful net-based applications using custom objects

That's right – we're going to get into some very cool stuff in this chapter. Ready? Good.

Server Object Overview

ASP's **Server** object is your window into the operations of the Web server. In the next few sections, we discuss the built-in methods and properties of this object and how to use them.

HTMLEncode()

HTML, like any other language, has a set of rules about what is and is not legal. Occasionally, you want to do something that HTML misinterprets. The **HTMLEncode()** method takes a given string and makes sure that it is properly encoded for display in an HTML page. Here's a good example.

Say you want to display the text *<output>* in your Web page. If you put that text in an HTML page and view it in a browser, your text will not appear. This is because of the way that HTML is structured.

All formatting commands in HTML are called *tags*. Each tag begins with a left angle bracket (<) and ends with a right angle bracket (>). For example, to display a piece of text centered on the page, you would write

```
<center> Your text goes here </center>
```

If you put the text *<output>* in your page, then your Web browser thinks that it is the beginning of an HTML tag. Therefore, it treats the text as a formatting command and does not display it. For example, the HTML code

```
This <output> is a <output> test.
```

is displayed by your browser as

```
This is a test.
```

The **HTMLEncode()** method, however, fixes this problem. The ASP code

```
<%
myString = Server.HTMLEncode("This <output> is a <output> test.")
%>

<% =myString %>
```

shows up in your browser as

```
This <output> is a <output> test.
```

As you can see, the **HTMLEncode()** method is a pretty handy feature to have. In fact, our rule of thumb is to run any dynamic output though this function, as long as we are not intending to embed HTML within it. You see a good use of this a little later in the chapter when we go over some of the examples.

URLEncode()

Just as the content within an HTML page has rules governing it, so do the actual URLs that point to a page. In the previous chapter, we touched upon how parameters are passed to a Web page via a URL. In this section, we discuss how to make sure that those parameters don't confuse your browser.

Say that you are entering data in an HTML form, and you type the string **The directory is /temp/files.** What do you think would happen if you tried to pass that information to a Web page via a URL such as the following?

```
Http://www.sweathog.com/test.asp?text=the directory is /temp/files
```

Assuming the browser didn't choke on the spaces in the URL, it would certainly get confused by the forward slashes (/). It would think that you are trying to reference a page within the /temp/files directory. Most likely, this would give you an error because that directory probably does not exist.

Fortunately, HTTP has a way to handle this. It is called the *URL encoding scheme*. Basically, this scheme defines a number of characters that are not legal in a URL and what characters can be used in their place. For example, in a properly encoded URL, spaces are represented by the plus sign (+). Therefore, the expression *this is a test* would be encoded as *this+is+a+test*. This, of course, means that the plus sign must also be encoded so as not to be confused with a space!

The way this substitution is accomplished is simple. Special characters are represented by a percent sign (%), followed by the hexadecimal number representing their value. For example, the previous code of

```
Http://www.sweathog.com/test.asp?text=the directory is /temp/files
```

is correctly encoded as

```
Http://www.sweathog.com/test.asp?the+directory+is+%2Ftemp%2Ffiles
```

NOTE: The hexadecimal representation of the forward slash character is 2F.

Normally, you would have to write logic to correctly encode this string. The **URLEncode()** method, however, takes care of this for you. For example, the previous string would be encoded with the following:

```
<% myString = Server.URLEncode("the directory is /temp/files") %>
<% =myString %>
```

This particular function is extremely important as you begin to generate HTML with embedded URL tags because it keeps your client browsers from getting hopelessly confused. (After all, nobody likes a confused browser!)

MapPath()

As you have already learned, every virtual path on a given Web server maps to a real directory on a hard drive. For example, the path */Scripts* may map to *c:\Webshare\Scripts*.

The **MapPath()** method returns the physical directory to which a given virtual directory is mapped. For example, the code

```
<% foo = Server.MapPath("/Scripts/whois.asp") %>
<% =foo %>
```

produces the output

```
c:\Webshare\Scripts\whois.asp
```

You may be wondering what practical application such a function has. Actually, this can be quite useful. For example, you want to have a button on your Web page that displays the ASP source code that generated the page. How do you do it? It's easy. You use the **MapPath()** function to return the real name of the script, and then you open it, use **HTMLEncode()** to encode it, and then print it to the screen. The following example shows you how:

```
<html>
<body>

<center><h1>The source code is... </h1></center>

<hr>

<%

sRealFile = Server.MapPath("/temp/urlTest.asp")

Set fs = Server.CreateObject("Scripting.FileSystemObject")
Set inFile = fs.OpenTextFile( sRealFile )

sAllText = inFile.ReadAll()

inFile.Close()

sOutput = Server.HTMLEncode( sAllText )

%>

<pre>

<% =sOutput %>

</pre>

</body>
</html>
```

This code is not as complicated as it may seem. The first seven lines print a header and a horizontal line. Next, we get the real path to the given ASP file using the **MapPath()** method. We then get a handle to that file and open it. Next, we read into a string the contents of the entire file. Finally, we encode the contents and display them.

It is not important that you understand everything going on in this script, just that you see the role that **MapPath()** plays. We cover some of the other things shortly.

CreateObject()

ASP has many helpful features built into it, which make it nice to use. The CreateObject() method, however, gives ASP so much additional power that it goes from being "nice" to use to "unbelievably cool" to use.

This particular function allows you to instantiate an OLE object within your ASP script.

"Huh?" you ask.

Okay, let's start from the beginning.

OLE AT A GLANCE

Several years ago, Microsoft invented a standard that allows one application to call the native functions of another application. For example, you can write a Visual Basic application that creates a Word document, without rewriting pieces of Word.

This is accomplished through a technology known as *Object Linking and Embedding* (OLE). It's a complex topic, but basically it boils down to this: When you create your application, you can choose to expose some of its internal structures and functions to other programs. You are, in fact, creating an *interface* to your application. This interface allows other applications to use key features of your program without having to re-invent them. This can be a huge time saver for a developer.

This process of controlling another application is called *OLE automation*. When your program allows such control, it is called an *OLE automation server*.

All OLE automation servers are assigned a globally unique string known as a *class ID* (CLSID). This string is typically something like {*000209FE-0000-0000-C000-000000000046*}.

As you can imagine, it would be terribly difficult to have to remember the CLSID for a given server. Fortunately, you can also reference a given server by its *program ID* (progID). The progID for a server is usually something more understandable, such as *Word.Document*.

With these concepts in mind, we are ready to talk about how OLE really fits in with ASP.

A Lot More OLE, A Little Later

If you are wondering how to write your own OLE components for ASP, we go over the process in great depth in Part IV of this book. It is surprisingly fun and simple. For now, though, you should concentrate on some of the more basic parts of ASP. They are more important to you in the long run.

APPLICATIONS IN ASP

The **CreateObject()** function allows you to create a handle to an OLE automation server. This means that not only can you use the built-in features of ASP in your program code, but you can use the capabilities of hundreds of other applications that allow this type of control. This gives you the ability to construct unbelievably powerful applications in a short period of time. You just have to pick and choose what features you want.

You may not realize it, but you have already used this feature. Remember the script we wrote to print out the source code to an ASP file? It contained the following line:

```
Set fs = Server.CreateObject("Scripting.FileSystemObject")
```

In this case, we have passed the progID of *Scripting.FileSystemObject* to the **CreateObject()** function. This means that the variable *fs* is actually an instance of the OLE object referenced by the progID *Scripting.FileSystemObject*. (This particular OLE component allows us to access a file from the hard disk.)

When you think about it, you can do many cool things with this particular function. For example, you can write a script that dynamically generates a usage summary for your site from data you store in a database. This can be done by instantiating (creating an instance of) an MS Word object and using its native functions to create a well-formatted report. You can even create an e-mail object to mail the report to your boss. Imagine . . . you can run all of this from a Web browser anywhere in the world!

Admit it: That's awfully compelling stuff.

The ScriptTimeout Property

Few things in life are guaranteed. Unfortunately, the existence of software bugs is one of them. No matter how good a job you do testing your applications, they are going to have bugs. Bugs in a Web program are nastier to deal with than errors in normal programs because they often lead to your server becoming unusable.

The most common occurrence of this is with runaway scripts. These chunks of program code execute for what seems like an infinite amount of time and chew valuable system resources. Unfortunately, they are unavoidable in a Web environment because too many factors are beyond your control as a programmer. If, for example, a few packets of data get lost on the way to your server, your application could hang while waiting for them.

This being the case, it would be nice to tell your server to terminate any scripts that have been running for longer than a specified maximum time. This is exactly what the **ScriptTimeout** property is for.

This attribute specifies, in seconds, how long a script can run before the system terminates it. However, you need to be aware of a couple things.

First, there is a restriction to the value you can assign here. Back in Chapter 1, we discussed the registry settings for ASP. We covered a setting named **ScriptTimeout**, which performs the same function as the **ScriptTimeout** property and has a default value of 90 seconds. You cannot set the **ScriptTimeout** attribute of the **Server** object to a value less than the value in that registry key. In other words, the registry key item holds the minimum amount of time to which any script can be limited.

The next caveat for using this property is that it not take effect while a component is running. In other words, the server waits until it is done running scripts that have already started before it sets this value. If it were not this way, then you could immediately terminate a script other than your own simply by setting this value to a number less than the number of seconds the other script has been running.

Some Truly Useful Examples

Now that we have covered all the basic parts of the **Server** object, it's time to go through some examples to help you put it all together.

NETUTILS.DLL

While writing this book, we decided to create our own ASP components for you to use. In fact, in Part IV, we show you how we did this. For now, however, we are just going to introduce these components so that you can begin using them.

The objects we talk about in this section are in a file named **netutils.dll**. You can find this file in the **\components** directory on the companion CD-ROM.

To install the components in this file, copy the **netutils.dll** file from the CD-ROM to the **\cmpnts** subdirectory of your ASP tree. For example, if you are using Windows 95, your directory is

```
c:\Program Files\Websvr\System\ASP\cmpnts
```

Once the file is copied, open a DOS box, go to that directory, and type

```
regsvr32 netutils.dll
```

That's all there is to it! You can now use these components in your scripts.

The TCPClient Component

The first component we want to talk about is the NETUTILS.TCPCLIENT component. This object lets you create a TCP/IP client connection to any host from within your ASP script. There are a number of useful things that this capability can do for you. For example, you can create a program that enables you to read your e-mail from within a Web browser. (In fact, we show you how to do that in another two sentences.)

Before we delve into our first example, we want to acquaint you with the various methods of this object and how to use them.

CONNECTWITH SERVER, PORT

This method connects you to a specific server and port and is the first one you call after you create an instance of this object. For example, the following snippet of code creates a TCP/IP client connection to the HTTP port of a remote machine:

```
<%
  set tcp = Server.CreateObject("NETUTILS.TCPCLIENT")
  tcp.ConnectWith "www.microsoft.com", 80
%>
```

ISCONNECTED()

This function returns 1 if you are currently connected to a machine, or 0 if you are not. For example, the following code:

```
<%
  set tcp = Server.CreateObject("NETUTILS.TCPCLIENT")

  Response.Write( "Connection status: " & tcp.IsConnected() )

  tcp.ConnectWith "www.microsoft.com", 80

  Response.Write( "Connection status: " & tcp.IsConnected() )
%>
```

prints:

```
Connection status: 0
Connection status: 1
```

This Is Odd

For reasons we don't quite understand, you cannot use parentheses with the ConnectWith function. If, for example, you try to do the following:

```
tcp.ConnectWith("www.microsoft.com", 80)
```

you get an error. We are not entirely sure why this is so, but we are leaning heavily towards calling it a bug in ASP. In any event, just be careful.

Only Sadists Type What They Can Steal!

All the source code for this and every other example in the book can be found in the appropriate sub-directory under the **\chapters** directory of the companion CD-ROM.

GET()

The **Get()** function returns, as a string, a line of data received from the connection. The following code gets the current date and time from a server running a Network Time Protocol Daemon (NTPD) process:

```
<%
 set tcp = Server.CreateObject("NETUTILS.TCPCLIENT")
 tcp.ConnectWith "jolt.eng.umd.edu", 13
 sTime = tcp.Get()
%>

The current date and time is: <% =sTime %>
```

The output of this script will be something like:

```
The current date and time is: Sat Jan 18 14:55:24 1997
```

SEND(DATA)

This function – as you may have guessed – sends a string of data to the server. Please note, however, that this function does *not* automatically append a carriage return/line feed pair. If you require that, then you have to add it yourself.

Example 1 – The WHOIS Client

Now that you have been formally introduced to the **NETUTILS.TCPCLIENT** component, it's time to put that knowledge to some good use. In this first example, we show you how to write a script that gets WHOIS information from the InterNIC.

A BRIEF EXPLANATION

The Internet is notorious for a lack of central control. There are, however, a few key exceptions. One of these exceptions has to do with domain name registration. There is a central authority, named the *Internet Network Information Center* (InterNIC), that keeps track of all domain names and makes sure that people don't get duplicate entries. Without this service, machines that translate the word-based names of servers (such as www.sweathog.com) into their specific IP addresses (such as 207.96.68.194) wouldn't know what to do when they got conflicts.

What's In A Name

In recent months, a number of organizations have challenged the InterNIC's right to be the central authority over domain names. They think that other organizations should also be able to assign that information. As we write this, there is a pitched battle going on to see if the InterNIC remains the sole central authority over this information.

The InterNIC maintains a server from which you can look up this information. This server is named *rs.internic.net,* and the protocol used to get the information is called the *WHOIS protocol.*

THE PROCESS
Getting WHOIS information is easy. All you do is connect to port 43 of the machine rs.internic.net and send it one line of data representing the string you want to look up. For example, if you want to look up the information about the domain sweathog.com, then you would connect to the InterNIC and send the string *sweathog.com.*

THE CODE
As you can see, the process by which you retrieve this information is very straight-forward. The code is just as simple. Say you want to write a script to get the domain information about the sweathog.com domain. The following script would do it for you:

```
<html>
<body>

<%
 CRLF = CHR(13) & CHR(10)

 set tcp = Server.CreateObject( "NETUTILS.TCPCLIENT" )
 tcp.ConnectWith "rs.internic.net", 43
 tcp.Send( "sweathog.com" & CRLF )

 Do While (tcp.IsConnected() = 1)
  sWhoisData = sWhoisData & tcp.Get() & CRLF
 Loop

%>

<plaintext>

<% =sWhoisData %>
```

Of course, this script needs a nicer interface in order to be truly useful.

In Case You Were Wondering

The *sweathog.com* domain to which we keep referring is actually owned by one of us. Which one? Go get the WHOIS information and see!

THE WHOLE SHEBANG

This kind of application really screams for a simple frames interface. In this part of the example, we walk you through creating it. The following picture (see Figure 4-1) shows what the application looks like when it's done.

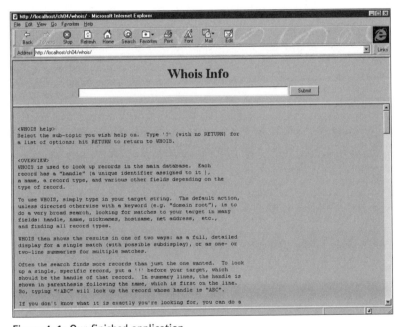

Figure 4-1: Our finished application

There is nothing particularly difficult about this interface. First, we need to construct the frames. This is accomplished using the following code:

```
<html>

<frameset rows=110,*>
  <frame name=EntryForm src=form.htm>
  <frame name=ResultArea src=whois.asp>
</frameset>

</html>
```

As you can see, we named the top frame **EntryForm** and are displaying the file **form.htm** in it. The bottom frame, named **ResultArea**, contains data from the **whois.asp** script. The source for **form.htm** is as follows:

```
<html>
<body>

<form method=GET target=ResultArea action=whois.asp>

<center>

<h1>Whois Info</h1>

<p>

<input name=lookup size=100></input> <input type=submit></input>

</center>

</form>
</body>
</html>
```

All this form does is accept a string in the **lookup** text box, call the code in **whois.asp,** and display the results in the **ResultArea** frame. The real meat of this application is in the **whois.asp** file. That code is as follows:

```
<html>
<body>

<plaintext>

<%
 CRLF = CHR(13) & CHR(10)

 set tcp = Server.CreateObject( "NETUTILS.TCPCLIENT" )
 tcp.ConnectWith "rs.internic.net", 43
 tcp.Send( Request.QueryString("lookup") & CRLF )

 Do While (tcp.IsConnected() = 1)
 sWhoisData = sWhoisData & tcp.Get() & CRLF
 Loop

%>

<% =sWhoisData %>
```

This code is identical to the code we described earlier, with one exception. The line that sends that actual request,

```
tcp.Send( Request.QueryString("lookup") & CRLF )
```

now gets the string to send from the **lookup** parameter. Other than that, it's the same code.

The E-Mail Component

The next component we want to introduce you to is the NETUTILS.EMAIL component. This object enables you to read, send, and delete Internet e-mail straight from your Web browser. This component has some interesting implications.

We wrote this component out of necessity. You see, we both work for a growing consulting firm and often have to travel to the offices of our clients. Most of the firms and agencies with which we deal have a firewall that allows only HTTP traffic. That means we cannot simply install an e-mail client because its packets never get to the outside world.

What we did instead was write this component so that we can connect to a Web page (through the normal HTTP port) and still read our e-mail. This gives us the ability to go anywhere there is a Web browser (since our primary line of consulting is the Internet, that's everywhere!), and we are guaranteed to be able to get and respond to our e-mail.

In the following sections, we explain all the pieces of this component and then take you through the steps to build a basic e-mail application on the Web.

CONNECT(SERVER, USERID, PASSWORD)

The first method of our component is the one that actually connects and authenticates users to their POP3 e-mail server. The following code snippet illustrates this:

```
<%
  set email = Server.CreateObject("NETUTILS.EMAIL")
  email.Connect "myMailServer.com" "jschmoe" "myPassword"
%>
```

Assuming that the parameters being passed are correct, this method establishes an active connection to the POP3 server.

MSGCOUNT()

After you successfully connect to the server, you need to know how many messages are waiting for you. You get this bit of information with the **MsgCount()** method.

POP What?

Post Office Protocol 3 (POP3) is the most common means by which e-mail is received over the Internet. This protocol, however, only provides the ability to read and delete e-mail. If you want to send e-mail, you have to use the Simple Mail Transfer Protocol (SMTP).

HEADER(MESSAGE, HEADER)

Each e-mail note has a set of lines at the beginning called the *header*. This information contains important data such as who sent the e-mail, what the subject is, what date and time the note was sent, and to whom the message was sent.

The **Header()** function lets you retrieve information specific to any of those items for a given e-mail note. For example, if you wanted to get the subject line for message number three, you would use the following line of code:

```
sSubject = email.Header(3, "SUBJECT")
```

The following list describes the most common items you want to retrieve:

◆ FROM. The person from whom the e-mail comes.

◆ TO. The person to whom the e-mail is addressed.

◆ SUBJECT. The subject line of the note.

◆ DATE. The date and time the note was sent.

NOTE: These items *must* be in capitals. If you send *Subject* instead of *SUBJECT*, you do not get any information back. Other than that, you can specify any field that exists within a normal e-mail header.

BODY(MESSAGE)

Once you have some basic information about a message, you probably want to read the body of it. This is done with the **Body()** method. This function takes a number representing the message you want to read and returns the entire contents of the message as a string. For example, the following line of code returns the body of message number three:

```
sBody = email.Body(3)
```

DELETE(MESSAGE)

Eventually, you want to delete messages you have read. The **Delete()** method deletes the message indicated by the number in the *Message* parameter. For example, to delete message number 3, simply type

```
email.Delete(3)
```

QUIT()

When you want to close the session with the e-mail server, call the **Quit()** method.

SENDMAIL(SERVER, SENDER, RECIPIENT, DATA)

As we mentioned earlier, POP3 provides no means by which to send an e-mail note. To do that, you have to connect to an SMTP server and use SMTP. The **SendMail()** method does just that. It connects to the server pointed to by the *Server* parameter, sends mail from *Sender* to *Recipient* containing the string pointed to by *Data,* and then disconnects. The following code illustrates this:

```
<%
 sData = "Great book! I loved it!"
 sServer = "jolt.eng.umd.edu"
 sSender = "jschmoe@noplace.com"
 sRecipient = "drensin@noblestar.com"

 set email = Server.CreateObject( "NETUTILS.EMAIL" )
 email.SendMail sServer, sSender, sRecipient, sData
%>
```

Your e-mail note can, of course, be as long as you want. We just chose a small one to make the code more readable. Also, because sending mail is one self-contained transaction, there is no need to call **Quit()**, **Connect()**, or any other method.

Example 2 – The POP3 Client

Now that you know the basics of using the **NETUTILS.EMAIL** component, it's time to construct something useful. The following application allows you to log in to any e-mail server on which you have an account and retrieve your mail. We do not add the ability to send or delete any mail until we cover the **Session** object in Chapter 6. For now, this program is read-only.

When the application is done, it will look like Figure 4-2.

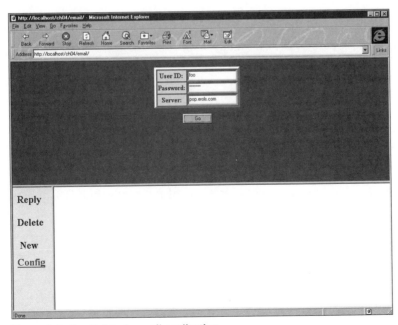

Figure 4-2: Our finished e-mail application

THE PARTS

There are several small pages that we have to construct for this application:

- ◆ **The Configuration page.** This page is where you enter your account information.

- ◆ **The Frame page.** This page sets up all the frames for this application.

- ◆ **The Headers page.** This page displays the headers for all your e-mail notes.

- ◆ **The Menu page.** This page contains the menu from which you can send, delete, or reply to e-mail. (Not all the options on this page are enabled until Chapter 6.)

- ◆ **The Body page.** This page displays the actual contents of a selected e-mail note.

In the next few sections, we cover each part of this application in some depth.

THE FRAME PAGE   This application is divided into three frames. To do this, you need to create a page with two frame sets. The following code illustrates this:

```
<html>

<frameset rows=50%,*>
 <frame name=headerFrame src=config.htm></frame>

 <frameset cols=100,*>
      <frame name=menuFrame src=menu.asp></frame>
      <frame name=bodyFrame src=body.asp></frame>
 </frameset>

</frameset>

</html>
```

After your frames are set up, you can move on to some of the other supporting pages.

THE MENU PAGE   The menu along the left side of the application is simple to generate. Here's the code:

```
<html>
<body bgcolor=yellow>

<center>

<h2>
```

```
<a href= >Reply </a> <br><br>
<a href= >Delete</a> <br><br>
<a href= >New </a> <br><br>
<a href=config.htm target=headerFrame>Config</a> <br><br>

</h2>

</center>

</body>
</html>
```

Notice that the first three items, *Reply, Delete,* and *New,* do not do anything yet. We get to them later. For now, the only important part is the last item, *Config.* When you click on it, it reloads the configuration screen in the top frame.

THE CONFIGURATION PAGE   The configuration page is where you enter your e-mail account information. This page is just an HTML table with three input boxes. Here's the code:

```
<html>
<body bgcolor=blue>

<form method=GET action=headers.asp>

<center>

<table border=5>

 <tr>
 <th bgcolor=cyan>User ID:</th>
 <td> <input name=userid> </input> </td>
 </tr>

 <tr>
 <th bgcolor=cyan>Password:</th>
 <td><input type=password name=passwd></input></td>
 </tr>

 <tr>
 <th bgcolor=cyan>Server:</th>
 <td><input name=server></input></td>
 </tr>

</table>

<br>
```

```
<input type=submit value=Go></input>

</center>

</form>
</body>
</html>
```

When the user clicks on the **Go** button, the form calls the **headers.asp** file with the parameters *userid, passwd,* and *server.*

Which brings you to the next page . . . the headers page.

THE HEADERS PAGE   On this page, things start to get interesting. In the first block of code, we are doing three basic things:

1. Retrieving the parameters passed from the configuration page

2. Connecting to the mail server

3. Getting a count of all the mail in our account

Once we have this information, we iterate through all the messages and get the sender and subject for each. We then use those facts to construct a row in a table for each message. It's all straightforward, with two exceptions.

First, there are two lines that seem to be constructing a hideously long string. What they are actually doing is constructing the HTML for each row of the table. The reason why they are so long is that they contain an HREF that passes all the necessary parameters to the body page. When we rewrite this code in Chapter 6, you see how we can cut out most of this nonsense by using session variables.

The second item that may seem out of place in this code is the use of a hitherto unmentioned object named **Response**. The **Response** object simply constructs data to be passed back to the browser. It is the subject of the next chapter, but for now you can think of that line of code as just printing the final HTML for each table row.

The complete script is as follows:

```
<html>
<body bgcolor=blue>

<%

CRLF = CHR(13) & CHR(10)

set email = Server.CreateObject("NETUTILS.EMAIL")

sServer = Request.QueryString( "server" )
sUserID = Request.QueryString( "userid" )
sPasswd = Request.QueryString( "passwd" )
```

```
email.Connect sServer, sUserID, sPasswd

mCount = email.MsgCount( )

%>

<center>

<table border=1>
<tr bgcolor=cyan><th colspan=2>From</th><th>Subject</th></tr>

<%

For i = 1 to mCount

 sSender = Server.HTMLEncode( email.Header( i, "FROM" ) )
 sSubject = Server.HTMLEncode( email.Header( i, "SUBJECT" ) )

 sGoTo = "body.asp?server=" & sServer & "&user=" & sUserID &
 "&password=" & sPasswd & "&message=" & i

 sHREF = "<a href=" & sGoTo & " target=bodyFrame><img src=mail.bmp
 width=25 height=25></img></a>"

 Response.Write( "<tr bgcolor=white><td>" & sHREF & "</td><td>" &
 sSender & "</td><td>" & sSubject & "</td></tr>" & CRLF )

Next

email.Quit( )

%>

</table>

</body>
</html>
```

THE BODY PAGE   The last part of this application is the code that retrieves the body text of a particular message. Once again, this is not difficult. All we do is get the parameters passed from the headers page, create a new e-mail object, connect to the server, and then get the body of the desired message.

The only interesting thing here is the use of an *If* statement. Any attempt to pass an empty server string to the **Connect()** method fails, and our next use of the e-mail object generates an error. We can prevent this problem by making sure that the *server* parameter is not empty.

Once again, the complete code is as follows:

```
<html>
<body bgcolor=white>
```

```
<%

sServer = Request.QueryString("server")
sUser = Request.QueryString("user")
sPassword = Request.QueryString("password")
iMsg = Request.QueryString("message")

If ( Len(sServer) > 0 ) Then

  set email = Server.CreateObject("NETUTILS.EMAIL")
  email.Connect sServer, sUser, sPassword

  sBody = email.Body( iMsg )

  email.Quit()

End If

%>

<plaintext>

<% =sBody %>
```

Summary

In this chapter, you learned about some important techniques to make your Web application more usable and stable. These techniques include ways to condition your data so as not to confuse your Web browser, as well as ways to use external software components to do things beyond the basic capabilities of ASP.

You were also introduced to some components that we have written (and which we eventually show you how to write), and you were shown how to use them to create some truly useful programs.

Chapter 5

The Response Object

IN THIS CHAPTER

The **Response** object is your tool for writing output to the HTTP client. Most output is handled through this object. There are a number of methods and properties to this object, because HTTP output can be fairly complex. You need a way to write to the HTTP headers as well as the HTTP body. Furthermore, it would be nice if you did not have to remember the syntax of all the HTTP header elements. The **Response** object handles all this for you.

In this chapter, we first discuss the pieces and syntax of the **Response** Object, and then we use it in some detailed examples. The main points we cover are:

- The architecture of HTTP headers

- An overview of the **Response** object structure

- The **Response** object methods

- The properties of the **Response** object

- The cookie collection of the **Response** object

- In-depth examples of using the **Response** object

The Response Object Overview

The **Response** object is structured a little bit differently than the **Request** object. The **Request** object is simply a collection of five other objects. In contrast, the **Response** object itself has many methods and properties. It contains only one object, the **Cookie** object, which is, in fact, a collection. We focus on the Response methods first.

Methods

By far, the most important method to the **Response** object is the **Write()** method, which outputs data to the HTML body. Entire applications can be written using just the **Write()** method of the **Response** object. Don't let the fact that we have listed all the methods of the **Response** object in alphabetical order confuse you. We do that so you can easily reference them as you need them.

AddHeader()

The **AddHeader()** method adds a new HTTP header to the response. This is helpful when you want to send an HTTP header that Internet Information Server (IIS) is not otherwise providing for you. The syntax is

```
Response.AddHeader name, value
```

For example, to include a "Transfer-Encoding" header, you do the following:

```
<% Response.AddHeader "Transfer-Encoding", "chunked" %>
```

Because you are sending a header to the client, you must make your calls to **AddHeader()** before you send any other HTML output to the client. For example, even this is no good:

```
<!DOCTYPE HTML PUBLIC "-//W3C//DTD HTML 3.2 Final//EN">
<% Response.AddHeader "Transfer-Encoding", "chunked" %>
```

You must call **Addheader()** first. This, however, is okay:

```
<%
Set Conn = server.createobject("ADODB.Connection")
Conn.open("My_ODBC_Datasource")
Response.AddHeader "Transfer-Encoding", "chunked"
%>

<!DOCTYPE HTML PUBLIC "-//W3C//DTD HTML 3.2 Final//EN">
```

AddHeader() does not override an existing header. For example, the following command does not work:

```
<% Response.AddHeader "Content-Type", "text/plain" %>
```

This command has no effect because the "Content-Type" header is already set elsewhere in ASP. (Refer to "ContentType," later in the chapter.)

AppendToLog()

If you need to write an entry to the IIS logs, you may do so with the **AppendToLog()** method. The syntax is

```
Response.AppendToLog string
```

where *string* is whatever you want to append to the log. For example:

```
<% Response.AppendToLog "This is a test of the AppendToLog method of
  the Response Object" %>
```

Because IIS buffers output to the log, you do not see this entry immediately. If you want, you can stop and start the IIS Service to force all log entries to be completed. The previous script causes a log entry something like this:

```
127.0.0.1, -, 1/26/97, 0:05:45, W3SVC, AFEDORCHEK_HOME, 127.0.0.1,
0, 244, 309, 200, 0, GET, /Response.AppendToLog.asp, This is test
of the AppendToLog method of the Response Object.
```

There are a couple important caveats here. First, you are limited to 80 characters, so be concise. Second, you cannot put any commas in your string. This is because IIS uses commas as delimiters in the log file.

The **AppendToLog()** method works equally well when you have configured IIS to log to an ODBC datasource. The string that you append appears in the *parameters* column of the log table. In SQL Server, this is created as a varchar(255) column. You might hope that both the restriction on comma use and the 80 character limit wouldn't apply for database logging, but no such luck. APS enforces the restrictions regardless of whether or not you are logging to a file.

BinaryWrite()

Everything we have shown you thus far in this book has revolved around sending text data back to the client browser. The truth is that many times you may want to send binary data, too. This is what the **BinaryWrite()** method is for. This function takes a variant as its only parameter. For example:

```
<% Response.BinaryWrite myBinaryVariable %>
```

At this point, you may be wondering just when you want to send binary data. Say that you decide that you want to write a Java applet that downloads files from your server. The easiest way to write this application is to use ASP to send the file to the client via the **BinaryWrite()** method. After all, why would you want to write a custom server module just to talk to your applet? You wouldn't. In fact, you can use this method to implement any file downloading scheme you may want. The point here is not to bore you with such details, but simply to point out that this function is more useful than it may at first appear.

Clear()

The **Clear()** method erases the HTML Buffer. This is useful if you have some custom error handling. In case of an error, you may want to show a custom error page. What, however, if you have already written out lots of HTML before you find the error? That's where **Clear()** comes into play. This method takes no parameters, so the syntax is merely

```
Response.Clear
```

For example:

```
<% Response.Buffer = TRUE %>
<!DOCTYPE HTML PUBLIC "-//W3C//DTD HTML 3.2 Final//EN">
<TITLE>Response.Clear</TITLE>
You should not see this text.
<% Response.Clear %>
This should be the first line.
```

Note that you must make sure that buffered output is on in order for the **Clear()** method to have any effect. (We get to that when we cover the properties of the **Response** object.)

End()

The **End()** method is a rather strange function to be buried in the **Response** object. It terminates the execution of your script, much like the end command in most programming languages, and flushes the output buffer (assuming you are using buffered output). **End()** takes no parameters. For example:

```
<!DOCTYPE HTML PUBLIC "-//W3C//DTD HTML 3.2 Final//EN">
<TITLE>"Response.End</TITLE>
This is before Response.End is called
<% Response.AppendToLog "This is before Response.End is called" %>
<% Response.End %>
This is after Response.End is called
<% REM The line below doesn't execute %>
<% Response.AppendToLog "This is after Response.End is called" %>
```

This complete script returns only the line "This is before Response.End is called" to the client browser. The second line of text is not sent, and the second Response.AppendToLog does not execute. The log contains only the "before" entry.

Flush()

Whereas **Clear()** deletes all HTML in the buffer, **Flush()** immediately sends it to the client. Like **Clear()**, it also takes no parameters. Here's an example:

```
<% Response.Buffer = TRUE %>

<!DOCTYPE HTML PUBLIC "-//W3C//DTD HTML 3.2 Final//EN">
<TITLE>Response.Flush</TITLE>

You will see this text.

<% Response.Flush %>
This line will not appear in the browser.
<% Response.Clear %>
```

If you have decided to use buffered output, **Flush()** gives you a way to push data to the client incrementally after you have done whatever checking you want to do.

Redirect()

The **Redirect()** method instructs the client browser to connect to another page. A good place to use this is in database updates. You may have a script that simply conducts some database transactions and then sends the browser to another ASP file. The syntax is

```
Response.Redirect URL
```

where *URL* is the Uniform Resource Locator to which you want to send the client browser. For example:

```
<% URL = Server.URLEncode("my_asp.asp?topic=Response Object")
Response.Redirect(URL) %>
```

This method causes the body content of your document to be ignored, so if you write

```
<!DOCTYPE HTML PUBLIC "-//W3C//DTD HTML 3.2 Final//EN">
<TITLE>"Response.End</TITLE>

This is before Response.Redirect is called

<% URL = Server.URLEncode("my_asp.?topic=Response Object")
Response.Redirect(URL) %>
```

then the client never sees "This is before Response.Redirect is called."

Write()

The **Write()** method sends its one parameter, a variant, to the current HTTP output. Therefore, the syntax is simply

```
Response.Write variant
```

where *variant* is the data that you want written to the HTTP output. For example:

```
<% Response.write "Hello World!" %>
```

As with all VBScript procedures, you may enclose your argument in parentheses, so the following commands are equivalent:

```
<% Response.write "Hello World!" %>
<% Response.write( "Hello World!" ) %>
```

> ## You Used To Be Able To Do This!
>
> The fact that **Redirect()** ignores your body text is a little annoying. What if you want to display a message to the user while your application is loading or a database transaction is processing? To do this, you need to use a little HTML chicanery. The following code illustrates:
>
> ```
> <META HTTP-EQUIV=REFRESH CONTENT="0; URL=myOtherPage.asp">
> <html>
> <body>
> 
> <h2>Loading the application ...</h2>
> 
> </body>
> </html>
> ```
>
> This code immediately loads the *myOtherPage.asp* page but displays the body until the output from the other page is ready. Pretty cool!

We are using string literals in the previous code, but you can use any variant, such as in this example:

```
<% Response.write "Your IP address is " & Request.ServerVariables
  ("REMOTE_ADDR") %>
```

Note the use of the concatenation operator & in the previous code. Because the **Write()** method accepts only a single parameter, you must concatenate multiple parameters into one variant.

ALTERNATE WRITE SYNTAX

The <%= %> ASP syntax for outputting a variant to the current HTTP output is merely a shorthand for the **Write()** method. Which you choose depends on your preference for creating readable code. When **Write()** is the only ASP command inside a string of HTML, the <%= %> is more readable:

```
<TABLE WIDTH=<%= site_width %> HEIGHT=100 BGCOLOR=<%= site_color %>
```

However, when you have just a bit of HTML inside of many scripting commands, **Write()** enhances your readability:

```
<%
do while not rs.eof
response.write rs("column1")
rs.movenext
loop
%>
```

You are also contrained to using only **Write()** when your scripts are contained in the <SCRIPT> ... </SCRIPT> HTML tags.

USING ESCAPE SEQUENCES

Write() is an ASP command, so it must be contained in the delimiters <% and %>. What if you want to pass %> as part of the variant to **Write()**? Clearly, this won't work:

```
<% REM the script below is wrong.
response.write "Here's what percent-greater than looks like: %>"
'More scripting commands here
%>
```

The %> embedded in the string terminates the ASP command; therefore, ASP doesn't see the final quote terminating the string, and so you get an error:

```
Microsoft VBScript compilation error '800a0409'
Unterminated string constant
/Response.asp, line 5
response.write "Here's what percent-greater than looks like:
————————-^
```

The correct approach is to use the \> escape sequence to include the %>:

```
response.write "Here's what percent-greater than looks like: %\>"
```

VBSCRIPT VARIANT LIMITS

Because VBScript limits static strings to 1,022 characters, you get an *Out of memory* error if you try to directly write a string, 1,023 characters or more. For example, the following code fails when you put 1,023 x's in it:

```
Response.write("xxx...xxx")
```

Instead, you must first assign the string to a variable, and then you can output it. Of course, you can't assign the entire string to a variable, either. Foo = "xxx...xxx" fails, where x is repeated 1,023 times. You have to split it in your assignment statements, too, such as the following:

```
foo = "some long string less than 1023 characters"
foo = foo + "some more text that makes foo longer than 1022"
```

JScript does not suffer this limitation.

WriteBlock()

If you are one of those people who has already read the online documentation for ASP, then you will, no doubt, notice that the **WriteBlock()** method appears nowhere in it. This is because it is completely undocumented. We found it by accident when we got a cryptic ASP error and began digging a little further. Needless to say, use of this function is not supported by Microsoft. That having been said, let's press on.

The **WriteBlock()** method prints a block of HTML from your script. A block is any text outside the ASP delimiters; in other words, something delimited by %> and <%. Blocks are identified by numbers, starting at 0. This method is not normally used within scripts themselves but is called implicitly. However, you can use it if you have a use for it. Consider the following example:

```
<!DOCTYPE HTML PUBLIC "-//W3C//DTD HTML 3.2 Final//EN">
<TITLE>"Response.Writeblock</TITLE>
<%%>This is
block 1. <%%>This is
block 2. <% Response.Writeblock(2)
Response.Writeblock(1)
%>
```

The output of this script is

```
This is block 1. This is block 2. This is block 2. This is block 1.
```

Properties

The **Response** object has five properties, each of which is set with the standard syntax:

```
Response.Property = value
```

You can retrieve the value of the property simply by referencing the property name:

```
Response.Property
```

For example, to display the current values of all the **Response** properties, you might use this simple ASP script:

```
<!DOCTYPE HTML PUBLIC "-//W3C//DTD HTML 3.2 Final//EN">
<TITLE>Response.Properties</TITLE>
<TABLE>
<TR><TD>Property<TD>Value
<TR><TD>The Response.Buffer<TD><%= Response.Buffer %>
<TR><TD>The Response.ContentType<TD><%= Response.ContentType %>
<TR><TD>The Response.Expires<TD><%= Response.Expires %>
<TR><TD>The Response.ExpiresAbsolute<TD><%= Response.ExpiresAbsolute
 %>
<TR><TD>The Response.Status<TD><%= Response.Status %>
</TABLE>
```

All the properties are writing to the HTTP header, so you must set them before you write any output.

Buffer

We have already touched upon the Buffer property in our discussion of **Clear()**, **End()**, and **Flush()**. You can choose to instruct IIS to send output to the client browser as it is produced by your script (non-buffered), or only when you say so (buffered). The advantage of buffered output is greater control, but it may result in longer delays on the client side in loading your pages. The **Buffer** property is either TRUE or FALSE:

```
Response.Buffer [= flag]
```

where flag is TRUE or FALSE. If you don't set the **Buffer** property, ASP uses the value of the registry setting "BufferingOn." Because buffering affects how the rest of the output is managed, the Response.Buffer command should be the first line of your script.

If you turn buffering on, the buffer writes to the client when one of the following occurs:

♦ You execute the **Flush()** command.

♦ You execute the **End()** command.

♦ Your scripts finish executing. If your scripts die because of a syntax error, that still counts as "finishing," and the buffer will be flushed.

You can clear the buffer with the **Clear()** method, in which case the client does not see it.

ContentType

The **ContentType** property gives you a way to send a content-type HTTP header to the current HTTP output. This header sets the media type you intend to use. The HTTP standard is that Media types are specified in this format:

```
media-type  = type "/" subtype *( ";" parameter )
```

Naturally, the default for ContentType is "text/html." Because you are setting a header, you must use this command before you write any page content. For example, this script:

```
<% Response.ContentType = "text/plain" %>
<!DOCTYPE HTML PUBLIC "-//W3C//DTD HTML 3.2 Final//EN">
<TITLE>Response.ContentType</TITLE>
<H1>The Response.ContentType is <%= Response.ContentType %></H1>
```

produces the following output in the client browser:

```
<!DOCTYPE HTML PUBLIC "-//W3C//DTD HTML 3.2 Final//EN">
<TITLE>Response.ContentType</TITLE>
<H1>The Response.ContentType is text/plain</H1>
```

Notice that none of the HTML commands were interpreted as HTML.

Expires

The **Expires** property allows you to specify how long, in minutes, a browser should cache a page. For example:

```
<% Response.Expires = 2 %>
```

This instructs a browser to display the cached version of the page that the user returns to it within two minutes. This works, of course, only if your browser is not set to check for a new version of the page on every visit.

ExpiresAbsolute

The **ExpiresAbsolute** property is similar to the **Expires** property, but it specifies a specific date and time when a page should expire, such as

```
<% Response.ExpiresAbsolute = #Feb 18,1998 13:26:26# %>
```

This instructs the browser to cache the Web page until Dave turns 26.

Status

The **Status** property controls the HTTP Status code sent to the client. It is "200 OK" by default. Whatever status you set may or may not be understood by the client browser. For example:

```
<% Response.Status = "401 Unauthorized" %>
```

will challenge the client for a password, but sending

```
<% Response.Status = "402 Payment Required" %>
```

has no effect, because at the time of this writing, status code 402 is reserved for future use in the HTTP 1.1 standard.

Collections

The one collection object within **Response** is the **Cookies** collection. With this collection, you can set client cookies (files the browser stores on your hard drive at the Web server's request), which you then read with the **Request** object. Because cookies are set in the HTTP header, the call to Response.Cookies must precede all HTML output. The syntax for accessing the **Cookies** collection is

```
Response.Cookies(cookie)[(key)|.attribute] = value
```

where *cookie* is the name of the cookie. For example, the following complete ASP script sets some cookies and then displays their values:

```
<% Response.Cookies("foo") = "bar"
Response.Cookies("today") = "Sunday" %>
<!DOCTYPE HTML PUBLIC "-//W3C//DTD HTML 3.2 Final//EN">
<TITLE>Response.Cookies</TITLE>
Here are your cookies:
<TABLE>
<TR><TD><B>cookie</B><TD><B>value</B>
<% For each x in Request.Cookies %>
<TR><TD><%= x %><TD><%= Request.Cookies(x) %>
<% next %>
</TABLE>
```

The entire cookie is, of course, a set of name value pairs. However, with the **Response** object, you can embed name value pair cookies within a single cookie using the *key* parameter. This gives you the option of creating cookies that are dictionary objects; that is, cookies that are themselves name value pairs. For example, if you previously collected someone's name in a form, you might write:

```
<% Response.Cookies("name")("first") = Request("name")
Response.Cookies("name")("last") = Request("name_last") %>
```

To find out if a cookie has keys, you can use the *haskeys* attribute. This is the only attribute that is readable for the **Cookies** collection. Note that so far we have been using the **Request** object to read the cookies, and you can query the haskeys attribute to find out if a cookie has keys, but the **Request** object is reading the HTTP header from the client browser. What if you want to determine if a cookie has keys as you are building the header? You don't have a client HTTP header to read yet. That's why Response.Cookies(cookie).HasKeys is necessary.

Summary

The **Response** object is your standard interface for sending output to the client. The one command that you use far and away the most is Response.Write, either explicitly or with the implicit <%= %> tags. However, the **Response** object gives you the flexibility to write information to the HTTP header, to cookies within the header, and even to terminate the execution of the ASP.

Chapter 6

Sessions, Applications, and the Global File

IN THIS CHAPTER

One of the biggest complaints about standard CGI programming is the lack of *session* and *state* management. Basically, this means that the usual way of writing Web applications lacks the capability to store what the user has done at a site while navigating from page to page. In this chapter, we cover how ASP addresses these problems. Specifically, we cover the following:

- Using the **Session** object to store persistent information about each user connection

- Defining the beginning and end of a user session

- Using the Application and Session level events to control resources on your server

- Creating global objects for use in all your sessions by all your users

- Modifying the e-mail example that we started in Chapter 4 to be more efficient and useful

By the time you finish this chapter, you will be able not only to create some very cool Web applications, but also to make them run effectively in your server environment.

The Application Object

In the last few chapters, we referred quite a bit to ASP *applications*. In this section, we define more formally what that means and how it impacts you.

What Is an Application?

An ASP application is defined as all the .asp files in a given virtual directory and its subdirectories. In reality, this means that an ASP application is a collection of logically related .asp files.

Why is this important, you ask? The concept of an application means that you can share things between users who are accessing related pages at the same time.

Sharing Things Amongst Users with the Application Object

Say you wanted to keep track of the number of users who access your ASP application. How would you do it? You could write information to a file or database table each time a new user came to a page, but that's awkward. Another way to do it is to update a variable that is shared between users of the same application. Because all users of the same application share a single **Application** object, it would be nice to somehow associate a variable with that object. Happily, you can.

ASP allows you to store both simple variables and objects within the **Application** object. The following code illustrates this:

```
<% Application("appCounter") = 1 %>
```

The application level variable named *appCounter* is now set to a value of 1 and is available to all the users of the current application.

Methods

This object only has two methods, but they can be extremely important. In this section, we cover them.

LOCK()

Having something available to multiple users can pose a problem. What if two or more users attempt to update the same application level variable at the same time? They undo one another's changes. This problem of simultaneous access to a shared resource is called *contention*.

ASP solves this problem with the **Lock()** method. This function locks the **Application** object and all of its variables until you specifically unlock them or the lock expires (more on this in just a little bit). The following code demonstrates:

```
<%
 Application.Lock()
 Application("myVar") = "This is a test"
 Application.Unlock()
%>
```

This code locks the object, sets the variable, and then unlocks the object. It's pretty straightforward and leads us nicely into our next point.

UNLOCK()

Obviously, if you need to have a way to lock something, then you also need a way to unlock it. The **Unlock()** method does just that.

Actually, ASP's locking scheme is somewhat interesting. If you do not explicitly unlock the **Application** object, then ASP does it for you when one of two situations occur: the script ends or the script times out. If the concept of a *timeout* is foreign to you, don't worry. We go over it in another couple paragraphs.

The Session Object

Dynamic Web applications are often called upon to interact in a complicated way with external applications such as databases and security managers. In order to do this effectively, the Web program must be able to track information specific to the particular instance a given user is using the program. In this section, we introduce you to the method by which ASP accomplishes this and how it can benefit you.

What Is a Session?

A *session*, in ASP, is defined as the time a particular user is using a specific application. This means that if 10 users are running the same application simultaneously, each of them has his or her own session.

This construct is extremely useful for a number of reasons. You can, for example, track users' passwords throughout the application and ask for them only once. You can also create components that the user needs for the entire life of the application just once. This has obvious performance and resource savings.

To this end, ASP implements a built-in item called a **Session** object. This object is unique to every session that your users' are within. It allows you to store information that you want to keep around while your user is in your application.

How It Used to Be Done

In traditional CGI programming, there was a way to pass simple data, such as strings and numbers, from form to form without storing them in any kind of persistent memory. This was accomplished with hidden fields in the HTML page. For example, the following HTML constructs a field named *password* that holds some string data that is never shown in the client browser:

```
<input type=hidden name=password value=myPasswordGoesHere> </input>
```

What happens is that one form collects this information and runs the designated CGI program. That program then generates HTML output for the user and embeds a hidden field for every item it wants to pass on. Unfortunately, there are two big problems with this approach:

1. The HTML generated to hold all the hidden fields is unwieldy and complicated.

2. You cannot pass anything more than simple data. This means that you cannot, for example, create an object and pass it from page to page.

Is This Safe?

One client said the following to us: "I don't want to store a password in a session variable because I don't want the password being passed back and forth over the network."

Fortunately, there is nothing to worry about. All the session variables are stored on the server. Only the session id passes back and forth.

Other techniques enable this to happen more efficiently, but they also lack the capability to store anything more than simple data types.

ASP's Answer

The ASP way to handle these problems is by using the **Session** object. The first time a user enters the first page of your ASP application, he or she is assigned a unique value known as a *session id*. This value uniquely identifies your current interaction with the application. The user's browser keeps this id and presents it to ASP each time a page is accessed. If the user goes to a page after the current session has timed out, a new id is issued.

In the following sections, we explore the methods and properties of this object and how you can effectively use them.

Storing Variables in the Session Object

One of the truly powerful features of this piece of ASP is that you can store variables and objects specific to a particular user session without having to pass them from within your HTML files. For example, the following code stores a password passed to an ASP page so that you can use it throughout the application without asking the user for it:

```
<%
 Session("password") = Request.QueryString("password")
%>
```

This storage doesn't apply only to simple variables, either. You can store objects for a session, too. For example, in Chapter 4 we showed you how to construct a simple e-mail application. The problem was that on every page you had to connect to the mail server. That is a costly process. You can, however, use the **Session** object to create the e-mail connection once and use it on every page within your application for a given session. The following code demonstrates:

```
<%
 sServer = Request.QueryString("server")
 sUserID = Request.QueryString("userid")
 sPassword = Request.QueryString("password")

 set email = Server.CreateObject("NETUTILS.EMAIL")
 email.Connect sServer, sUserID, sPassword
 set Session("emailObject") = email
%>
```

The important code in this example is the line in boldface. Notice that it is syntactically the same as the previous example, with one exception — we had to use the **Set** keyword. In VBScript, the use of this keyword is required when setting a variable to an object. Other than that, the example is basically the same.

Now you can reference the existing connection from any page within the application with the following code:

```
<%
 set newEmail = Session("emailObject")
 newEmail.Body(15)
 … etc …
%>
```

Actually, you don't need to assign the session level object to a new variable before you use it. You can reference it directly, like so:

```
<%
 Session("emailObject").Body(15)
 … etc …
%>
```

With these things in mind, we can begin to explore some of the other parts of the **Session** object.

The Abandon Method

The **Session** object has only one method associated with it — **Abandon**. This function destroys all objects associated with the current session and frees their memory. If you do not explicitly call this method yourself, then ASP does it when the session times out, as defined in the **Session.Timeout** method. For example, the following code:

```
<%
 Session("test") = "this is a test"
 Response.Write( "The value is: " & Session("test") & "<br>" )
 Session.Abandon()
 Response.Write("The value is: " & Session("test") & "<br>" )
%>
```

prints the following output:

```
The value is: this is a test
The value is:
```

This brings up an important point. If you try to access data stored within the **Session** object after the session has been destroyed, your return value will be empty.

Properties

If you think the methods of the **Session** object are important, wait until you read about the properties! In this section, we cover them.

SESSIONID

You have already learned that each user's interaction with your ASP application is encompassed by a session. Each session, in turn, has a unique number that identifies it to the system. This identifier is called a *session id*. The **SessionID** property of the Session object stores that unique value. The following code displays it for you:

```
<html>
<body>

ID: <% =Session.SessionID %>

</body>
</html>
```

Interestingly enough, this value is nothing more than a large number, which makes it easy to use. There are some caveats, however.

First, the SessionID property is only guaranteed to be unique for each run of the server. In other words, it is possible to stop and restart the server and later get a previously used session id. For this reason, using this property as the primary key of a database table is a bad idea.

Second, you cannot change the value of this property. It is a protected member of the Session class. If you try, you get an error in your ASP code.

As long as you realize these facts, this property can provide a lot of good use to you.

Well . . . almost.

A BIG HAIRY BUG!

Remember how we promised to tell you the truth about ASP? Well, here it is. There is a bug with the SessionID property, and here's how to reproduce it.

First, stop and restart your server. Then create an ASP script that consists of the following:

```
<html>
<body>

<%

 Response.Write( "ID: " & Session.SessionID & "<br>" )
' Session("a") = "b"
' Session.Abandon()
%>

</body>
</html>
```

After you create this script, go ahead and run it. Hit your refresh button a few times. Notice something? That's right, the number keeps incrementing! This is definitely *not* what is supposed to happen. Wait, though; things get odder. Uncomment line seven so that it reads:

```
Session("a") = "b"
```

Now run the program and hit reload a few times. Notice that the number doesn't increment any more. Very strange.

You're not quite done yet. Recomment line seven and uncomment line eight. The lines should look like so:

```
' Session("a") = "b"
Session.Abandon()
```

Go ahead and run this (you don't need to hit refresh). This code destroys the Session level variable named "a" that we created in the earlier step. When you are done, recomment line eight so that the file looks as it did in the beginning. Run the code and again hit the refresh button a few times. Now the numbers increment again.

As near as we can tell, the SessionID increments inappropriately as long as there are no session level variables assigned. The only workaround we know is to create a dummy variable in the **Session_OnStart** event. Don't worry; we cover this in just a few more pages. We just didn't want you to think that you were doing something wrong.

TIMEOUT

For all the similarities between conventional Windows applications and Web applications, there are a few differences. One of the most important is the fact that an application written in ASP has no way of knowing for sure when the user is done with it.

For example, nothing keeps users from going through half the pages in your application and then surfing to another site. If ASP were to wait forever for those users to return, it would waste a lot of memory storing Session variables and other system-level resources. This problem can easily bring a frequently visited server to its knees.

To get around this issue, ASP imposes a time limit on how long it waits for a user's input in an application. By default, this limit is 20 minutes. The **Timeout** property allows you to change that default for the current session. For example, the following code sets the session timeout to one minute:

```
<% Session.Timeout = 1 %>
```

There is something important to note here. The finest granularity of time you can get is one minute. There is no way to set the **Timeout** property in increments any finer than one minute. The following code, for example, does not set this property to 1.6 minutes. Instead, it rounds up to 2 minutes:

```
<% Session.Timeout = 1.6 %>
```

Even worse, this next example returns an error because ASP attempts to set the timeout value to zero:

```
<% Session.Timeout = .4 %>
```

In our opinion, this limitation is a little too constraining. Sometimes you may want to limit a particular session to just a few seconds. Any solution you might try to accomplish this (and there are a couple of possibilities) is not guaranteed to always work. We grant you that this is not a critical omission, but, in our opinion, it is somewhat annoying.

Events

If you have ever done any Windows programming, the concept of events should be quite familiar. ASP implements a limited event model to allow you to take advantage of event-driven programming. In this section, we cover the way ASP does this and how you can use it to your advantage.

A Quick Overview

If you are not familiar with event-driven programming, don't worry. The ideas are simple.

When you do anything within an application in the Windows environment, the operating system sends a signal to the application that tells it what you have done. For example, if you click on a button, Windows tells your application that the button has been clicked. The person who wrote the application most likely has written code to trap that signal and do something with it.

The triggering action (the button click) is called an *event*. The signal that Windows sends to the application is called the *event message,* and the code in the application to respond to the event is called the *event handler.*

Application Events

An application, as you may recall, is defined in ASP as a series of related pages in the same virtual path. In order to give you some control over the initialization and de-initialization of your application, ASP defines two application level events — **Application_OnStart** and **Application_OnEnd.** In the next two sections, we discuss these events.

APPLICATION_ONSTART

An ASP application starts when the first user accesses any page within it. Knowing this, there are some things you may want to do to initialize your application. For example, you may want to create an application level variable to track the number of users who run the program.

ASP allows you to do this by creating an **Application_OnStart** subroutine. ASP automatically calls this function, which you define, when your application starts. The following code demonstrates:

```
<SCRIPT LANGUAGE=VBScript RUNAT=Server>

Sub Application_OnStart

 Application("appCounter") = 0

End Sub

</SCRIPT>
```

This code is placed in a special file named **global.asa.** In this file you put the event handlers for all application and session events.

There are a few important things to notice in the code. First, the entire subroutine is enclosed within the HTML *<SCRIPT>* and *</SCRIPT>* tags. This is different from the usual <% and %> pair.

Second, we did not use the **Lock()** and **Unlock()** methods. This is because the **Application_OnStart** event is called before the requested page and is run only once during the life of an application. It is impossible for another script in the same application to be running while this event is being handled. This means that there is never a contention issue.

Finally, you need to keep in mind what is and is not available from within this script. Only the **Server** and **Application** objects are available to you from within this event. If you try to reference the **Request, Response,** and **Session** objects, ASP gives you an error.

APPLICATION_ONEND

An ASP application ends when the Web server is shut down. At that time, ASP looks for a user-defined subroutine named **Application_OnEnd** and executes it. Again, this code must be declared in the **global.asa** file and has a few restrictions placed upon it.

As you may have guessed, the only objects that this script can reference are the **Server** and **Application** objects. In addition, this code cannot call the **MapPath()** method of the **Server** object.

In our previous example, we initialized a counter in the **Application_OnStart** event that holds the number of users who have run the application. Because that variable will be lost when the server shuts down, it may be a good idea in this event to save the contents of that variable back to a column in a database table.

Session Events

Just as ASP defines events at the application level, it also defines the same events at the session level. The only difference is that session level events are called for each user who runs the application.

SESSION_ONSTART

As its name implies, the **Session_OnStart** event is called when a new **Session** object is created. This is a great place to create any objects that you want to be persistent throughout the entire session. For example, in Chapter 4 you constructed an e-mail application that was forced to create a new connection to the mail server for each page in the application. A more efficient way to accomplish this is to create one e-mail connection in this event. For example:

```
<SCRIPT LANGUAGE=VBScript RUNAT=Server>

Sub Session_OnStart
  Set Session("emailObject") = Server.CreateObject("NETUTILS.EMAIL")
End Sub

</SCRIPT>
```

Unlike application level events, session level events have no restrictions on what objects they can or cannot reference. There is, however, an important caveat to using them. If backwards contemptibility, er, compatibility, is important to you, then session level events can pose a problem.

Who Thinks of These Things, Anyway?

The Internet etymology of the term *cookie* is an issue of some debate. Some people claim that it comes from an old Dungeons and Dragons game, while other claim that the term is completely contrived by the folks at Netscape. Still others think that cookies are part of a government plot to peek into our private lives. (After all, what would the Internet be without a good conspiracy theory or two!) In any event, the exact origin of the term is unknown.

"C" IS FOR COOKIE . . .

Earlier in this chapter, we told you that ASP keeps track of what session you are in by asking your browser to store the session id. When you access a new page in the application, ASP retrieves that value from the browser and determines whether you need a new session. That stored value is called a *cookie.*

The problem with cookies is that some older browsers don't take them, and some Internet surfers keep them disabled because they feel that cookies pose a security risk. If the person surfing your application falls into either of these categories, ASP creates a new session id each time they access a new page in your program. This means that the **Session_OnStart** event is fired for every page. This also means that storing session level variables and objects is useless. About the only thing you can do to prevent this is to include a big warning on your first page telling users that they *must* use a cookie-capable browser with that particular feature enabled. If it's any consolation to you, the latest versions of Netscape Navigator and Microsoft Internet Explorer fully support cookies.

SESSION_ONEND

A session ends when one of three things happens: the session times out, the **Abandon()** method is called, or the server is shut down. When any of these situations occur, ASP looks in the **global.asa** file for a subroutine named **Session_OnEnd** and executes it.

This script is a good place to clean up any session level variables or objects that may be lying around. In our e-mail example, for instance, this event would be an ideal place to call the **Quit()** method of the NETUTILS.EMAIL object:

```
<SCRIPT LANGUAGE=VBScript RUNAT=Server>

Sub Session_OnEnd
  Session("emailObject").Quit()
End Sub

</SCRIPT>
```

Session Objects, Application Objects, and the <OBJECT> Tag

In all of our previous examples, we have showed you how to create session and application level objects with the following construction:

```
<% set Session("objName") = Server.CreateObject("someProgID") %>
```

There is another way to do it. You can use the *<OBJECT>* tag from within the **global.asa** file. The syntax of this tag is as follows:

```
<OBJECT RUNAT=Server SCOPE=Scope ID=Identifier
  {PROGID="progID"|CLASSID="ClassID"}>
```

As you can see, there are a few parameters here. In the next few sections, we explain them.

RUNAT

Currently, the only supported option for this parameter is **Server**. The assumption is that it may be possible someday to say *RUNAT=Client* to signal that certain code is to be run on the client machine.

Scope

This parameter dictates what scope the created object will be. Supported values are **Session** and **Application**.

ID

This parameter sets the name by which you refer to the object from within your code. For example, the following code creates a session level e-mail object named *myEmail*:

```
<OBJECT RUNAT=Server SCOPE=Session ID=myEmail
  PROGID="NETUTILS.EMAIL"> </OBJECT>
```

PROGID

This parameter specifies the English name of the component to be created. For example, a PROGID of *"NETUTILS.EMAIL"* creates an instance of the e-mail object we have been using. If you use this parameter, you cannot use the **CLASSID** parameter.

CLASSID

This parameter specifies the CLSID of the component to create. For example, a CLASSID of "{6DDF0161-70B4-11D0-83D2-0080C765AB10}" creates an instance of the NETUTILS.EMAIL object. You cannot use this parameter if you use the **PROGID** parameter.

The Benefit of the <OBJECT> Tag

Using the <OBJECT> tag may seem a little pointless when you can simply create session and application level objects from within your ASP code. There are, in fact, two benefits to using this construct.

First, you get to reference your session level object with a slightly easier syntax. For example, say you code the following:

```
<% set Session("test") = Server.CreateObject("NETUTILS.EMAIL") %>
```

In order to do anything with that object, you have to do something similar to the following:

```
<% Session("test").Body(10) %>
```

If, on the other hand, you create your session level object using the <OBJECT> tag in the **global.asa** file, like so:

```
<OBJECT RUNAT=Server SCOPE=Session ID=test PROGID="NETUTILS.EMAIL">
 </OBJECT>
```

you can refer to the object from within your scripts with a slightly easier construction:

```
<% test.Body(10) %>
```

The other benefit that makes the <OBJECT> tag attractive is that it gives you a slight performance boost. This is because the object is not actually created until it is first referenced in an ASP script. This means that you do not incur the penalty of using the extra resources without deriving the benefit of the component. For a really busy site, this reason alone may be enough to use this tag.

The Modified E-Mail Example

Back in Chapter 4, we helped you create a simple e-mail reading program. In this chapter, we help you make that program much more efficient and useful.

New and Improved

The last incarnation of the e-mail application suffered from two main problems:

1. Inefficiency
2. Lack of features

The program was inefficient because it had to connect to the mail server on every page. This wasted a lot of time and system resources. The application also lacked important features such as the capability to create, reply, or delete messages.

In the following sections, we show you how to use what you have learned in this chapter to fix those problems. Specifically, we go over the necessary changes to the e-mail application to make it much better.

Global.asa

The easiest way to overcome the program's inefficiencies is to create a session level e-mail object that is used by all the pages in the application. Of course, the best place to do this is in the **Session_OnStart** event handler. Following are the contents of the **global.asa** file. This file defines code to both initialize and clean up each user session. Here's our finished file:

```
<SCRIPT RUNAT=Server LANGUAGE=VBScript>

Sub Session_OnStart
 set Session("email") = Server.CreateObject("NETUTILS.EMAIL")
 Session("isConnected") = 0
 Session.Timeout = 60
End Sub

Sub Session_OnEnd
 Session("email").Quit()
End Sub

</SCRIPT>
```

Default.htm

Because this application is frame based, it needs a default page to construct the frames and display the default data. The following version of the **default.htm** file is nearly identical to the one used in the example in Chapter 4:

```
<html>

<frameset rows=50%,*>
 <frame name=headerFrame src=config.asp></frame>

 <frameset cols=100,*>
```

```
        <frame name=menuFrame src=menu.asp></frame>
        <frame name=bodyFrame src=body.asp></frame>
  </frameset>

</frameset>

</html>
```

Menu.asp

In the original e-mail application, the only implemented features were the capabilities to read a message and reconfigure the login information. This new version of the **menu.asp** file also adds the capability to delete, reply to, and send new messages. The new HTML code is as follows:

```
<html>
<body bgcolor=yellow>

<center>

<h2>

<a href=reply.asp target=bodyFrame >Reply </a> <br><br>
<a href=delete.asp target=bodyFrame >Delete</a> <br><br>
<a href=new.asp target=bodyFrame >New </a> <br><br>
<a href=config.asp target=headerFrame>Config</a> <br><br>

</h2>

</center>

</body>
</html>
```

Config.asp

The configuration screen in this version of the application has remained largely unchanged. The only difference is the addition of a few lines of logic in the beginning. This code checks for an already active connection and kills it. This is needed so that you do not create excess connections each time you try to reconfigure your login parameters. Here are the final file contents:

```
<html>
<body bgcolor=blue>

<%
  If ( Session("isConnected") = 1 ) Then
  Session("email").Quit()
  set Session("email") = Nothing
  set Session("email") = Server.CreateObject("NETUTILS.EMAIL")
  End If
```

```
    Session("isConnected") = 0
%>

<form method=GET action=headers.asp>

<center>

<table border=5>

 <tr>
 <th bgcolor=cyan>User ID:</th>
 <td> <input name=userid> </input> </td>
 </tr>

 <tr>
 <th bgcolor=cyan>Password:</th>
 <td><input type=password name=passwd></input></td>
 </tr>
<tr>
 <th bgcolor=cyan>Server:</th>
 <td><input name=server></input></td>
 </tr>

</table>

<br>

<input type=submit value=Go></input>

</center>

</form>
</body>
</html>
```

Headers.asp

By far, the biggest changes to this application occur in the **headers.asp** file. First, there is a little logic in the beginning to make sure that an existing valid connection is available. If so, the application uses it instead of creating a new one.

The next change to this code is the addition of a **Reply** button to the visible interface. The Reply button reloads this screen with the *server, userid,* and *passwd* parameters and is the reason that a form is declared right before the main table. You should also notice that the use of session level variables has made the individual *HREFs* for each table row much smaller. The finished code is as follows:

```
<html>
<body bgcolor=blue>

<%

CRLF = CHR(13) & CHR(10)
```

```
Session("server") = Request.QueryString( "server" )
Session("userid") = Request.QueryString( "userid" )
Session("password") = Request.QueryString( "passwd" )

If ( Session("isConnected") = 0 ) Then
 Session("email").Connect Session("server"), Session("userid"),
 Session("password")
 Session("isConnected") = 1
End IF

mCount = Session("email").MsgCount()

%>

<center>

<form method=get action=headers.asp?server=<% =Session("server")
 %>&userid=<% =Session("userid") %>&passwd=<% =Session("password")
 %>

<table border=1>
<tr bgcolor=cyan>
 <th colspan=2>From</th>
 <th>Subject</th>
 <td rowspan=<% =mCount + 1 %> valign=middle><input type=submit
 value=Refresh></input></td>

</tr>

<%

For i = 1 to mCount

 sSender = Server.HTMLEncode( Session("email").Header( i, "FROM" ) )
 sSubject = Server.HTMLEncode( Session("email").Header( i, "SUBJECT"
 ) )

 sHREF = "<a href=body.asp?message=" & i & " target=bodyFrame><img
 src=mail.bmp width=25 height=25></img></a>"

 Response.Write( "<tr bgcolor=white><td>" & sHREF & "</td><td>" &
 sSender & "</td><td>" & sSubject & "</td></tr>" & CRLF )

Next

%>

</form>

</table>

</body>
</html>
```

Body.asp

The code to display the body of an e-mail message doesn't change much in this version of the application. The most important thing to notice is that we are now tracking which message currently displays and what its body text is. This is a critical part of implementing additional features. Here's our new script:

```
<html>
<body bgcolor=white>

<%

Session("message") = Request.QueryString("message")

if ( Session("isConnected") = 1 ) Then
  Session("bodyText") = Session("email").Body( Session("message") )
Else
  Session("bodyText") = ""
End If

%>

<plaintext>

<% =Session("bodyText") %>
```

Delete.asp

The ability to delete an e-mail message is new in this version of the application. The code is simple. First the current message is deleted, and then a small notice is displayed to the screen. Here's the code:

```
<%
 Session("email").Delete( Session("message") )
%>

<html>
<body>

<center>
<h2>
Message <% =Session("message") %> deleted ...
</h2>
</center>

</body>
</html>
```

New.asp

The ability to compose a new message is also new to the application in this version. The HTML may seem a little complicated because we are using a table to keep everything correctly aligned on the page. In fact, the only logic on this page is the construction of the **From** address. This is assumed to be your login id plus an *at* sign (@) plus your mail server machine name. When you finish filling out this information, the **sendmail.asp** file is run. The complete listing is as follows:

```
<html>
<body bgcolor=cyan>
<form method=get action=sendMail.asp>

<%
 sFrom = Session("userid") & "@" & Session("server")
%>

<table border=0>
<tr>
 <th align=right valign=top>
 To: <input name=sendTo></input><br>
 From: <input name=sentFrom value= <% =sFrom %> ></input><br>
 Subject: <input name=Subject></input><br>
 <hr>
 <center> <input type=submit value=OK></input> </center>

 </th>

 <td rows=20>
 <textarea name=messageText rows=20 cols=100></textarea>
 </td>

</tr>
</table>

</body>
</html>
```

Reply.asp

Replying to an e-mail message requires almost the same process as composing a new one. Instead of presenting blank fields to the user, this code fills in a few things. For example, it assumes that the subject of the reply is *RE:* plus the subject of the original message. This code also assumes that you are replying to the person who sent the original message. The code is as follows:

```
<html>
<body bgcolor=cyan>
<form method=get action=sendMail.asp>
```

```
<%
CRLF = CHR(13) & CHR(10)

sFrom = Session("userid") & "@" & Session("server")
sTo = Server.HTMLEncode( Session("email").Header(
Session("message"), "FROM" ) )
sSubject = Server.HTMLEncode( Session("email").Header(
Session("message"), "SUBJECT" ) )
sBody = Server.HTMLEncode( Session("bodyText") )

sSubject = "RE: " & sSubject
sBody = CRLF & CRLF & CRLF & "————————————————" & CRLF &
sBody
%>

<table border=0>
<tr>
<th align=right valign=top>
To: <input name=sendTo value="<% =sTo %>" ></input><br>
From: <input name=sentFrom value="<% =sFrom %>" ></input><br>
Subject: <input name=Subject value="<% =sSubject %>" ></input><br>
<hr>
<center> <input type=submit value=OK></input> </center>

</th>

<td rows=20>
<textarea name=messageText rows=20 cols=100><% =sBody %></textarea>
</td>

</tr>
</table>

</body>
</html>
```

Sendmail.asp

The last piece of the new and improved mail application is the code to send an e-mail note. The logic is simple. It gathers the sender, recipient, subject, and text from the data passed to it; constructs the appropriate e-mail data; and calls the e-mail object's **SendMail()** method to send the note. Here is the final logic:

```
<html>

<%
CRLF = CHR(13) & CHR(10)

sFrom = Request.QueryString("sentFrom")
sTo = Request.QueryString("sendTo")
sSubject = Request.QueryString("Subject")
sMessage = Request.QueryString("messageText")
```

```
sData = "Subject: " & sSubject & CRLF & CRLF & sMessage & CRLF

Session("email").SendMail "jolt.eng.umd.edu", sFrom, sTo, sData
%>
```

```
</html>
```

Summary

Session and application level events and variables can play a huge role in making your ASP application leaner and more functional. In this chapter, you have seen how to use these things to enhance the example we began in Chapter 4. You have also learned about the potential pitfalls of these techniques and how to avoid them.

Part III

The External ASP Components

Chapter 7

The Database Access Component

IN THIS CHAPTER

Using a database in tandem with a Web site is one of the hottest areas in Web technology. Web pages provide information. What better way could there be to organize that information than in a database?

The tough question is how to get the information from the database to the HTML pages. ASP has a database component to make this easy for you, and that's what we want to discuss in this chapter.

One could easily write a whole book on ADO (hmm . . . maybe we should talk to our publisher about that). However, there is a lot about ADO that isn't particularly helpful for ASP. In this chapter, we confine ourselves to those ADO features that we use with Web site generation. Therefore, you do not find an exhaustive list of ADO features in this chapter. For that we refer you to the online documentation.

This chapter covers three basic concepts:

♦ How to connect to an RDBMS from ASP with ADO

♦ How to retrieve your records once you have this connection

♦ Other considerations, especially debugging concerns

One more word before we start. Almost every client we have who uses ASP uses SQL Server. It only makes sense. If you are using ASP, you have probably invested heavily in Microsoft products, so you are going to use either SQL Server or MS Access. Of the two, only SQL Server can be seriously expected to handle large volumes of data, many concurrent users, or security issues. And you probably already have a copy of Windows NT, so you have a place to put SQL Server, too.

Unfortunately, the ASP to SQL Server bridge escapes most Web developers, many of whom have limited database experience. While we would love to see you invest in a copy of our *SQL Server 6.5 Secrets* (IDG Books Worldwide), we owe it to you to give you what you need in this book to get up and running with ASP. Therefore, we delve heavily into some SQL Server-specific information in this chapter, though the concepts apply to all Relational Database Management Systems (RDBMSs).

ADO

Those of you who have been using Microsoft products for several years have heard of *Data Access Objects* (DAO) and *Relational Data Objects* (RDO). Microsoft is now replacing both of these with *Active Data Objects* (ADO). ADO is an object-oriented (OO) interface to database servers. With ASP, you use ADODB, which is an implementation of ADO optimized for Microsoft OLE DB providers, such as ODBC.

The reasons for wanting an OO database interface are many:

- ◆ You get the advantages that OO should bring to a good design, such as modular code and ease of maintenance.

- ◆ Your database access is consistent with your method for manipulating all other parts of your programs.

- ◆ ADO spares you somewhat from learning SQL.

- ◆ ADO insulates you from the differences in various vendor's database implementations.

ADO Hierarchy

The centerpiece of the Database Access Component is the **Recordset** object. The Recordset object represents the records of an RDBMS query or stored procedure. It includes all kinds of features for retrieving and updating the database records.

To create a Recordset, you must access the database, which typically involves specifying where the database is, your userid and password, and the query that specifies the result set. For example, when you want information from SQL Server, you must first authenticate with a login and password. You then have a connection to SQL Server, which stays open until you or your application closes it. If you constantly re-authenticate to SQL Server every time you want a Recordset, you incur too much connection overhead. Fortunately, there is a better way.

Connection Object

To alleviate the overhead of continuously connecting and disconnecting with RDBMS, ADO allows you to create a **Connection** object. This object represents a unique session with your RDBMS. What it means and what it can do varies with the RDBMS you choose. For SQL Server, the **Connection** object represents an active database process (what you see in the sysprocesses table.)

As with any object, you must first create an instance of the **Connection** object:

```
<% set conn = server.createobject("ADODB.Connection") %>
```

Now the variable named *conn* is a **Connection** object. At this point, you have not yet connected it to any particular RDBMS; you just have a blank slate.

Open Method

The first thing you may want to do with the **Connection** object is connect it to an actual RDBMS. The **Open** method sets this up for you. The syntax is

```
connection.Open ConnectionString, UserID, Password
```

Table 7-1 lists the pieces of the **Open** method syntax.

TABLE 7-1 OPEN METHOD SYNAX

Part	Description
Connection	A connection object
ConnectionString	A connection string or Data Source Name (DSN)
UserID	Optional Username
Password	Optional Password

The only tricky piece here is the DSN. To use an RDBMS, you must have an ODBC data source defined on the Web server machine for that RDBMS.

CREATING AN ODBC DATA SOURCE

To set up an ODBC data source, you start with the control panel and select the ODBC icon. Select the System DSN tab. You see the dialog box in Figure 7-1.

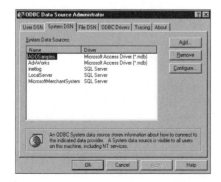

Figure 7-1: Remember to use System DSNs for ASP

These are data source names that you define for the machine. (User DSNs are specific to your logon, which is of no help to IIS.) Click on the Add button and select the appropriate driver. For example, if you are setting up a SQL Server driver, you would choose *SQL Server*. See the dialog box in Figure 7-2.

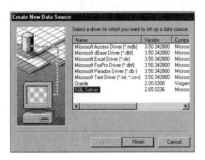

Figure 7-2: Choose the appropriate driver for your RDBMS

Click on Finish to get to a setup box specific to the driver you selected. The SQL Server setup box appears in Figure 7-3. If you are setting up a SQL Server driver, you probably want to use the Options button to specify a database name. The only two mandatory entries on this page are the Data Source Name and Server. The server name is a bit tricky. SQL Server keeps a list of names of servers in the Registry, under HKEY_LOCAL_MACHINE\SOFTWARE\Microsoft\MSSQLServer\Client\ConnectTo. When you type in the name of a server, SQL Server looks here first.

Figure 7-3: Remember to fill out the Options in ODBC SQL Server setup

If you are connecting to a SQL Server via TCP/IP, you can just type in the IP address for the server name, but you must type **DBMSSOCN** for the Network library. This makes an entry for you in the Registry key listed previously. Alternatively, you can run the SQL Server Client Configuration Utility by choosing it in the Microsoft SQL Server 6.5 folder or by typing **WINDBVER.EXE** at the command prompt. The

Advanced tab of this utility shows the Registry key listed previously and allows you to add, modify, and delete entries.

REMOTE ODBC DSN CREATION

The fascinating question is: What if you must set up an ODBC data source remotely? Suppose you are located in Massachusetts, and you lease your Web server from a company in Virginia. What should you do then? You don't want to have to call the company holding your lease every time you want to change an ODBC data source. One solution is to use the Registry Editor. A better solution is to get an ASP component to change it. You can find such components on the Web, but you are merely installing something that is changing the Registry for you, so you may as well know how to do it yourself. No doubt you have heard all the dire warnings from Microsoft about how you can completely mess up your machine when you use the Registry Editor, and we echo that here. We use the Registry Editor all the time and haven't trashed a machine yet, but we provide you this advice without any guarantees. If you toast your machine, you have to fix it.

You have only three keys to worry about as you set up the DSN, all of which are under HKEY_LOCAL_MACHINE. One key is for SQL Server, and two are for ODBC.

SOFTWARE\MICROSOFT\MSSQLSERVER\CLIENT\CONNECTTO   Assuming that you are using TCP/IP, since you are performing a remote setup, you need to enter a registry value with the server name and a string that is DBMSSOCN,*IP address*. For example, to use a server named FOO whose IP address is 207.68.137.100, you would create a value named FOO and use the string DBMSSOCN,207.68.137.100.

SOFTWARE\ODBC\ODBC.INI\ODBC DATA SOURCES   In this key, we specify that we want a DSN named FOO_DSN, and that FOO corresponds to a SQL Server RDBMS. Therefore, we make this entry for the ODBC DSN, with *SQL Server* as the string:

```
Value X
  Name: FOO_DSN
  Type: REG_SZ
  Data: SQL Server
```

SOFTWARE\ODBC\ODBC.INI\FOO_ DSN   Finally, you must make a whole new key with the name you supplied above, in our case FOO_DSN. The entries in this key must include, at a minimum, the following:

```
Value 2
  Name: Driver
  Type: REG_SZ
  Data: C:\WINNT\System32\sqlsrv32.dll

Value 6
  Name: Server
  Type: REG_SZ
  Data: FOO
```

You will typically find many other entries when the key is created by the ODBC applet, but by telling the Registry which DLL and which SQL Server machine to use, you are all set.

PINGING YOUR ODBC DATA SOURCE

Save yourself hours of frustration later by verifying now that your ODBC DSN is valid. Microsoft SQL Server ships with a utility that verifies *any* ODBC data source — SQL Server or otherwise. It is called ODBCPING, and the syntax is simply

```
ODBCPING [-S Server | -D DSN] [-U Login Id] [-P Password]
```

For example, to check our source above we would execute this command:

```
ODBCPING -D "FOO DSN" -U IUSR_OURSERVER -P the_password
```

OPTIONAL USERID AND PASSWORD

You may have noticed that the userid and password are *optional* parameters on the **Connection** object. This should make you raise your eyebrows. With any robust RDBMS, such as SQL Server, the userid isn't optional. You must log in as someone so that SQL Server knows what permissions you have. There are two reasons why the userid can be optional when you connect to SQL Server:

1. SQL Server can use an authentication mechanism called *trusted connections,* in which SQL Server determines who you are from your Windows NT login.

2. SQL Server supports guest accounts so that a large number of users can access SQL Server under a userid named "guest."

It is to your advantage to use SQL Server's trusted connections and omit the userid and password from the connection string. In so doing, you ensure that the password for the database account is not stored in a text file that someone may potentially see. Furthermore, with SQL Server trusted connections, the password becomes irrelevant. You can set it to some unreasonable string that no one can remember, such as 53*(61d135euid.p%ud53@##. SQL Server gives IIS access based on NT Security.

If, for some reason, you must store your password in the text of your ASP file, you of course want to follow the usual security methods, such as frequently changing the password. Consider also these options if you are using SQL Server:

◆ Include unprintable characters in the password. With the sa account of SQL Server, you can set passwords such as the following:

```
declare @password varchar(16)
select @password = char(9) + char(10) + char(11) + char(13)
sp_password null, @password, 'foo'
```

You have now created a userid whose password includes a tab and carriage return. This is perfectly legal in SQL Server and sets up an extra layer of frustration for a would-be hacker.

♦ Use triggers to restrict write access to the IIS machine. In SQL Server, you can write a snippet of code called a *trigger* that runs each time someone changes data in a table. This code then rejects the change. If data is to be changed solely through the Web interface, you can use the trigger to demand that only the IIS machine be allowed to alter data:

```
create trigger trig_name on tbl_name for insert, update,
delete as
begin
 if select hostname from master..sysprocesses where spid =
@@spid rollback tran
end
```

WHAT TO DO WHEN THE OPEN METHOD FAILS

If the open method fails, read the previous section about ODBCPING. In most situations in which ODBCPING works but ADO can't successfully use the **Open** method, you have a typo in your ASP script. Remember to use the same userid and password with ODBCPING that you are using in ASP. If you have specified no userid in ASP, you are using the default IIS userid, which is initially set to IUSR_*SERVER-NAME*, where *SERVERNAME* is the name of your server.

Quick Check Connection

If you are running SQL Server on the same machine as IIS, you may be able to connect with this command:

```
<%
set conn = server.createobject("ADODB.Connection")
conn.open "LocalServer", "probe", ""
%>
```

This is a cheat, but a fascinating one. When you install SQL Server, an ODBC datasource named "LocalServer" is created for you. Furthermore, SQL Server includes a userid for system use named "probe" that has no password. Most folks never change this, so it's a good bet that you can connect this way. If you are having trouble connecting to SQL Server, try the previous script. If it works, you might compare the "LocalServer" DSN to your own and see where you went wrong.

Minimizing Connection Overhead

There is overhead associated with connecting to and disconnecting from an RDBMS such as SQL Server, so you would prefer not to do this all the time. In particular, any visitor to your site will hopefully take the time to see many different pages in one visit. You want to establish one connection to the database for the duration of this visit. If you don't, each new page the user requests requires your Web server to reconnect (and reauthenticate) to the RDBMS. Fortunately, there are mechanisms for solving this issue. The best way is to use connection pooling.

CONNECTION POOLING

ODBC 3.0 supports *connection pooling.* Here's how it works. When you disconnect from an ODBC data source, ODBC 3.0 does not immediately disconnect from the server. Instead, it waits a certain period of time, 60 seconds by default. Should you happen to come back within this time period and request a new connection to the server with the same userid and password, ODBC 3.0 simply gives you the connection that it held open.

To enable connection pooling for SQL Server, you must use the Registry Editor (yes, this is how Microsoft recommends you do it) and set the value of this key to 1:

```
Key Name:
SYSTEM\CurrentControlSet\Services\W3SVC\ASP\Parameters
Value 20
  Name: StartConnectionPool
  Type: REG_DWORD
  Data: 0
```

To verify that connection pooling is working, you can use the SQL Trace utility of SQL Server, SQLTRACE.EXE. Simply set up a filter on the account that IIS is using and watch. Without connection pooling, you see a million connect and disconnect statements. With connection pooling, this is no longer the case.

USING SESSION VARIABLES

Your other choice for minimizing connection overhead is to use session variables, which we discussed in Chapter 6. You simply save your database connection in a session variable. The difference here is that each session takes 20 minutes to time out, so if you have a high traffic site, you have too many idle connections to your RDBMS.

Recordset Object

The key to ADO is the **Recordset** object. The **Recordset** object represents either the results of a SQL statement that you have executed or the entire records of a table in your database. You use the **Recordset** object to retrieve and display data.

To retrieve records from a database, you must have an active connection. The **Recordset** object creates a connection for you if you do not have one open, but we don't recommend that you do that. Go ahead and create your own **Connection** object. It takes only two extra lines of code, and then you have it for whenever you need it.

Assuming that you have already created a **Connection** object, you can create a **Recordset** object with the execute method of the **Connection** object, like so:

```
Set Recordset = connection.Execute(CommandText, RecordsAffected,
  Options)
```

The only mandatory parameter is CommandText, which can be a SQL statement, a table name, or a stored procedure. RecordsAffected is a variable in which you hope the RDBMS places the number of records affected by the operation. The optional Options parameter tells ADO whether you are sending SQL, a table name, or a stored procedure.

For example, suppose you have a connection open to SQL Server, and you want to find some information about your connection. Use the following code:

```
set rs = conn.execute( "select user_name() user, dbname() db" )
```

In this case, we have created a **Recordset** object named *rs,* which contains the results of the previous query. We didn't include the Options parameter, so ADO assumes that we have sent SQL. Now suppose that we want to retrieve the sysobjects table for our analysis. We use the following code:

```
set my_rs = conn.execute( "sysobjects", x, adCmdTable )
```

By using the adCmdTable constant, which happens to be 2, we tell ADO that "sysobjects" is a table name, not a stored procedure. Had we left out this third parameter, ADO would first have to send a query to the RDBMS to determine whether "sysobjects" was a table or stored procedure. Next, ADO could actually execute the query. By supplying the parameter, we avoid a call to the database. Furthermore, in the case of a system table such as we have used here, ADO does not correctly identify CommandText as a table, so without the Options parameter, the Recordset creation fails.

The Need for Speed

Here's a curious little fact that we stumbled upon. When using ADO, retrieving data from SQL Server using SQL SELECT statement is *a lot* slower than using a stored procedure. This is because the ODBC driver goes to the server for each row of data. When using a stored procedure, however, the driver gets all the data in one connection and gives it to you as you ask for it. As near as we can tell, this is not the case with other DBMSs and is specific to the particular ODBC driver we are using for SQL Server. The important thing to remember is that you may get better performance by passing a SQL Server stored procedure name instead of a SELECT statement to ODBC.

Being able to retrieve an entire table by specifying just the table name is a neat trick, but you can never be sure in which order the RDBMS gives you the rows. You should always use the SQL *ORDER BY* clause to request a particular order from the RDBMS.

STORED PROCEDURE EXECUTION

A stored procedure is a set of one or more SQL commands that are pre-compiled in the RDBMS. SQL Server provides its own extended version of SQL called Transact-SQL. This allows you to include control of flow commands in stored procedures so that they can quickly become mini-programs. Here's an example. Suppose we have the following Recordset in ASP:

```
set rs = conn.execute( "select name, user_name(uid) user" & _
"from sysobjects" & _
"where type = '" & request("type") & "'" & _
"order by 1, 2" )
```

We can create a procedure in SQL Server to replace this SQL:

```
create proc sp_object_list @type char(1) = 'u' as
select name, user_name(uid) user
 from sysobjects
 where type = @type
 order by 1, 2
go
grant execute on sp_object_list to IUSR_SERVER
```

Now we can create our Recordset as simply

```
set rs = conn.execute( "sp_object_list '" & request("type") & "'" )
```

We want to point out several things about this quick example:

♦ You can pass parameters to stored procedures. Notice that you must send string parameters to SQL Server with quotes around them.

♦ Stored procedures allow you to set up default values for your parameters. In the previous example, type defaults to 'u.'

♦ Remember to grant permissions on your procedure. If you have done your job correctly, IIS is logging onto SQL Server with the minimum privileges that it needs. Please, do not use the sa account with ASP. If anyone manages to compromise your security and gets hold of the sa password, you are completely vulnerable. Assuming that you have set up an account for IIS named IUSR_SERVER, you must give this account permission to use the procedure.

Retrieving Data From Your Recordset

The **Recordset** object has a Fields collection of **Field** objects. Each **Field** object has these properties: ActualSize, Attributes, DefinedSize, Name, NumericScale, OriginalValue, Precision, Type, UnderlyingValue, and Value. Of these, you use Value the most, and it is the default property of the **Field** object. You can access individual **Field** objects with the Fields collection by name or by number. For example, if you want to display all the columns of our Recordset, you would write

```
for j = 0 to rs.fields.count - 1
  response.write( rs(j) )
next
```

However, if you want to display only the column named "foo," you should address it as rs("foo"). Even if you know the column number for foo, it is better to address it by name. This way, if the column order of the query changes, then your code still works.

The Type property is helpful if you are creating an HTML form and want to know what input type to use. For example, here is a script to create an HTML form for editing a record of any Recordset:

```
<FORM ACTION="foo.asp">
<%
for j = 0 to rs.fields.count - 1
  if rs(j).type = adBoolean then
  response.write( rs(j).name & "<INPUT TYPE=CHECBOX" )
  else
  response.write( rs(j).name & "<INPUT TYPE=TEXT" )
  end if
%>
NAME="<%= rs(j).name %>"
VALUE="<% rs(j).value %>"
SIZE=<% rs(j).actualsize %>
MAXLENGTH=<% rs(j).definedsize %>
>
<%
next
%>
</FORM>
```

Scrolling Through Your Recordset

ADO creates all **Recordset** objects as cursors. When you refer to any of the properties mentioned in the previous section, such as the name or value of a field, you get information about the current record of a cursor. To retrieve information from other rows, you adjust your position in the **Recordset** with the cursor. ADO supports four types of cursors: Dynamic, Keyset, Static, and Forward-only. Dynamic is the most robust. You can move any which way you like through the Recordset, you can update records, and you can see changes made by other users. Keyset is similar, but you can't see changes made by other users. Static is read-only, and Forward-only is read-only and only supports movement in one direction.

The default cursor is Forward-only, which turns out to be exactly what you want for the vast majority of all Web pages. Typically, you are retrieving records and listing them on your page. Period. You don't need to update the records. After you have written a record to the HTTP output, you usually don't need to refer back to it. The performance is fastest on Forward-only cursors, so use them unless you need the extra functionality of a Dynamic, Keyset, or Static cursor. In fact, the ODBC drivers provided by some RDBMS makers support only forward-only cursors. This is their way of forcing you to use native drivers instead.

With Forward-only cursors, there is only one method for advancing through the Recordset – the **MoveNext** method. The syntax is simply

```
recordset.movenext
```

For example:

```
do while not rs.eof
  response.write( "<TD>" & rs(0) & "</TD>" )
  rs.movenext
loop
```

This loop outputs Field 0 for every record in the Recordset. An easy mistake to make is forgetting the MoveNext command, which results in an infinite loop if your loop test is the End Of File (EOF). EOF is one of the properties of the **Recordset** object. It is a Boolean value that ADO sets to true when you call MoveNext on the last record of the Recordset.

Good Housekeeping

Your mother was right to tell you to put away your toys when you finish playing with them. The same applies to database objects. When you are finished with a Recordset or a Connection, you should call the Close method. This frees up your connection to the database and any locks you may have been holding on the tables that you were using. Although calling the Close method is not mandatory for the Recordset object, it's still a good habit to get into. As it turns out, the Recordset object closes any open connections when it goes out of scope.

Multiple Recordsets

You can have any number of connections or Recordsets open that you need. However, don't make this common mistake:

```
set conn = server.createobject( "ADODB.Connection" )
conn.open "MY_DSN"
set rs1 = conn.execute( "sp_A" )
set rs2 = conn.execute( "sp_B" )
```

This leads to a cryptic error about being busy with another connection. What's going on here is this: rs1 is using the connection variable for its cursor. This is going to keep the connection tied up until you close rs1. However, rs2 needs the connection concurrently for the results of stored procedure B, and so the creation of rs2 fails. Either you must close rs1 before you open rs2:

```
set conn = server.createobject( "ADODB.Connection" )
conn.open "MY_DSN"
set rs1 = conn.execute( "sp_A" )
' Do whatever you need to do with rs1
rs1.close
set rs2 = conn.execute( "sp_B" )
```

or you must create two connections:

```
set conn1 = server.createobject( "ADODB.Connection" )
set conn2 = server.createobject( "ADODB.Connection" )
conn1.open "MY_DSN"
conn2.open "MY_DSN"
set rs1 = conn1.execute( "sp_A" )
set rs2 = conn2.execute( "sp_B" )
```

Another option for multiple Recordsets is to store a Recordset in an array. This might be appropriate for records that you intend to use repeatedly. Rather than holding a connection open to the database, you can put all the records of the Recordset into an array. The Recordset option provides a GetRows method to save you from looping through the Recordset to populate the array. The syntax is simply

```
Set array = recordset.GetRows(Rows, Start, Fields)
```

Rows, of course, is the number of rows that you want to retrieve. The default, -1, requests all rows. *Start*, of course, is the first row that you want retrieved, and it defaults to your current position in the Recordset. Thus, if you have already fetched five rows before you call GetRows, then you will start with the sixth row. *Fields* is an array holding either the names or column numbers of the columns that you want to retrieve. By default, you get them all.

Updating Data in the Database

Unfortunately, updating data with ASP is not as simple as we would like. Sure, ADODB gives you all kinds of operations for posting changes from a Recordset to a database, but these methods are of little value to you as the Web site developer.

Your database changes will be coming from the input of HTML forms. In this section, we discuss how to post that data back to the database.

The ASP that updates your database is the ASP that is named in the ACTION tag of the HTML form the user filled out. The data that must go into the database is therefore in the name value pairs of the **Request** objects. Hopefully, you will at least do yourself the favor of naming the columns in your HTML forms with the same names that the database is using. If not, you have to create a **Dictionary** object to map the HTML form names into the database names. We assume in this section that the name value pairs of the **Request** object are the actual database column names.

Following is a generic ASP script for updating any table, assuming that you pass the special parameters shown in Table 7-2.

TABLE 7-2 PARAMETERS FOR UPDATE-TABLE ASP SCRIPT

Parameter	Meaning
table_name	The name of the table or view that you plan to update
table_columns	A comma-delimited string of the columns that you want to update
what_is_text	A comma-delimited string indicating which table_columns are strings
primary_key	The name of column to be used in the where clause, typically the primary key

```
<%
set conn = server.createobject("adodb.connection")
conn.open "my_dsn"

sql = "update " & request("table_name") & " set "
foo = split( request("table_columns"), "," )
bar = split( request("what_is_text"), "," )
for i = 0 to ubound(foo)
     x = foo(i)
     if bar(i) = "Y" then
             sql = sql & x & " = '" & replace( request( x ), "'",
"''" ) & "', "
     else
             sql = sql & x & " = " & request( x ) & ", "
     end if
next
sql = replace( sql, " = ,", " = null," )
sql = sql & "- end "
sql = replace( sql, ", - end", " where " & request("primary_key") &
" = " & request(request("primary_key")) )
```

```
conn.execute( sql )
%>
```

There are a number of important points in this script:

♦ We are using a trusted connection to SQL Server. No userid or password appears in the ASP file.

♦ We use the split function to convert a comma-delimited string into an array. VBScript's split function doesn't support regular expressions like PerlScript's split does, but it is still quite useful.

♦ We loop through the columns to build the update statement. Passing a string of the column names isn't necessary, strictly speaking. We could get this information by querying the RDBMS, but that would be less efficient.

♦ String data must be enclosed in single quotes in an update statement, hence the need for special handling.

♦ Because string data is enclosed in quotes, we have a bit of a problem if the value itself contains quotes. For example, suppose we want to set the column foo to the string "don't." When we write 'don't,' SQL Server sees "don" as the string value, and "t" appears as a syntax error. The ANSI standard for coping with this is to escape a single quote with another single quote. Hence, we would write **foo = 'don''t.'** Note that this escape is *only* for the single quote character.

♦ A null value is displayed as an empty string on an HTML form, and this is how nulls appear in our Request object – as empty strings. When we update numbers, this won't work because we send commands like "set foo = ," to the RDBMS. Therefore, we change the SQL to read "set foo = null,." For our strings, we have "set foo = ''," which is legal. Here we have a bit of problem. We could change this to "set foo = null," also, but suppose the user really wanted the column to hold the value '' instead of null? The trouble lies in our original HTML form. We would have to supply a check box for each nullable string column to let the user indicate if the column is null.

♦ We build the update string with a comma after each column name-value pair, but the last column can't have such a comma. Therefore, we take it back with a replace function, and at the same time we append our where clause.

To make this example complete, we simply need to tell the client browser where to go once our update is complete. The best way to handle this is to pass a go_back_to value to the form:

```
Response.Redirect( go_back_to )
```

Inserting New Records

What about inserting new records? The method is similar, except that we need to create an insert statement instead of an update statement. There are at least two additional curve balls regarding inserts. First, you presumably have some required fields. You owe it to yourself to write some client-side JavaScript to check that the user fills them out. However, you still have to check for this on the server side, because not everyone is going to have a browser that understands your JavaScript. The other tricky part is dealing with automatically generated surrogate keys. Here is an ASP to insert a row into any table, given the same HTML form parameters as in the update example:

```
<%
 sql = "insert " & request("table_name") & " ( " &
 request("Non_key_name") &" ) values ( "
 foo = split( request("Non_key_name"), "," )
 bar = split( request("what_is_text"), "," )
 req = split( request("what_is_required"), "," )

 for i = 0 to ubound(foo)
     x = foo(i)

     missing = ""
     if req(i) = "Y" then
             val = request( x )
             val = replace( val, " ", "" )
             if len(val) = 0 then missing = missing & "missing=" &
 x & "&"
         end if
         if ( missing <> "" and request("what_is_required") <> "" )
 then
                 response.redirect( request("fail") & "?" & replace(
 missing & "-end", "&-end", "" ) )
         end if

         if bar(i) = "Y" then
                 sql = sql & "'" & replace( request( x ), "'", "''" ) &
 "', "
         else
                 sql = sql & request( x ) & ", "
         end if
 next
 sql = replace( sql, " on,", " 1," )
 sql = replace( sql, ", ,", ", null," )
 sql = replace( sql, ", ,", ", null," )
 sql = sql & ") - end"
 sql = replace( sql, ", ) - end", " )" )

 set conn = server.createobject("adodb.connection")
 conn.open "my_dsn"
 conn.execute( sql ) %>
```

```
set rs = conn.execute( "select @@identity global_identity" )
global_identity = rs("global_identity")
rs.close

if request("sql") <> "" then
      sql = request("sql")
      sql = replace( sql, ", ,", ", null," )
      sql = replace( sql, ", ,", ", null," )
      sql = replace( sql, "@@identity", global_identity )
      conn.execute( sql )
end if

go_back_to = replace( go_back_to, "@@identity", global_identity )
%>
```

All the comments about the update ASP apply to this ASP as well, but here we have a few additional considerations:

◆ We passed a hidden value in the form named "what_is_required." The ASP code is looking for a comma-delimited string of Y and N letters. The first letter tells us if the first column is required, the second letter tells us if the second column is required, and so on. Therefore, a string such as "Y,N,N,Y,Y," tells us that the first, fourth, and fifth columns are required. This is *not* something that we could necessarily get from the RDBMS. We loop through the columns looking for empty values for required fields, and we count a string of spaces as being empty. After we make a list of columns that came up empty, we pass the ball to the ASP named in the "fail" parameter for further processing. In this ASP, you might give the user a polite error message and tell the user which columns were omitted.

◆ Bit fields in the RDBMS hold the values 0 and 1, as you would expect. Regrettably, these appear as 0 and -1 in ODBC, an important point to remember when writing if-then statements. To make matters more confusing, you most likely display bit fields as check boxes. A check box passes the value "on" in its name value pair, so we must convert this to a 1.

Once we send the SQL statement to the RDBMS, we aren't quite done. Most RDBMSs support the creation of *surrogate keys,* numbers that the RDBMS creates that uniquely identify records. When you have inserted a row, you may want to know the key number that the RDBMS picked for you. We discuss how to do this for SQL Server; methods for other RDBMSs vary.

SQL Server provides surrogate keys with identity columns. The proper way to check the identity value that SQL Server gave you is to query a global variable named *@@identity.* Any other method might lead to trouble. For example, it isn't enough to simply find the maximum surrogate key value and assume that you got the next number in line. Another user might perform an insert in the millisecond between your query of the maximum surrogate key and your insert. Furthermore,

SQL Server allows identity increments to be set by the table creator, so the keys might increment by 2, or 10, or even -1!

Therefore, we query @@identity in the ASP immediately after we make the insert. Allowing for the fact that we may want to take some action with this @@identity, we test to see if the form included a SQL parameter. If it did, we replace the string "@@identity" in that SQL with the true value of the surrogate key and execute the SQL. We also pass the value of the surrogate back in the URL, should we happen to need it.

Trapping for Errors

During development, it would be convenient if all errors from the RDBMS were sent straight to the HTML output. Probably the most common mistake is forgetting to include the correct spaces in your CommandText. For example:

```
set rs = conn.execute( "select * from foo where c1=" & _
request("c1") & "and c2=" & request("c2") & "order by 1" )
```

If c1 = 1 and c2 = 2, send this text to the RDBMS:

```
select * from foo where c1=1and c2=2order by 1
```

In this SQL statement, *1and* and *2order* are syntax errors, and SQL Server sends an error message back to ODBC to that effect. Yet in your HTML output, you are likely to see something like this:

```
Invalid operation on closed object
```

Huh? Here's what's happening. ADO takes the error messages from SQL Server, silently stores them in the **Error** object, and let's your script keep running. This is a feature. However, you don't have a valid **Recordset** object because the Execute method failed. Therefore, any attempt to use your **Recordset** object, such as rs.eof, rs(0), or even rs.close fails.

The **Connection** object contains an Errors collection composed of **Error** objects. The count property of the Errors collection tells you how many **Error** objects are currently in the Errors collection. The Clear method of the Errors collection removes all the **Error** objects.

The **Error** objects themselves contain information about the errors, such as the descriptions and so on. Therefore, the best way to handle your Recordsets is like this:

```
conn.errors.clear 'Clear the errors just in case
set rs = conn.execute( sql )
if conn.errors.count = 0 then
'Do all your Recordset processing here
```

```
 rs.close 'Note that the close is in this branch of the if-then
 'If the Execute failed there is no Recordset to close.
else
 response.write( "<BR>Connection Errors Encountered:<BR>" )
 for j = 0 to conn.errors.count - 1
 response.write( conn.errors(j).description & "<BR>" )
 next
 conn.errors.clear 'This is where the clear should go
end if
```

Summary

ADO provides a simple, object-based interface to any ODBC-compliant RDBMS. All you need to do is instantiate the ADODB.Connection object, call its Open method to connect to an RDBMS, and then use the Execute method to create a Recordset. You then have an object holding the results of a SQL statement, a base table, or an RDBMS stored procedure. Not only does the **Recordset** object give you the data, but it provides data dictionary information such as column names, datatypes, and defined lengths. The errors from the RDBMS are placed in a special errors object so that you can proactively manage the connection.

Chapter 8

The Advertisement Rotator

IN THIS CHAPTER

Money makes the world go 'round. It's one of the oldest and truest adages in life. Life on the Internet is no exception. The fastest growing segment of Internet business — in terms of dollars of revenue — is advertising.

Before we begin, we should let you know that one of us (the one writing this chapter) has a degree in business, reads *The Wall Street Journal* every day, and actually enjoys doing competitive market analysis summaries. This chapter, therefore, covers much more than just the mechanics of Web advertising. It also details how to apply those principles to earn revenue from your Web site. No, this is not a plug for another Internet-get-rich-quick scheme. Instead, it's a recipe for applying usage data to more effectively deal with your site and your customers.

This chapter, then, is about much more than just how to put ads into your Web site. We cover the following:

◆ How to put ads onto a page

◆ How to give preference to certain advertisements

◆ How to track your users' interest in those advertisements so that you can decide advertisement rates

Go to any search engine and look at the top of the page. No doubt, you will see an advertisement banner that differs from visit to visit. Have you ever wondered why those ads are there?

Think about it. It costs money — *a lot* of money — to run a heavily visited Web site. Yet most sites don't charge you anything. How are they making money? It's simple. They make it the same way your local TV station makes it — through advertising.

Until now, much effort was needed to maintain all those ad links on a site. They have to be scheduled, formatted, and metered, which are no small tasks. Fortunately for you, ASP's Ad Rotator component does all this for you.

The *Ad Rotator* component automates the rotation of advertisement images on a Web page. Each time a user opens or reloads the Web page, the Ad Rotator component displays a new advertisement based on a schedule that you set. This scheduling information is kept in a special file called the *Rotator Schedule File*. All you need to do is create the component on your page and point it to your file. After that, the rest is up to ASP. For example, the following code instantiates the **AdRotator** object, gets an ad from the scheduler file, and prints to the client:

```
<%
 Set NextAd = Server.CreateObject("MSWC.AdRotator")
 AdHTML = NextAd.GetAdvertisement("/ads/schedule.txt")
 Response.Write(AdHTML)
%>
```

This code creates the Ad Rotator object, retrieves the HTML for the next ad in the schedule, and displays that HTML. That's all there is to it!

The Schedule File

By far, the most important part of this component is the schedule file. This is where you specify which ads you want to run, in which order, and how often. The basic structure of this file is as follows:

[REDIRECT URL]

[WIDTH numWidth]

[HEIGHT numHeight]

[BORDER numBorder]

*

adURL

adHomePageURL

Text

impressions

This file is really in two sections. The first section—everything up to the asterisks—contains global parameters that apply to all the ads. The second section contains the information about each individual ad. In the following sections, we discuss what each piece means and how to use it.

REDIRECT URL

The idea behind the rotator is that when you click on an ad, your browser is redirected to the home page of the sponsoring company. There are two ways to accomplish this:

1. ASP can do it automatically.

2. You can implement the redirection yourself.

If ASP were to perform this operation automatically, you couldn't track statistics relative to which ads were attracting the most attention. Therefore, ASP gives you the option to implement your own redirection file. Basically, this file is any .asp, .dll, or .exe file that can implement redirection. For example, a basic .asp file to do this is

```
<% Response.Redirect(Request.QueryString("url")) %>
```

On the other hand, if you do not include the *Redirect* parameter, then ASP simply performs the redirection for you. Don't worry, we go into more depth about what you can do with a redirection file later in the chapter.

WIDTH numWidth

This parameter specifies, in pixels, the width of the advertisement. If you omit it, ASP defaults to 440 pixels.

HEIGHT numHeight

This parameter specifies, in pixels, the height of the ad. Should you opt to leave it out, ASP uses a default of 60.

BORDER numBorder

This parameter sets the width, in pixels, of the border surrounding the ad. If you leave this parameter out, ASP uses a default of 1. If you don't want any border surrounding your ad, set this value to 0.

adURL

Each advertisement on your page consists of an image on which the user can click. The *adURL* parameter specifies the URL to that image for a particular ad. Keep in mind that this URL doesn't necessarily have to point anywhere within your site. It can point to *any* URL you choose.

adHomePageURL

If users are interested in the advertisement they are seeing, then they click on it to get more information. The *adHomePageURL* parameter specifies the URL to which users should be taken when they click on the ad. If you do not want them to go to another page for this specific ad, you can simply enter a hyphen (-) for this parameter. This tells ASP not to redirect the user's browser.

Text

Believe it or not, some users still use browsers that do not support graphics or have graphics disabled. The *Text* parameter holds the text to be displayed instead of the ad graphic for those users unable to view images.

impressions

Not all advertisers are created equal. Some pay you more money to display their ads more frequently to your users. The *impressions* parameter specifies a number between 0 and 4,294,967,295 that indicates the relative weight of the advertisement.

For example, if you have three ads with impressions set to 2, 3, and 5, the first advertisement is displayed 20 percent of the time, the second 30 percent of the time, and the third 50 percent of the time.

An Example

The following sample schedule file gives you an idea of how a normal schedule file looks when you are done. It defines two ads that run with equal frequency.

```
REDIRECT /scripts/adredir.asp
WIDTH 440
HEIGHT 60
BORDER 1
*
http://www.goodDeals.com/images/ad1.gif
http://www.goodDeals.com
Great Deals On Stuff You Don't Need
20
http://www.delta1.org/~pewter/ad.gif
http://www.delta1.org/~pewter
The Best Pewter Sculptures On The Net!
20
```

Redirection File

In our opinion, the *most* important part of the whole advertisement process is the redirection file. This is where you can keep statistics about which ads are getting the most attention.

The redirection file receives two parameters from ASP — *url* and *image*. The *url* parameter contains the URL of the Web page associated with the displayed ad, and the *image* parameter contains the URL of the image displayed in the ad.

At a minimum, a redirection file should send the user to the page associated with the displayed ad. For example, the following code is the minimum required for this file:

```
<% Response.Redirect(Request.QueryString("url")) %>
```

Beware the Extra Spaces!

This one bit us hard the first time we ran across it. If you have extra spaces at the end of any of the lines in the schedule file, then your ad may not display. It took us a while to figure this out the first time we witnessed this behavior, so please be careful.

Of course, a redirection file that simple doesn't buy you much. Instead, you probably want to keep some statistics about what ads are interesting to your users.

Example 1 – The Simple Ad Meter

In this section, we show you how to create a simple ad meter that stores click statistics in a small Access data table. Of course, you can set up this table in something more robust than Access (like SQL Server), but for now, Access will do fine.

The adCounter Table

First, you need to define what your table is going to be like. For the purposes of this example, we call our table *adCounter*. Table 8-1 shows how we define it.

TABLE 8-1 THE SCHEDULE FILE PARAMETERS

Field Name	Field Type	Primary Key?	Has Index?
AdURL	Text	Yes	Yes
Clicked	Number	No	No
Client	Text	No	No
Description	Text	No	No
ImageURL	Text	No	No
Impression	Number	No	No

The *adURL* field contains the URL to which the user was redirected, and the *clicked* field contains a running total of the number of users who have clicked on the ad. An explanation of the remaining fields are deferred until later in the chapter.

The example1.asp File

The next piece of this example is the main ASP file – example1.asp. It is a simple script that loads the next ad from the schedule file. Here's the code:

```
<html>
<body>

<%
 Set NextAd = Server.CreateObject("MSWC.AdRotator")
 AdHTML = NextAd.GetAdvertisement("/temp/schedule.txt")
%>

<% =AdHTML %>

</body>
</html>
```

As you can see, all we are doing here is creating the rotator object, getting the HTML for the next ad, and displaying that ad.

The Schedule File

The next piece of this example is the schedule file. For the purposes of this example, it is also simple.

```
REDIRECT /ch08/adredir.asp
BORDER 1
*
http://gov.noblestar.com/gif/gov_bar.gif
http://gov.noblestar.com
Noblestar Systems Corp. - Government Systems Division
10
http://et.noblestar.com/images/nslogo.gif
http://et.noblestar.com
Noblestar Systems Corp. - Emerging Technologies Division
10
```

This file defines two ads. The first is for Noblestar's Government Systems Division (the place where Dave works). The second ad is for Noblestar's Emerging Technologies Division (the place where Andrew works). These ads are set to show equally.

The Redirection File

The final, and most important, piece of this example is the redirection file itself. First we show you the code, and then we explain it.

```
<%
 URL = Request.QueryString("url")
```

```
set conn = Server.CreateObject("ADODB.Connection")
conn.Open "dsn=ASP Book"

SQLQuery = "SELECT count(*) as count FROM adCounter WHERE adURL =
'" & URL & "'"
set RS = Conn.Execute(SQLQuery)

If (RS("count") = 0) Then

SQLQuery = "INSERT INTO adCounter VALUES ('" & adURL & "'," & _
"1,'','',10,'')"
Else
SQLQuery = "UPDATE adCounter SET clicked = clicked + 1" & _
" WHERE adURL = '" & URL & "'"
End If

set RS = Conn.Execute(SQLQuery)
Response.Redirect(URL)

%>
```

Again, this code is very straightforward. First, we get the URL to which to direct the user. Next, we open a connection to the ODBC data source that references our database. (In this case, we called that source "ASP Book.") Next, we figure out if there is currently a record in the *adCounter* table that references our target URL. If not, we add one and give it a clicked count of one. Otherwise, we simply increment its clicked counter by one. Finally, we redirect the user's browser to the referenced Web page. See, we told you it was simple! Later in this chapter, we expand on this example to show you how to track these statistics to create advertising rates.

The GetAdvertisement Method

The Ad Rotator component has only one method – GetAdvertisement(). This function gets an advertisement from a specific schedule file. For example, this code:

```
AdHTML = NextAd.GetAdvertisement("/temp/schedule.txt")
```

retrieves an ad from the schedule file */temp/schedule.txt.*

Properties

The Ad Rotator component also has a number of properties associated with it. In this section, we discuss each of them.

Border

The *Border* property determines what size border ASP displays around the ad. For example, the following code displays no border:

```
Ad.BorderSize(0)
```

Clickable

The *Clickable* property determines whether the user can click on the particular ad being shown. A value of TRUE allows the user to click on the ad, while a value of FALSE disallows it.

TargetFrame

As you have seen in Chapters 4 and 6, an HTML page can consist of many frames, within which other HTML pages can be shown. The *TargetFrame* property of the Ad Rotator component specifies in which frame the linked URL (that is, the page that the user will be redirected to) will show. For example, the following code loads the referenced URL into the frame named *AdFrame* if the user clicks on the ad:

```
<%
Set ad = Server.CreateObject("MSWC.AdRotator")
ad.TargetFrame("AdFrame")
%>

<%= ad.GetAdvertisement("/temp/schedule.txt") %>
```

You can also use the standard HTML-reserved frame words for this attribute:

- ◆ _TOP. Always load this link at the top level.
- ◆ _NEW. Always load this frame as a new window.
- ◆ _SELF. Always load this link over yourself.
- ◆ _PARENT. Always load this link over the parent frame.
- ◆ _BLANK. Always load this link into a new, unnamed window.

Example 2 – Schedule Maintenance

As you may have guessed, there can be a lot of effort involved in effectively using the Ad Rotator component. Most of this effort involves tracking hits and maintaining the schedule file. In this section, we present an example of a program you can use to perform those functions. When it's done, this schedule maintenance application looks like Figure 8-1.

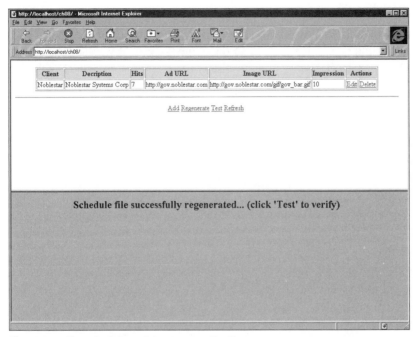

Figure 8-1: The schedule maintenance application

No need to worry about the underlying database as we are going to use the same *adCounter* table as from the previous example.

Default.htm

You first need to write the default page. All this page needs to do is set up the frames for the application. Here's the code:

```
<html>

<frameset rows=50%,*>
 <frame name=topFrame src=example2.asp></frame>
 <frame name=bottomFrame src=generate.asp></frame>
</frameset>

</html>
```

The top frame loads our next file, example2.asp, and the bottom frame automatically regenerates the schedule file.

Example2.asp

The heart of this application is its capability to view the information for each schedule entry and edit it. This is done in the following code. Essentially, this script is just creating an HTML table that holds all the records in the *adCounter* table. The steps are as follows:

1. ASP generates the header:

```
<html>

<head>
 <title>Example 2</title>
</head>

<body bgcolor=white>

<center>
```

2. Next, we open a database connection and create a Recordset that contains all the rows from the *adCounter* table:

```
<%
set conn = Server.CreateObject("ADODB.Connection")
conn.Open "dsn=ASP Book"

SQLQuery = "SELECT * FROM adCounter"
set RS = Conn.Execute(SQLQuery)

%>
```

3. Finally, we create the heading for our table:

```
<table border=1 bgcolor=white>
<tr bgcolor=cyan>
<th>Client</th>
<th>Description</th>
<th>Hits</th>
<th>Ad URL</th>
<th>Image URL</th>
<th>Impression</th>
<th colspan=2>Actions</th>
</tr>
```

Once all this preliminary stuff is out of the way, we get into the meat of the code. In this segment, we iterate through all the rows in the Recordset and create a corresponding row in our HTML table. The only thing to note here is the construction of HREFs for the edit and delete functions. Here's the code:

```
<%

Do While (RS.EOF = FALSE)

client = RS("client")
description = RS("description")
adURL = RS("adURL")
imageURL = RS("imageURL")
impression = RS("impression")
clicked = RS("clicked")

editHREF = "<a target=bottomFrame href=edit.asp?adURL=" & _
Server.URLEncode(adURL) & ">Edit</a>"

deleteHREF = "<a target=bottomFrame href=delete.asp?adURL=" & _
Server.URLEncode(adURL) & ">Delete</a>"


Response.Write("<tr><td>" & _
client & "</td><td>" & _
description & "</td><td>" & _
clicked & "</td><td>" & _
adURL & "</td><td>" & _
imageURL & "</td><td>" & _
impression & "</td><td>" & _
editHREF & "</td><td>" & _
deleteHREF & "</td></tr>")

RS.MoveNext

Loop

%>
```

After all that is finished, we close the table and add links for regenerating the schedule file, testing the ads, adding a new ad, and refreshing the display. Here's the code:

```
</table>

<hr>

<a href=add.asp target=bottomFrame>Add</a>
<a href=generate.asp target=bottomFrame>Regenerate</a>
<a href=test.asp target=bottomFrame>Test</a>
<a href=example2.asp>Refresh</a>

</center>

</body>
</html>
```

In terms of pure logic, this particular script is the most complex in the application. Once you understand it, the rest is simple.

Delete.asp

You can perform three basic operations on a row of data in a data table – *delete*, *edit*, and *add*. Of these, the delete operation is the simplest and, therefore, the one we cover first.

Delete.asp is passed the adURL from the clicked row in the **example2.asp** file. Because that piece of information is the primary key of the *adCounter* table, we can use it to delete the concerned record. The final script looks like this:

```
<%

 adURL = Request.QueryString("adURL")

 set conn = Server.CreateObject("ADODB.Connection")
 conn.Open "dsn=ASP Book"

 set RS = Conn.Execute("DELETE FROM adCounter WHERE adURL = '" & _
 adURL & "'")

%>

<html>
<center>
<h2>Record deleted... (click 'Refresh' to update display)</h2>
</center>
</html>
```

Edit.asp

Editing an existing record is a little tricky, but still not difficult. In this section, we walk you through it.

In the first chunk of code, we set up the headers and the form for the page:

```
<html>

<head>
 <title>Example 2</title>
</head>

<body bgcolor=white>

<form method=get action=update.asp>
```

Next, we retrieve all the columns for the record we are going to edit. It's important to note that we are storing the original adURL information *before* the record is edited. This is critical because it is possible to edit the adURL on this page. If we don't store the original value, then we have no way to change the record in the table!

```
<%

  adURL = Request.QueryString("adURL")

  set conn = Server.CreateObject("ADODB.Connection")
  conn.Open "dsn=ASP Book"

  SQLQuery = "SELECT * FROM adCounter WHERE adURL = '" & adURL & "'"
  set RS = Conn.Execute(SQLQuery)

  client = Server.HTMLEncode( RS("client") )
  description = Server.HTMLEncode( RS("description") )
  adURL = Server.HTMLEncode( RS("adURL") )
  imageURL = Server.HTMLEncode( RS("imageURL") )
  impression = Server.HTMLEncode( RS("impression") )

  Session("adURL") = adURL

%>
```

The rest of this code is easy. All we are doing is constructing the form elements for each item in the record:

```
<center>

<table border=1 bgcolor=cyan>

<tr><th align=right>Client:</th>
 <td>
 <input name=client size=96 maxlength=255 value=<% =client %>
 </input>
 </td>
</tr>

<tr><th align=right>Description:</th>
 <td>
 <textarea cols=100 rows=5 name=description><% =description %>
 </textarea>
 </td>
</tr>

<tr><th align=right>Ad URL:</th>
 <td>
 <input name=adURL size=96 maxlength=255 value=<% =adURL %>
 </input>
 </td>
</tr>

<tr><th align=right>Image URL:</th>
 <td>
```

```
<input name=imageURL size=96 value=<% =imageURL %>
</input>
</td>
</tr>

<tr><th align=right>Impression:</th>
<td>
<input name=impression size=96 value=<% =impression %>
</input>
</td>
</tr>

</table>

<hr>

<input type=submit value=OK></input>

</center>

</form>
</body>
</html>
```

Add.asp

The script to add a new record to the table is virtually identical to the code to edit an existing record. There is only one significant difference – the stored session variable is empty. You will see why in the next section when we explain the code to update the table. Here's the final script:

```
<html>

<body bgcolor=white>

<form method=get action=update.asp>

<%

 Session("adURL") = ""

%>

<center>

<table border=1 bgcolor=cyan>

<tr><th align=right>Client:</th>
 <td><input name=client size=96></input></td>
</tr>

<tr><th align=right>Description:</th>
 <td><textarea cols=100 rows=5 name=description></textarea></td>
```

```
</tr>

<tr><th align=right>Ad URL:</th>
 <td><input name=adURL size=96 value="You MUST put a value
 here!"></input></td>
</tr>

<tr><th align=right>Image URL:</th>
 <td><input name=imageURL size=96></input></td>
</tr>

<tr><th align=right>Impression:</th>
 <td><input name=impression size=96 value=10></input></td>
</tr>

</table>

<hr>

<input type=submit value=OK></input>

</center>

</form>
</body>
</html>
```

Update.asp

Whenever you either edit or add a record to the *adCounter* table, the update.asp file is invoked. This code handles all the correct data manipulation for you. Here are the steps.

First, we get all the edited/added values from the previous page, and we get the original URL for the record. Then we open a database connection. Here's the code:

```
<%

 adURL = Request.QueryString("adURL")
 client = Request.QueryString("client")
 description = Request.QueryString("description")
 imageURL = Request.QueryString("imageURL")
 impression = Request.QueryString("impression")
 clicked = 0

 oldURL = Session("adURL")

 set conn = Server.CreateObject("ADODB.Connection")
 conn.Open "dsn=ASP Book"
```

When updating an existing record in a table, we have two choices. The first is to figure out what has changed in the row and construct a SQL UPDATE statement. The other choice is to delete the record and insert a new one with the new data.

This second option is much easier than the first and can also be used to add new records.

With this option, we first check to see if we are updating an existing record or inserting a new record. We do this by checking to see if the session variable we have been using is empty. If it is not empty, then we know we are editing an existing row. Because we have decided to use a DELETE/INSERT method instead of an UPDATE method, we must delete the existing information. Before we do that, however, we must first get any columns that we want to preserve (in this case the "clicked" column). Here's the code:

```
If ( Len(oldURL) > 0 ) Then

SQL = "select clicked from adCounter where adURL = '" & _
oldURL & "'"

set RS = Conn.Execute(SQL)

clicked = RS("clicked")

SQL = "DELETE FROM adCounter WHERE adURL = '" & oldURL & "'"

set RS = Conn.Execute(SQL)

End If
```

After we make all the necessary deletions, we can insert the new information:

```
SQL = "INSERT INTO adCounter VALUES ('" & adURL & "'," & _
clicked & ",'" & client & "','" & imageURL & _
"'," & impression & ",'" & description & "')"

set RS = Conn.Execute(SQL)

%>
```

Finally, we print a small message to tell the user that all is right in the world:

```
<html>
<center>
<h2>Record updated... (click 'Refresh' to update display)</h2>
</center>
</html>
```

Generate.asp

An application that maintains ad information in a database isn't much use unless it can also generate a new schedule file. The generate.asp code does exactly that. Although this script is not complicated, it is important to note that two lines of this code have hard-coded paths in them. All you need to do is alter them for your site.

Here's the entire script:

```
<%

Set fs = CreateObject("Scripting.FileSystemObject")
Set a = fs.CreateTextFile("c:\temp\schedule.txt", True)

a.WriteLine("REDIRECT /temp/adredir.asp")
a.WriteLine("BORDER 1")
a.WriteLine("*")

set conn = Server.CreateObject("ADODB.Connection")
conn.Open "dsn=ASP Book"

SQLQuery = "SELECT * FROM adCounter"
set RS = Conn.Execute(SQLQuery)

Do While (RS.EOF = FALSE)

description = RS("description")
adURL = RS("adURL")
imageURL = RS("imageURL")
impression = RS("impression")

a.WriteLine(imageURL)
a.WriteLine(adURL)
a.WriteLine(description)
a.WriteLine(impression)

RS.MoveNext

Loop

a.Close

%>

<html>
<center>

<h2>
 Schedule file successfully regenerated... (click 'Test' to verify)
</h2>

</center>
</html>
```

Test.asp

After you have modified your data and regenerated your schedule file, you certainly want to test your links. The following script runs your ads each time you load it. Once again, you need to beware of a hard-coded path in this script:

```
<html>
<body>

<%
 Set NextAd = Server.CreateObject("MSWC.AdRotator")
 AdHTML = NextAd.GetAdvertisement("/temp/schedule.txt")
%>

<% =AdHTML %>

</body>
</html>
```

Adredir.asp

Finally, you need some code to update the hit counter for each link. You should recognize this script as the same one we used in the previous example, except that we removed the code to insert a new row in the table. There is no need to have that code here because you will never run the following code for an ad that isn't already in the *adCounter* table:

```
<%
 URL = Request.QueryString("url")

 set conn = Server.CreateObject("ADODB.Connection")
 conn.Open "dsn=ASP Book"

 SQLQuery = "UPDATE adCounter SET clicked = clicked + 1 WHERE adURL
 = '" & URL & "'"

 set RS = Conn.Execute(SQLQuery)
 Response.Redirect(URL)

%>
```

Summary

Money is an inescapable force in our lives. As long as Web sites cost money to maintain, Web maintainers have to find new ways to raise funds.

In this chapter, we have shown you how to implement advertisements on your site and track their usage. Certainly, you can greatly expand the application we have provided you to gather statistics such as what pages are most visited or which times of the day are the most popular. With a little effort, you can even automate your rate and billing processes.

Chapter 9

Further Components in ASP

IN THIS CHAPTER

This chapter covers the remaining ASP components that ship with ASP. After this chapter, we discuss how to write your own components, but before you reinvent the wheel, let's look at the rest of what Microsoft has invented. We want to explore the **File Access, Browser Capabilities,** and **Content Linking** components. Each component presents an object or objects to perform tasks that would be awkward, cumbersome, or even impossible otherwise.

- ◆ The File Access component, an object for reading and writing files on your Web server

- ◆ The Browser Capabilities component, an object that streamlines and simplifies the headaches of creating Web pages to use the capabilities of specific browsers

- ◆ The Content Linking component, an object to quickly and easily link together a series of Web pages to be viewed sequentially

File Access Component

Absent from our discussion of scripting thus far has been any conversation about disk I/O. We can retrieve data from databases with the Data Access component, but how do we read and write to ordinary files? ASP provides the **File Access** component for that. This is actually two objects: a **FileSystemObject** object and a **TextStream** object. The **FileSystemObject** simply creates or opens a file, returning a **TextStream** object. The **TextStream** object exposes properties and methods to perform typical file manipulation operations, such as reading in a line, checking for End of File (EOF), and so forth.

FileSystemObject Object

The **FileSystemObject** creates or opens a file for your use. It has no properties and only two methods, one for creating a file and one for opening an existing file. The logical question to ask at this point is how to test for the existence of a file, so that you know which method to use. Regrettably, the **File Access** component fails to provide the means to do this, other than the two methods just mentioned. We discuss how to handle the issue of determining the existence of a file in the section "OpenTextFile Method."

The syntax for creating a FileSystemObject in VBScript is simply

```
Set fs = Server.CreateObject( "Scripting.FileSystemObject" )
```

With that, you are ready to use either of the two methods that the object exposes, CreateTextFile and OpenTextFile.

CREATTEXTFILE METHOD

The **CreateTextFile** method creates a file and returns a **TextStream** object that you can use to read or write from the file. The syntax is

```
object.CreateTextFile(filename[, overwrite[, unicode]])
```

The object here is your **FileSystemObject**. The filename is, of course, the name of the file. You have two Boolean flags, one to indicate if you want to overwrite the file and the other to specify ASCII (false) or Unicode (true). Contrary to what the ASP documentation would have you believe, *the overwrite flag defaults to true.* Make sure you explicitly specify the value of the overwrite flag in all code that you write!

Here's an example of using CreateTextFile:

```
Set fs = Server.CreateObject( "Scripting.FileSystemObject" )
Set ts = fs.CreateTextFile( "CreateTextFile_test.txt", false )
```

In the example code, we are being sloppy and not giving a full path to the file, which drops the file into the current directory – \WINNT\system32 – if no other directory were specified.

If you set overwrite = false and the file exists, then your script terminates with an error. It's up to you to catch this with On Error Resume Next in VBScript or with an eval() in JScript.

OPENTEXTFILE METHOD

The **OpenTextFile** method opens a text and returns a **TextStream** object that you can use to read from or append to the file. If the file doesn't exist, you can opt to create it. If the file does exist, you will be appending to it, not overwriting it.

The syntax is

```
[object.]OpenTextFile(filename[, iomode[, create[, format]]])
```

The parameters in this syntax are

> **object** The name of a FileSystemObject object
>
> **iomode** Either ForReading or ForAppending
>
> **create** A Boolean specifying whether or not to create the file if it doesn't exist
>
> **format** A Tristate value to indicate how to open the file — TristateTrue for Unicode, TristateFalse (default) for ASCII, TristateUseDefault to use the system default

In order to use named constants in your VBScript, such as ForReading, you must include the adovbs.inc file to define them. There is a corresponding adojavas.inc file for JavaScript.

Here is an example of using OpenTextFile:

```
Set fs = Server.CreateObject( "Scripting.FileSystemObject" )
Set ts = fs.OpenTextFile( "\Projects\ASP\test.txt" )
```

TextStream Object

The **TextStream** Object allows you to read and write from a file. The syntax is

```
TextStream.{property | method}
```

We discuss each property and method in detail. All **TextStream** properties are read-only. For the purposes of this discussion, assume that we have already created a **TextStream** object named *ts*.

ATENDOFLINE PROPERTY
The **AtEndOfLine** property returns true when the file pointer is pointing to a new line character. This property is only available for files opened for reading.

ATENDOFSTREAM PROPERTY
The **AtEndOfStream** property returns true when the file pointer has reached the end of a file. The following script demonstrates both the **AtEndOfLine** and **AtEndOfStream** properties. It simply reads a file character by character and prints it out with periods between characters and <HR> tags between lines. The script is as follows:

```
<%
 Set fs = Server.CreateObject( "Scripting.FileSystemObject" )
 Set ts = fs.OpenTextFile( "\Projects\ASP\test.txt" )
```

```
        do while ts.AtEndOfStream = false
             do while ts.AtEndOfLine = false and ts.AtEndOfStream = false
                  foo = ts.Read(1)
                  Response.write( foo & "." )
             loop
             ts.ReadLine
             Response.write( "<HR>" )
        loop
        ts.Close
%>
```

In the inner loop, we check for both a new line and EOF, because the file may not end in a new line.

CLOSE METHOD
The **Close** method closes a file. The syntax is simply

```
object.close
```

Since ts is our TextStream object, we would write

```
ts.close
```

COLUMN PROPERTY
The **Column** property gives the current column location of the file pointer, whether you are reading or writing. For the first character of a line, column = 2, so column = 1 means that you are at the beginning of a fresh line. Stated another way, when the **Column** property returns 2, the next character you write is the second character in the line.

LINE PROPERTY
Similar to the **Column** property, the **Line** property tells you which Line is the current line of the file pointer. Again, we have the cryptic convention that Line is equal to 1 before anything is written to the first line. The following script reads a file character by character and shows the column and line numbers. Note that we print the column and line numbers before beginning each loop to see when the properties equal 1. The script is as follows:

```
<%
  Set fs = Server.CreateObject( "Scripting.FileSystemObject" )
  Set ts = fs.OpenTextFile( "\Projects\ASP\test.txt" )

  Response.write( ts.line & "<HR>" )
  do while ts.AtEndOfStream = false
       Response.write( ts.column )
       do while ts.AtEndOfLine = false and ts.AtEndOfStream = false
```

```
            foo = ts.Read(1)
            Response.write( foo & ts.column )
        loop
        ts.ReadLine
        Response.write( "<BR>" & ts.line & "<HR>" )
    loop
    ts.Close
%>
```

If test.txt = "Hello\nWorld," the output would be

```
1
1H2e3l4l5o6
2
1W2o3r4l5d6
2
```

Notice that **Line** equals 2 for both lines. This is because the file doesn't end in a new line. If it did, Line would be 3 as we read the last line.

READ METHOD
The **Read** method reads a specific number of characters from a file and returns the result as a string. A new line counts as one character. If you request more characters than remain in the file, you simply get the rest of the file. The syntax is

```
object.Read(characters)
```

For example:

```
ts.Read( 100 )
```

READLINE METHOD
The **ReadLine** method reads from the current location in the file to the next new line character and returns a string. The new line is not included in the string, but the current position of the file is set to the first character after the new line. The syntax is

```
object.ReadLine
```

Assume that test.txt is just three characters: *a\nb*. Consider the following code fragment:

```
Set ts = fs.OpenTextFile( "\Projects\ASP\test.txt" )
foo = ts.ReadLine
bar = ts.Read(1)
```

In this case, foo = *a* and bar = *b*.

SKIP METHOD

The **Skip** method is like the **Read** method, but it discards the characters by skipping over them instead of returning them in a string. This is useful for bypassing a large volume of data. The syntax of the **Skip** method is

```
object.Skip(characters)
```

Assume this time that test.txt is "Hello\nSkipThisWorld." Here is a complete script to demonstrate the **Skip** method:

```
<%
 Set fs = Server.CreateObject( "Scripting.FileSystemObject" )
 Set ts = fs.OpenTextFile( "\Projects\ASP\test.txt", 1 )
 foo = ts.ReadLine
 ts.Skip(8)
 foo = foo + ts.ReadLine
 Response.write( foo )
 ts.Close
%>
```

The output is "HelloWorld."

SKIPLINE METHOD

If you have been following the list of **TextStream** methods, you can already guess what the **SkipLine** method does and what its syntax is. Sure enough, it skips a line of input and discards it, and the syntax is simply

```
object.SkipLine
```

WRITE METHOD

The **Write** method writes a string to a text file. With the **Write** method, we cross over from reading a file to writing to a file. The first point to bear in mind is that you can't do both. When you open a file, you have to specify whether you plan to read it or append it. The second point to consider is that you have to write sequentially to the file. You can't back up and insert or overwrite in the middle of the file.
    The syntax is

```
object.Write(string)
```

The following script is a complete example of using the **Write** method:

```
<%
 Set fs = Server.CreateObject( "Scripting.FileSystemObject" )
 Set ts = fs.OpenTextFile( "\Projects\ASP\test.txt", 2 )
 ts.write( "Write method test" )
 ts.Close
%>
```

VBScript doesn't offer the standard C escape sequences such as \t or \n, but you can put such characters into your strings with the chr() function. For example, suppose that earlier we had written

```
ts.write( "Write" & chr(13) & "method" & chr(9) & "test" )
```

The file test.txt would contain what a C programmer recognizes as "Write\nmethod\ttest." To avoid at least the new line problem, the **TextStream** object provides a special method.

WRITELINE METHOD

The **WriteLine** method does the same thing that the **Write** method does, and it puts a new line at the end of the file. We recommend using this method instead of using the chr() function because you leave all the work of figuring out when to use \n and when to use \r\n to **WriteLine**. The syntax is

```
object.WriteLine(string)
```

Refer to the **Write** method for example code.

WRITEBLANKLINES METHOD

If you want only the new line characters, then you want the **WriteBlankLines** method. It takes an integer parameter and writes that number of new lines to your file. The syntax is

```
object.WriteBlankLines(lines)
```

A File Access Example Script

One example of using the **File Access** component is to display ASP source code. The Adventure Works sample application included with ASP has a file named code.asp, which does exactly that. Instead, we write a file that shows the first four lines of each file named in a list.

One drawback (or feature, depending on your point of view) of the **File Access** component is that it provides no directory information. Using the following DOS command, we create a file that lists files:

```
dir /b *.asp > dir.txt
```

Then we read that file to open each file in turn:

```
<%
 path = "\Projects\ASP\JScript\"
 lft = chr(13)+chr(9)
 Set fs = Server.CreateObject( "Scripting.FileSystemObject" )
 Set ts_dir = fs.OpenTextFile( path & "dir.txt" )
```

```
Response.write( "<DL>" )
do while not ts_dir.AtEndOfStream
      file_name = ts_dir.ReadLine
      Set ts = fs.OpenTextFile( path & file_name )
      Response.write( lft & "<DT>" & file_name & "</DT>" )
      Response.write( lft & "<DD>" & ts.Read( 256 ) & "</DD>" )
      ts.close
loop
Response.write( chr(13) & "</DL>" )
ts_dir.Close
%>
```

Browser Capabilities Component

A common problem for Web developers is dealing with differences in browser capabilities. You may want to use features of JavaScript 1.2 in your client-side scripting, but you know that there will be users with versions of Internet Explorer and Netscape Navigator that don't support JavaScript 1.2. Moreover, even if you know which browser each of your clients has, how do you keep track of which browsers support frames or VBScript or background sounds? The **Browser Capabilities** component takes care of most of this work for you.

Client browsers send a USER_AGENT HTTP header to servers with their HTTP requests. The **Browser Capabilities** component reads this header to retrieve an ASCII string naming the browser, such as

```
Mozilla/4.0b2 (WinNT; I)
```

The **Browser Capabilities** component then searches for this string in a special file named browscap.ini. When it finds a match, the properties of the **Browser Capabilities** component reports what the browser does. If not, the properties default to unknown. You can change these defaults to a value of your choice.

In our example, HTTP_USER_AGENT, we are using Beta 2 of Netscape Navigator, which shipped well after ASP. Ah ha, you point out. What good is a browscap.ini file filled out sometime late in 1996? Microsoft has already thought of this and regularly posts updated browscap.ini files on their Web site. You can get the latest file at `http://www.microsoft.com/iis`. At the time of this writing, you can find browscap.ini files under Using IIS⇨Developing for IIS⇨Updates for IIS. You must save this file in the same directory as the browscap.dll, which should be \WINNT\system32\inetsrv\ASP\Cmpnts.

Browser Properties

The browscap.ini file that ships with ASP reports at least the properties shown in Table 9-1.

TABLE 9-1 COMMON BROWSER PROPERTIES

Property	Specifies
ActiveXControls	Whether the browser supports Active X Controls
backgroundsounds	Whether the browser supports background sounds
beta	Whether the browser is beta software
browser	The name of the broswer (Netscape, IE, and so on)
cookies	Whether the browser supports cookies
frames	Whether the browser supports HTML frames
javaapplets	Whether the browser supports javaapplets
javascript	Whether the browser supports javascript
majorver	The major version number of the browser
minorver	The minor version number of the software
parent	The parent browser, as defined in browscap.ini
platform	The user's operating system
tables	Whether the browser supports HTML tables
vbscript	Whether the browser supports VBScript
version	The full version number of the browser

The following code tests most of the properties of a given browser:

```
<% bc = Server.CreateObject("MSWC.BrowserType") %>
<table border=1>
<TR><TD>AK</TD><TD><%= bc.AK %></TD></TR>
<TR><TD>AOL</TD><TD><%= bc.AOL %></TD></TR>
<TR><TD>ActiveXControls</TD><TD><%= bc.ActiveXControls %></TD></TR>
<TR><TD>SK</TD><TD><%= bc.SK %></TD></TR>
<TR><TD>Win16</TD><TD><%= bc.Win16 %></TD></TR>
<TR><TD>backgroundsounds</TD><TD><%= bc.backgroundsounds
 %></TD></TR>
<TR><TD>beta</TD><TD><%= bc.beta %></TD></TR>
<TR><TD>browser</TD><TD><%= bc.browser %></TD></TR>
<TR><TD>cookies</TD><TD><%= bc.cookies %></TD></TR>
<TR><TD>crawler</TD><TD><%= bc.crawler %></TD></TR>
<TR><TD>frames</TD><TD><%= bc.frames %></TD></TR>
<TR><TD>javaapplets</TD><TD><%= bc.javaapplets %></TD></TR>
```

```
<TR><TD>javascript</TD><TD><%= bc.javascript %></TD></TR>
<TR><TD>majorver</TD><TD><%= bc.majorver %></TD></TR>
<TR><TD>minorver</TD><TD><%= bc.minorver %></TD></TR>
<TR><TD>parent</TD><TD><%= bc.parent %></TD></TR>
<TR><TD>platform</TD><TD><%= bc.platform %></TD></TR>
<TR><TD>tables</TD><TD><%= bc.tables %></TD></TR>
<TR><TD>vbscript</TD><TD><%= bc.vbscript %></TD></TR>
<TR><TD>version</TD><TD><%= bc.version %></TD></TR>
</table>
```

Run on IE 3.0, this script yields the following:

```
AK 0
AOL 0
ActiveXControls -1
SK 0
Win16 0
backgroundsounds -1
beta 0
browser IE
cookies -1
crawler Unknown
frames -1
javaapplets -1
javascript -1
majorver 3
minorver 01
parent IE 3.0
platform WinNT
tables -1
vbscript -1
version 3.01
```

However, on Netscape Navigator 4.0b2, the result is the following:

```
AK Unknown
AOL Unknown
ActiveXControls 0
SK Unknown
Win16 Unknown
backgroundsounds 0
beta -1
browser Netscape
cookies -1
crawler Unknown
frames -1
javaapplets -1
javascript -1
majorver 4
minorver 00
parent Netscape 4.00
platform WinNT
```

```
tables -1
vbscript 0
version 4.00
```

Testing for the Unknown

Before presenting some practical uses of the **Browser Capabilities** component, we want to emphasize that any or all properties might return "Unknown." Therefore, you can't write if-then logic that assumes that a value will be true or false, or even that a value will be a number. You must either test for "Unknown" or set a default that fits with your if-then logic. We discuss how to set defaults in "Editing browscap.ini."

The **Browser Capabilities** component lets your site be all things to all people. Instead of putting a link on your site that says "click here for a no frame version," you can simply write a script like this:

```
<%
bc = Server.CreateObject("MSWC.BrowserType")
 if bc.frames = 0 then
REM no frames version here
 elseif bc.frames = -1 then
REM frame version here
 else
REM ask the user if he has frames and redirect according
 end if
%>
```

An even better use of the **Browser Capabilities** component is to test for JavaScript-enabled browsers. Rather than messing with all kinds of fancy JavaScript hiding tricks, you can simply include your client-side JavaScript this way:

```
<%
bc = Server.CreateObject("MSWC.BrowserType")
 if bc.javascript = 0 then
REM give them the vanilla version
 else
REM JavaScript version
REM If bc.javascript is unknown, we'll give them the benefit of the
REM doubt and send the JavaScript code.
 end if
%>
```

We recommend that you make note when you encounter an unknown browser. You can either make a note of this in a file or append it to the server log. We prefer to append it to a file:

```
<%
 if bc.browser = "Unknown" then
 Set fs = Server.CreateObject("Scripting.FileSystemObject")
 Set ts = fs.OpenTextFile("\wherever\unknown_browser.log", 2)
```

```
For Each name In Request.ServerVariables
ts.Write(name& '=')
ts.WriteLine( Request.ServerVariables(name) )
Next
End if
%>
```

Check this log for holes in your browscap.ini file. What you should do about these holes is our next topic.

Editing browscap.ini

There are three good reasons to edit browscap.ini:

◆ Your site is being used by a browser not listed in Microsoft's latest browscap.ini file.

◆ You want to add your own default values for certain properties.

◆ You want to add more properties to browsers listed in your .ini file.

In this section, we discuss the structure of browscap.ini so that you feel comfortable changing it. The good news is that your changes are reflected immediately; you don't have to stop and restart your Web server. The syntax for browscap.ini is

```
; comments
[HTTPUserAgentHeader]
parent = browserDefinition
property1 = value1
...
propertyN = valueN
```

The syntax requires some explanation, but here's an example to clarify what's going on:

```
;;; Netscape 4.0

[Netscape 4.00]
browser=Netscape
version=4.00
majorver=#4
minorver=00
frames=TRUE
tables=TRUE
cookies=TRUE
backgroundsounds=FALSE
vbscript=FALSE
javascript=TRUE
javaapplets=TRUE
ActiveXControls=FALSE
beta=True
```

```
[Mozilla/4.0b1 (Win95; I)]
parent=Netscape 4.00
platform=Win95

[Mozilla/4.0b1 (WinNT; I)]
parent=Netscape 4.00
platform=WinNT
```

Semicolons denote comments, but only at the beginning of a line. In the previous text, the "; I)]" after WinNT is not a comment.

The HTTP User Agent Header must appear in square brackets. All text after that up to the next set of square brackets should be properties. You can use the * wildcard in the User Agent Header to denote zero or more characters. For example, rather than adding separate blocks for each new beta version of Navigator 4, we could write the following:

```
[Mozilla/4.0b* (Win95; I)]
parent=Netscape 4.00
platform=Win95

[Mozilla/4.0b* (WinNT; I)]
parent=Netscape 4.00
platform=WinNT
```

This then matches 4.0b1, 4.0b2, and so on.

The properties are listed as name value pairs in the format property = value. Property names must start with a letter and cannot be more than 255 characters. Happily, properties are not case-sensitive. Even if you are using JScript, which is a case-sensitive scripting language, the properties still aren't case sensitive. You can write *Version* in your file and still access it as *object.version* within JScript.

The parent property is special. By specifying a parent, you allow a browser to inherit all the properties of the parent. Therefore, Mozilla/4.0b2 still reports true for javascript and javaapplets, even though these properties are not listed in the [Mozilla/4.0b*] section. Explicitly specifying a property overrides the parent. For example:

```
[Mozilla/4.0Gold (WinNT; I)]
parent=Netscape 4.00
platform=WinNT
beta=False
```

We have overridden the beta property for the gold code version of Navigator 4.0.

ADDING PROPERTIES

The browscap.ini only provides a true/false value for javascript. In our opinion, that's inadequate. Which version of JavaScript is the client using? It could be 1.0, 1.1, or 1.2. We add a property to capture this.

Happily, the parent browser is all we need to determine the JavaScript version, so we add the following code indicated to each parent:

```
[IE 3.0]
javascriptversion = 1.1

[IE 4.0]
javascriptversion = 1.1

[Netscape 2.0]
javascriptversion = 1.0

[Netscape 3.0]
javascriptversion = 1.1

[Netscape 3.01]
javascriptversion = 1.1

[Netscape 4.00]
javascriptversion = 1.2
```

Now our newly created javascriptversion property is available to any ASP script you write:

```
<% Set bc = Server.CreateObject("MSWC.BrowserType")
Response.write( "Your JavaScript version is " & _
 bc.javascriptversion ) %>
```

DEFAULT PROPERTIES

Our javascriptversion property shown in the last section isn't quite ready for production. First of all, we ignored the [Oracle 1.5] parent, which supports JavaScript. Second, we made no attempt to address the issue of browsers without parents. Rather than spend hours carefully editing browscap.ini, we just declare a default. Any scripts we write should first check the javascript property to see if a browser has JavaScript at all. Assuming that it does, we'll play it safe and default to Version 1.0.

The syntax for declaring defaults is

```
[Default Browser Capability Settings]
defaultProperty1 = defaultValue1
```

We could add the following two lines anywhere in our browscap.ini that we would normally put a User Agent Header, but we prefer to put them at the beginning of the file for clarity:

```
[Default Browser Capability Settings]
javascriptversion=1.0
```

Now all browsers default to javascriptversion=1.0, unless the browser or its parents specifies otherwise.

Content Linker Component

Some sites have a string of HTML files that are best read sequentially. The easiest way for a user to read these files is to scroll forward and backward with *next* and *previous* buttons, and you also want to have such features as a table of contents. If you have a large number of files, a table of contents is a pain to set up and even more of a pain to maintain. Inserting a page in the middle requires changing links on other pages, and reordering the pages is a nightmare.

ASP, in combination with the **Content Linker** component, makes this a breeze. The idea is that instead of straight HTML, you will have ASP files for each page. These ASP files use the **Content Linker** methods to determine what URLs to use on their next and previous buttons. One text file lists the desired order of the ASP files and an optional description for each ASP page. If you change this text file, your links are automatically correct.

Our approach here is to discuss the methods of the **Content Linker** first, so that you have an idea of what it can do. Then we investigate creating a Content Linking List file. Finally, we pull it all together with an example script.

The syntax for creating a **Content Linker** object is

```
Set NextLink = Server.CreateObject("MSWC.Nextlink")
```

Content Linker Methods

Most of the **Content Linker** methods have the following syntax:

```
Object.Method(listURL)
```

The location of the Content Linking List file is listURL. Remember to use a virtual path to specify listURL. Two methods, **GetNthDescription** and the **GetNthURL**, use an additional parameter.

Many of the **Content Linker** methods are intended to be called from an ASP page that is on the Content Linking List. The calling ASP page is referred to as the *current page,* so that *next* and *previous* are always relative to the page invoking the method.

GETLISTCOUNT
The **GetListCount** method returns the number of pages listed in the Content Linking List file.

GETLISTINDEX
The **GetListIndex** method returns the index of the current page in the Content Linking List file. The first page is numbered 1, not 0. **GetListIndex** returns 0 when the page invoking the method is not in the Content Linking List file. **GetListIndex** is helpful for displaying page numbers:

```
Page <%= NextLink.GetListIndex( "nextlink.txt" ) %>
```

GETNEXTDESCRIPTION

The **GetNextDescription** method returns a string holding the description of the next page listed in the Content Linking List file. Remember that *next* is relative to the called page. If the calling page isn't in the Content Linking List, then **GetNextDescription** returns the description of the last page on the list.

GETNEXTURL

The **GetNextURL** method returns a string of the next URL in the Content Linking List file. This is one of the methods you use to create links:

```
<A HREF="<%= NextLink.GetNextURL( "nextlink.txt" ) %>">Next</A>
```

GETNTHDESCRIPTION

The **GetNthDescription** method gives the description of the Nth page listed in the Content Linking List file, counting from the first page at the top of the file. This is an absolute reference, not a relative one. The **GetNthDescription** and the **GetNthURL** methods are the two methods that take a second parameter. The syntax of **GetNthDescription** is

```
Object.GetNthDescription( listURL, N )
```

GETNTHURL

The **GetNthURL** method returns the URL of the Nth page listed in the Content Linking List file. Combined with **GetListCount,** you can use **GetNthURL** to create *Home* and *End* links:

```
the_end = NextLink.GetListCount( "nextlink.txt" )
<A HREF="<%= NextLink.GetNthURL( "nextlink.txt", 1 ) %>">Home</A>
<A HREF="<%= NextLink.GetNthURL("nextlink.txt",the_end) %>">End</A>
```

GETPREVIOUSDESCRIPTION

The **GetPreviousDescription** method returns a string that is the description of the previous page listed in the Content Linking List file.

GETPREVIOUSURL

The **GetPreviousDescription** method returns a string that is the URL of the previous page listed in the Content Linking List file.

Content Linking List File

The Content Linking List file specifies the files that you want to display. The order of the filenames is the order in which they are displayed. The syntax is

```
Web-page-URL [ text-description [ comment]]
```

A new line character must terminate each line. Because you are putting a text description for each line, characters such as commas and semicolons can't be used to separate the items. Therefore, the **Content Linker** component looks for a tab between the Web-page-URL, text-description, and comment items.

The Web-page-URL must be local to the server and accessible from a virtual path. The Content Linker ignores fully qualified URLs starting with *http://* and network files in the format *\\server name\file path*. The text-description can be whatever you want, as long as it does not contain tabs or new lines. Remember that this text is returned by some of the methods of the **Content Linker**. The comment is a comment for your reference.

Following is the Content Linking List file from the Adventure Works site:

```
/AdvWorks/excursions/Alaska.asp      Alaska Invitation
/AdvWorks/excursions/Washington.aspWashington Excursion
/AdvWorks/excursions/Patagonia.asp Patagonia Adventure
```

Using the Content Linker in a Script

We now have the tools to put the Content Linker to use for us. In this example, we take an arbitrary group of HTML files and translate them into ASP files for use with the Content Linker. Each file has the same header, which we insert with a server-side include.

To exploit as much of the Content Linker functionality as possible, our header displays the following:

- The page number of the current page

- The total number of pages

- The description of the next page, with a link

- The description of the previous page, with a link

- The description of the last page, with a link

- The description of the first page, with a link

The code we want is as follows:

```
<% Set NextLink = Server.CreateObject ("MSWC.NextLink") %>
<% the_end = NextLink.GetListCount( "nextlink.txt" ) %>

Page <%= NextLink.GetListIndex( "nextlink.txt") %>
 of <%= the_end %><BR>

<a href="<%= NextLink.GetNthURL( "nextlink.txt", 1 ) %>">
First</a> page:
<%= NextLink.GetNthDescription ("nextlink.txt", 1) %><BR>
```

```
<a href="<%= NextLink.GetPreviousURL( "nextlink.txt" ) %>">
Previous</a> page:
<%= NextLink.GetPreviousDescription ("nextlink.txt") %><BR>

<a href="<%= NextLink.GetNextURL( "nextlink.txt" ) %>">
Next</a> page:
<%= NextLink.GetNextDescription ("nextlink.txt") %><BR>

<a href="<%= NextLink.GetNthURL( "nextlink.txt", the_end ) %>">
Last</a> page:
<%= NextLink.GetNthDescription ("nextlink.txt", the_end ) %><BR>
```

When we are done, we see something like this at the top of each page:

```
Page 7 of 26
First page: Component Reference
Previous page: Connection Pooling
Next page: Content Linking List File
Last page: File Access Component
```

Warning: Geeky Stuff Ahead

The work in the next example is in converting the HTML files to ASP files and creating the Content Linking List. This requires some heavy-duty text manipulation, and there simply is no better choice for this task than Perl. Since many of you are CGI programmers accustomed to Perl, we feel comfortable including this. For those of you who are not, you may want to skim this section.

CONVERTING HTML TO LINKABLE ASP

The following script is a complete Perl script (not to be confused with PerlScript) for converting HTML to linkable ASP:

```
# This script facilitates linking HTML files
# as ASP scripts with ASP's Content Linker.
# Written by Andrew M. Fedorchek, 1997
# Distribute and use this to your heart's content.
# usage: ContentLinker.pl "compref*"
# links all files named "compref*.htm"

use strict;

# Load an array HTML files
my @files = (<$ARGV[0].htm>);
```

```perl
# If you don't want to sort alphabetically,
# supply your own sort routine.
my @sorted_files = sort @files;

open( NEXTLINK, ">nextlink.txt" ) || die "Phooey! ";

# We will open each file in turn,
# Writing it out to an ASP file with our ssi.
# We'll also snag the title as our description

my $file;
for $file(@files) {
 open( HTM, $file ) || die "Phooey! ";

 # The ASP file has the same name
 # with an .asp extension
 my $asp = $file;
 $asp =~ s/\.htm/.asp/i;
 open( ASP, ">$asp" ) || die "Phooey! ";

 while (<HTM>) {

        # Copy the line to the ASP file
        print ASP;

        # Look for the description
        if ( /<TITLE>(.+)<\/TITLE>/i ) {
                print NEXTLINK "$asp\t$1\n";
        };

        # We drop the ssi in right after the <BODY> tag
        if ( /<BODY/i ) {
                print ASP '<!-#include file="ContentLinkerHeader.asp"-
>';
        };
 };
};
```

For the non-Perl programmers, here's what's basically happening:

◆ The script takes an argument, a wildcard that corresponds to a list of htm filenames. For example, to link all files named comp*.htm, you pass the parameter *comp**. To link every last file in the directory, you simply use "*" as your argument.

◆ We load an array of filenames and sort it alphabetically. This is probably not the order you want, but the great part about the Content Linker is that you can change the order around.

◆ We open each HTML file one by one. Line by line, we copy the contents to an ASP file.

♦ We look for the tags <TITLE> ... </TITLE> and call whatever is in between the description. If the Title tags aren't on the same line, then this ASP isn't going to make the list, though the ASP is still created.

♦ On the first line after the string "<BODY," we insert our ssi. If there is a multiline body tag, the new ASP files aren't going to come out right.

If any of the files that you are linking contain frames, then those pages won't work right because the <FRAMESET> tags precede the body tags.

Summary

In this chapter, we explored three more ASP components. The **File Access** object provides access to the file system of the server. It provides methods to create and open files. Once you have an open file, you can read it by any number of techniques. You can read a specific number of characters, a whole line, or the entire file. For large files, you may want to skip a certain number of characters or lines for the sake of efficiency. The **File Access** object likewise lets you write characters and lines.

The **Browser Capability** component takes the guesswork out of dealing with various browsers. Capabilities such as support for frames or VBScript are captured as properties of an object. The **Browser Capability** component reads a master file of browsers that ships with ASP. Regularly getting free updates of this file from Microsoft saves you work. When you do need to tinker with the file yourself, you have much flexibility. Adding new browsers is as simple as inserting a few lines of text. New versions of existing browsers are particularly easy because you can declare a parent and then override specific properties. The **Browser Capability** component lets you specify default properties and invent your own properties.

The **Content Linker** is designed to be a major maintenance saver for linking together ASP files. When you have a group of files that should be read in a specific order, you need to at least be able to specify what's next. To make life easy on your users, you may also want to includes links to the previous page, the first page, the last page, and the description for each page. Without the **Content Linker,** inserting or removing pages or otherwise changing the order would require you to edit many links. The **Content Linker** allows a page to look itself up in a list and find out who its neighbors are and return that information to you.

Part IV

Writing Your Own ASP Components

Chapter 10

Writing Your Own ASP Component in Visual Basic

IN THIS CHAPTER

Throughout this book, we have shown you how to use ASP components in your Web applications. We are sure, though, that as you have been experimenting, you have thought of additional components that would be useful to you. In this chapter, we show you how to write your own components in both Visual Basic 4 and 5. Right off the bat, we assume that you are at least familiar with this tool. We are not going to spend much time orienting you to the Visual Basic environment. In this chapter, we cover the following:

- ◆ What is an ASP component?

- ◆ The basics of OLE automation

- ◆ How ASP handles OLE servers

- ◆ Writing your first components

As you may guess, a fair amount of explanation is needed before we can get into the how-tos of creating your own components. This is important stuff, and we strongly encourage you to resist the urge to blow past it. That having been said, let's get to it!

Two for the Price of One

By the time you read this, Visual Basic 5 will be a new tool on the market. When writing this chapter, however, we had a dilemma. Do we write it for the established VB4 or for the new VB5? In our usual decisive style, we did both! If you have never created an OLE automation component in VB, then read the *whole* chapter. Little has changed from VB4 to VB5 in this department, and we cover those changes near the end of the chapter.

What Is an ASP Component, Anyway?

Basically, an ASP component is an OLE automation server. The real question is: What is an OLE automation server? For that, we need briefly to discuss OLE.

A Short Tour of OLE

Not too many moons ago, the engineers at Microsoft thought it would be a good idea if users could drag documents from one application and drop them into documents of another application. For example, they wanted users to be able to drag a section of an Excel spreadsheet into an open Word document. Everyone agreed that this would be a neat idea, so they wrote it. Eventually, this capability became known as the Object Linking and Embedding (OLE) 1.0 standard.

A few years later, the folks at Microsoft revisited the OLE standard and decided to update it. Because object-oriented programming techniques and languages were coming into vogue, they thought that perhaps they should recast the OLE standard into more OO-friendly terms. Essentially, they wanted to give users the ability to drag functional segments from one application into the workspace of another application. Instead of simply having applications share documents, they wanted applications to share entire functional capabilities. This work eventually became the OLE 2.0 standard.

No discussion of OLE is complete without at least a cursory review of objects and object-oriented principles. If you are already familiar with these concepts, you can skip ahead to "OLE Automation." Otherwise, read on.

In our daily lives, we constantly manipulate objects. We drive cars, spend money, eat food, and so forth. Each of these objects has certain characteristics that describe it and its certain function. For example, an alarm clock can be black – a characteristic – and sound a buzzer at a certain time – a function. In object-oriented terms, we call these characteristics *properties* and the functions *methods.*

So far, with the exception of some new terms, this should be pretty simple. So what's the big deal?

Until recently, most computer languages were unable to describe things in these terms. They had no way of associating methods and properties with a common thing – an *object.* Instead, programmers had to go to great lengths to write software that worked around this fundamental limitation. By writing software in a language that supports object-orientation and by following good modeling and design principles, programmers can now avoid many of the headaches that used to plague them. For example, do you care about the particular mechanics by which your alarm clock sounds its buzzer? Of course not. All you care about is that it sounds at the appropriate time. The same is true in programming. You, as a developer, shouldn't have to worry about how a particular object implements its methods. You should only care that it performs the requested service.

Knowing that people would be developing and using components of software through OLE, the developers at Microsoft designed the standard to be inherently object-oriented. In fact, you have already seen the benefits of this design. Consider this: You have already used the **Server.CreateObject()** method to create an instance — a.k.a. *instantiate* — of an ASP component and have used it without any regard to how it handles your requests. As you see later, you can use these same components in development environments other than ASP. In fact, you can use them in any environment that supports OLE. This means that you can build a library of pre-built components that you can plug into your code, no matter what language you are writing in.

OLE Automation

Now that you have had the nickel tour of objects, it's time to talk more about OLE. The process by which one application uses the capabilities of another application is called *automation*. In order for a program — for example, Excel — to allow another program to control it, it must be written to be an *automation server*. This term makes sense. The controlling program is called the *client*, and the program being controlled is called the *server*. Servers, however, come in two distinct flavors: *in-process* and *out-process*.

IN-PROCESS SERVERS

An in-process server actually runs in the same memory space as the program calling it. These servers are contained in .DLLs and yield the best performance for an application because they don't incur the overhead of starting another process.

OUT-PROCESS SERVERS

Out-process servers, on the other hand, run in their own memory and process space and are contained in .EXEs. Since you already know that in-process servers perform better, you may be wondering why anyone would write an out-process server. The answer is convenience. It is possible for you to write an application that has a graphical interface (such as Word) and also is an automation server. In this case, it's easier to create the program as an out-process server and keep all the code wrapped up in one executable file. Otherwise, you have to write an .EXE for the program and a .DLL for its OLE services.

Using Out-Process Servers in ASP

By default, ASP does not allow you to use out-process servers with the **Server.CreateObject()** method. If you need to do this, you have to change the **AllowOutOfProcCmpnts** key in the ASP Registry tree to 1. For further reading on this, please refer back to Chapter 1.

Writing an OLE Server in Visual Basic 4

By far, Visual Basic is the easiest tool in which to write OLE automation servers. In fact, only a few simple steps are involved. Remember, even if you are using VB5, read this section!

An Overview

In order to author your first OLE server in VB, you only need to create two small files and flip a couple of switches. The first file you create is a generic module file. The only reason this file exists is so you can put your main subroutine in it. In fact, the file only contains the following two lines:

```
Sub Main
End Sub
```

The second file you need to create is a class file. A *class* is simply the template for an object. In fact, *object* is the term assigned to the particular instance of a class. For example, you could write a segment of code that describes an alarm clock. That segment, or template, is a class. When you actually create an instance or occurrence of that class, you have created an object.

After you create these two files, you can create your server.

STEP 1: CREATE A NEW PROJECT

From within the Visual Basic environment, select the File⇨New Project menu option. Click on **OK** to create the project.

STEP 2: DELETE THE DEFAULT FORM

Because the server we are going to create does not have a visual component, there is no need to keep the blank form that VB gave to us. Select the File⇨Remove File option to get rid of it.

STEP 3: SET THE PROJECT PROPERTIES

Okay, now that you have a clean slate, you can begin to create your server. First, you need to set a couple properties about this project. To do this, select the Tools⇨ Options menu item and click on the **Project** tab. The dialog box shown in Figure 10-1 should open.

First, give your project a decent name. Change the project name from *Project1* to *ASPBook*.

Next, tell VB that you want your application to be an OLE server. Do this by selecting the *OLE Server* radio button in the *StartMode* section.

Finally, give your project a description. Enter this in the text box labeled *Application Description*. When you are done, your dialog box should look something like Figure 10-2.

Figure 10-1: The Project properties

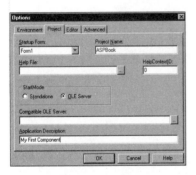

Figure 10-2: The complete Project properties

STEP 4: CREATE YOUR MAIN MODULE

After you set your project properties correctly, you need to create your main code module. Select the **Insert⇨Module** menu option. The screen shown in Figure 10-3 should appear.

This screen shows a blank code module. You first (although it's not strictly necessary) should rename this module to something more useful than *Module1*. You do this by changing the module's name in the properties window. For the sake of this example, name your piece *MainCode*.

Next, create an empty main subroutine in this module. Do this by typing **Sub Main** in the empty module window.

VB automatically adds the **End Sub** line and formats your code. It should look like Figure 10-4.

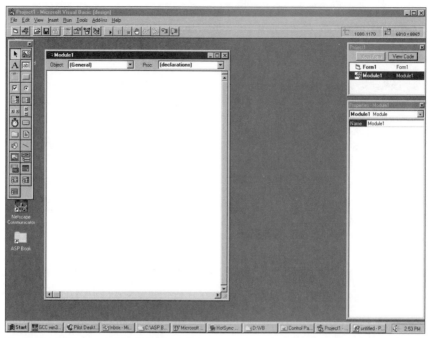

Figure 10-3: Your new, blank code module

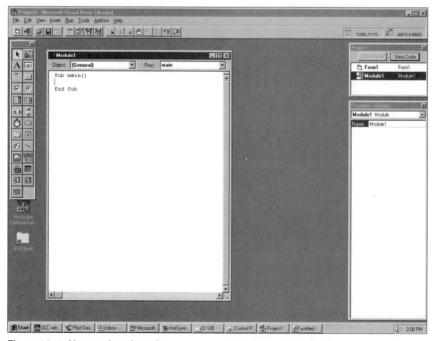

Figure 10-4: Your main subroutine

If you've gotten this far, then you're doing well. Go ahead and close this window.

STEP 5: CREATE YOUR FIRST CLASS

Now the fun begins. You need to know a couple things about the class you are about to create. First, it needs to be a *public* class. This means that it has to be accessible by programs other than the one that creates it.

When you instantiate an object, such as the **ADODB.Connection** object, you are actually creating an instance of a public class named **Connection**. Okay, if a class can be *public*, can it be *private*? You bet. A private class just means that it is accessible only by the program that created it.

Second, the class must also be able to have multiple instances. This simply means that memory for the class must be allocated in such a way as to allow for more than one client at a time to create it. That having been said, it's time for you to create your first class.

Select the **Insert⇨Class Module** menu item. The screen shown in Figure 10-5 appears.

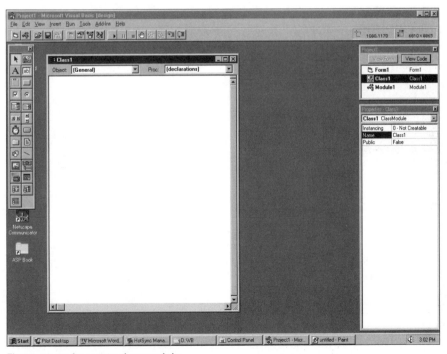

Figure 10-5: An empty class module

You first need to change some of this module's properties. First, change the name to something better than *Class1*. Try something more original, such as *MyFirstClass*.

Next, set the *Public* property to *True*. Otherwise, your class will not be visible to other programs or ASP.

Finally, change the *Instancing* attribute to *Creatable MultiUse*. This means that more than one program can instantiate this class at one time. After you set up the correct properties, it's time to create your code.

Type the following code into your module window:

```
Public Function Test() As String
 Test = "Hello World."
End Function
```

This code creates a public function named **Test()** that returns a string.

STEP 6: SAVE YOUR WORK

Now that you've gone to all this trouble, we think you should save your work. Trust us. Nothing is worse than losing your work because you forgot to save it!

STEP 7: CREATE THE .DLL

Create your .DLL by selecting **File⇨Make OLE DLL File**. The dialog box shown in Figure 10-6 appears.

Figure 10-6: DLL compilation

It's important to give your .DLL a meaningful name. It winds up being the first half of your object's progID. We name ours *example1.dll*. After you settle on a name, click on OK.

STEP 8: REGISTER YOUR COMPONENT

ASP ships with a program named **regsvr32.exe**. This program registers OLE automation servers in the registry of your machine. Where you can find this application depends entirely on where ASP was installed. Sometimes you can find it in your *windows\system* directory, as well. Your best bet is to use the Find command from the Start button to find this program. Once you find **regsvr32.exe**, you use it with the following command to register your server:

Regsvr32 *yourdll.dll*

You should get a message indicating a successful registration. Congratulations! You have just created your first ASP component.

STEP 9: TEST YOUR COMPONENT

All that's left is to test your component. For example, the following code tests our example component:

```
<html>
<body>

<%
 set myObject = Server.CreateObject("example1.MyFirstClass")
 Response.Write( myObject.Test() )
%>

</body>
</html>
```

Interfacing with the ASP Server

Certainly, creating your own ASP components is fascinating. What if we told you, however, that you also interact with internal ASP objects from within your component? That's just plain cool! In this section, we show you how.

THE SCRIPTINGCONTEXT OBJECT

When any particular ASP script runs, it is said to have a *scripting context*. This context encapsulates all the things known to the script – variables, session data, application data, and so forth. In order for your ASP component to utilize the internal ASP objects, your component must be able to manipulate the scripting context for the script that called your object.

Okay, so how do you *get* the scripting context for a given script? Easy. When ASP loads your component, it looks for a method named **OnStartPage().** ASP passes a *ScriptingContext* object to this method as a parameter. The *ScriptingContext* object (which we haven't mentioned until now) exists for the sole purpose of giving you access to ASP's internal components. In fact, this object has only five methods:

◆ **Application( )** returns a copy of the current Application object.

◆ **Request( )** returns a copy of the current Request object.

◆ **Response( )** returns a copy of the current Response object.

◆ **Server( )** returns a copy of the current Server object.

◆ **Session( )** returns a copy of the current Session object.

The following code should help bring all of this into focus. As we said earlier,

OnEndPage()

When ASP finishes processing a given page, it calls the **OnEndPage()** method for each object not declared in the Application scope. This means that you should put any cleanup code you need for your object in this method, because it is always the last method invoked for your component.

ASP looks for a method in your object named **OnStarPage()** and calls it when your object loads. The following code, to be declared in *MyFirstClass*, prints some HTML when the component is loaded:

```
Public Function OnStartPage(myScriptingContext As object)

 set myResponse = myScriptingContext.Response()
 myResponse.Write "<CENTER><H1>INSIDE COMPONENT!</H1></CENTER>"

END Function
```

This is straightforward stuff. The scripting context for the calling script is passed to the function, which, in turn, uses it to get a copy of the current **Response** object. Then it uses the **Write()** method to write some HTML out to the client. Of course, you don't have to limit yourself to using the **ScriptingContext** object from within this particular method. You can assign it to a global variable that you have created and use it in any method.

Writing an OLE Server in Visual Basic 5

You know all those steps you performed earlier? Well, they're still valid. In fact, there are only a few differences in writing components with VB5. In this section, we review them.

First of all, when you first create a new project, you are presented with a dialog window, shown in Figure 10-7.

This window is a nice enhancement to the tool. You want to select **ActiveX DLL**. Once you do, notice that VB has already created your first class for you and named it *Class1*. See Figure 10-8.

Figure 10-7: A new VB5 project

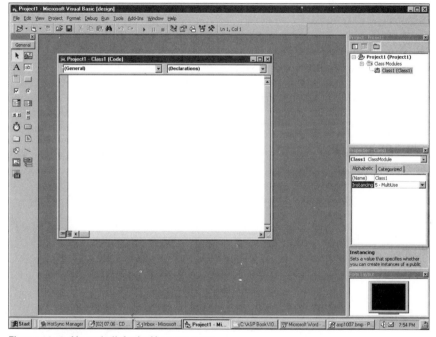

Figure 10-8: Your shell ActiveX component

In fact, VB has just performed the first five steps of creating a component for you! All you have to do now is add your application-specific code (as before), compile, and register. That's it! As we said, the steps are 99 percent the same.

Your Second Component – Data2HTML

Now that you are somewhat familiar with the ins and outs of writing an ASP component in Visual Basic, it's time to put that knowledge to productive use. In this section, we show you how to write a component that will serve you well for a long time.

Overview

Perhaps the easiest way to represent database data in a Web page is through the use of a table. The Data2HTML component takes a **Recordset** object and formats its contents into a nice HTML table.

Pieces

There are only two pieces to this puzzle: the actual component and the ASP code that calls it. We explain each.

THE COMPONENT CODE

The Data2HTML component is actually very simple. The first thing you should do is follow the steps outlined in the beginning of the chapter to create an OLE DLL with the following properties:

- ◆ Name the project **Data2HTML**

- ◆ Create a class named **TableFromData**

The TableFromData class should have a method named **Transform** that contains the following code:

```
Public Function Transform(r As Variant, iBorder As Integer) As
  String

' ****** SECTION 1 *********

Set rs = r

CRLF = Chr(13) & Chr(10)

iCnt = rs.Fields.Count


' ****** SECTION 2 *********

sHTML = "<table border=" & Str$(iBorder) & ">" & CRLF & "<tr>"


' ****** SECTION 3 *********

For i = 0 To iCnt - 1
sHTML = sHTML & "<th>" & rs(i).Name & "</th>"
Next

sHTML = sHTML & "</tr>" & CRLF
```

```
' ****** SECTION 4 *********

Do While (rs.EOF = False)

sHTML = sHTML & "<tr>"

For i = 0 To iCnt - 1
sHTML = sHTML & "<td>" & rs(i) & "</td>"
Next

sHTML = sHTML & "</tr>" & CRLF

rs.MoveNext

Loop


' ****** SECTION 5 *********

sHTML = sHTML & "</table>" & CRLF

Transform = sHTML

End Function
```

This code probably warrants a little explanation. First, this function takes two parameters. The first is a **Recordset** object, which holds the data to format, and the second is an integer that indicates how wide to make the table border. For the sake of this explanation, we have broken this code up into five sections.

Section one performs the basic initialization for this routine. The first line:

```
Set rs = r
```

is interesting. When the **Recordset** object is passed to this function from the ASP script, it is passed as a variant. In order to use it in the code, however, it needs to be cast into an object. This line creates an object named **rs** that holds the contents of the parameter **r**. This is really just a way of forcing the parameter into a form the script can use.

The next two lines:

```
CRLF = Chr(13) & Chr(10)

iCnt = rs.Fields.Count
```

create a string variable named *CRLF*, which holds a carriage return/line feed pair, and an integer named *iCnt* that holds the number of columns in the result set.

Section two has only one line of code, which begins the table definition. The important thing to note here is the use of the *iBorder* parameter.

The fun really starts in section three. This segment of code creates the headers for the resulting table. Pay close attention to the construction *rs(i).Name*. This retrieves the column name for the column represented by i.

Section four is the meat of this code. This snippet loops through all the rows in the Recordset and constructs the appropriate HTML for a row in a table.

Finally, in section five, we finish our table definition and return the resulting string.

After you successfully create this object (or copy it off the CD-ROM), you must register it with the *regsvr32.exe* program.

THE ASP CODE

Now that you have a correctly registered component, it's time to use it. The following short ASP script shows you how:

```
<html>
<body>

<%
 set conn = Server.CreateObject("ADODB.Connection")

 conn.Open("Inventory")
 set rs = conn.Execute("select prod_desc from Inventory ")

 set data2HTML = Server.CreateObject("Data2HTML.TableFromData")
 sHTML = data2Html.Transform(rs,1)
%>

<% =sHTML %>


</body>
</html>
```

As you can see, there's not much to it. First, you create a **Recordset** object via the normal method. Next, you create an instance of the Data2HTML object and call the **Transform()** method. Finally, you display the results. Of course, you need to alter this script to use an ODBC data source that exists on your server, but you get the idea.

As you were reading the code for the **Transform()** method, you were probably wondering why we went to so much effort to put in CR/LF pairs in the HTML. The answer is that we did it so that the resulting HTML would be readable to the human eye. For example, the generated source for the above document is as follows:

```
<html>
<body>

<table border= 1>
<tr><th>prod_desc</th></tr>
```

```
<tr><td>Canondale 800</td></tr>
<tr><td>Canondale 820</td></tr>
<tr><td>Canondale 830</td></tr>
<tr><td>Canondale 810</td></tr>
<tr><td>Shirt-short Sleeve R</td></tr>
<tr><td>Shirt-Long Sleeve bl</td></tr>
<tr><td>Shirt-short Sleeve w</td></tr>
<tr><td>Shirt-short Sleeve R</td></tr>
</table>

</body>
</html>
```

Not bad, eh?

Summary

Now admit it, writing ASP components in Visual Basic is simple. In fact, we had a programmer proofread this chapter, and he commented, "Jeez. I always thought OLE was hard. If this is all there is to it, then I'm going home and writing a few components right now!" (Really, this did happen!)

Anyway, we hope you had the same reaction. The truth is that writing these components *is* easy in Visual Basic. In fact, unless you have to perform some fairly sophisticated system-level programming, Visual Basic may be the only tool you ever use to write OLE Automation components. On the other hand, if you find you need something with more depth, then continue to the next chapter.

Chapter 11

Writing a Basic ActiveX Component in Visual C++

IN THIS CHAPTER

These days, 4GL languages and tools such as Visual Basic seem to dominate the programming world. It's no wonder! These tools are relatively simple to use and create some powerful applications. Sometimes, however, they aren't enough. Sometimes you have to go deeper and use C++.

In this chapter, we teach you how to create your own ASP components using Microsoft Visual C++. In fact, the structure of this chapter is similar to the structure of the last chapter. We even construct the same examples. This way, you get a good idea of the differences in each approach. More specifically, though, we cover the following:

- ◆ An overview of OLE automation in VC++
- ◆ How to access ASP internals from C++ code
- ◆ Microsoft's recommendation for interfacing with ASP
- ◆ Our recommendation for interfacing with ASP

Some Assumptions

For the duration of this chapter, we make a few assumptions about you. First, we assume that you are fairly familiar with C++ programming in a Windows environment. If you are not, then you will be lost here. Second, we assume that you know enough about Visual C++ to find help on any classes that may be new to you. We use many MFC objects and definitions in this code and do not spend much time explaining how they work. (MFC is a complicated topic and is the subject of a multi-volume set of books by Microsoft.) Finally, we assume that you know enough about VC++ to navigate around it. Although there is some brief discussion on how to use tools such as the ClassWizard, we do not spend any serious time on the VC++ IDE interface. Ready? Good, let's go!

The ATL Shunned!

As you read through this chapter, notice that we have not included any discussion of Microsoft's Active Template Library (ATL). We have done this for a couple reasons. First, in our experience, it's easier to teach someone how to create OLE components using the MFC. Tools such as ClassWizard do much of the work for you and also keep you from having to learn IDL syntax. Second, a proper discussion takes at least another two chapters. To be perfectly honest, we don't have the time, and the ATL is a topic better suited for a book on COM/DCOM.

Why Write an ASP Component in Visual C++?

This is a good question. Actually, the question should really be: Why write *anything* in Visual C++? After all, easier tools such as Visual Basic grow in features daily. It certainly takes less time to write most things in VB, so the question is this: What value is VC++?

Simple. No matter how many features Visual Basic gets, there are still tasks for which VC++ is better suited. For example, Visual Basic doesn't allow you to create individual threads. As an experienced programmer, you know that correctly using threads greatly helps the performance of complicated applications. This is, of course, just one example. The point is this: VC++ affords you a level of control that other simpler tools do not.

OLE Automation in VC++

Okay, so you've decided to write your component in VC++. How do you do it? In this section, we give a step-by-step overview on creating such creatures with this tool.

Step 1: Create a New Project

The first thing you need to do when creating your component is create a new VC++ project. To do this, select the File⇨New menu option and select the Projects tab. The dialog shown in Figure 11-1 appears.

In the last chapter, we explained why it is better to use in-process components rather than out-process components. This being the case, you want to select *MFC AppWizard(dll)*. This creates a .dll rather than an .exe.

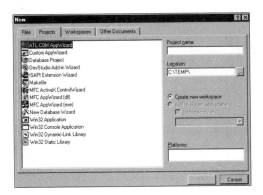

Figure 11-1: Create a new project

Next, you want to name your component and choose the directory for your project. For the time being, please name your project *vcTest*. When you are done, click on the OK button. The dialog shown in Figure 11-2 appears.

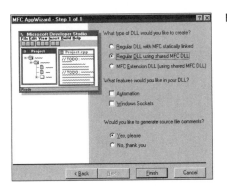

Figure 11-2: DLL options

Your first decision is to choose what type of .dll to create. Choose the option marked *Regular DLL using shared MFC DLL*. You also want to enable *OLE Automation*. This is *very* important. Without it, you are not able to expose the methods of your classes to ASP. When you are done, click on the Finish button. A new dialog appears to show you your chosen options. Click on OK.

Step 2: Add Your Class with the ClassWizard

At this point, you have created a bare-bones .dll that does absolutely nothing of value. What you really need to do is add your own classes. This is best accomplished via the ClassWizard. To invoke the ClassWizard, select View⇨ClassWizard from the main menu. (You can also use the keyboard shortcut Ctrl+W.) The dialog shown in Figure 11-3 appears.

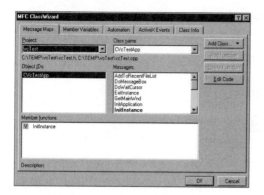

Figure 11-3: The ClassWizard

CREATE A BASIC CLASS

If you are not already familiar with the ClassWizard, you are missing a great tool. You can use it to simplify many otherwise complicated tasks. In this case, you want to add a new class. Click on the Add Class button and select the New option. The New Class dialog appears, as shown in Figure 11-4.

Figure 11-4: A new class

    Here you define the basic properties of your new class. For the time being, please fill in the information as we tell it to you.

    In the Name edit box, enter a value of **Test**. Next, select the option marked *CCmdTarget* from the Base class list box. The reason you are inheriting your new class from this particular base class is that it already supports OLE automation. If you did not, you would have to add it by hand. (Trust us, that is a difficult and ugly process!) Next, under the Automation section, select the *Createable by type ID* radio button. Notice that a value of *VCTEST.TEST* has already been filled in. Unless changed, this is the *ProgID* of your class.

    Finally, click on Create. If all goes well, you should be back at the MFC ClassWizard dialog.

ADD METHODS AND PROPERTIES TO YOUR CLASS

After you create the basic shell for your class, it's time to add specific methods and properties. Click on the OLE Automation tab. Your dialog should look like Figure 11-5.

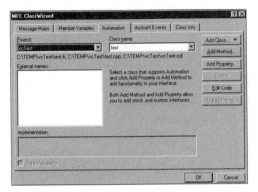

Figure 11-5: Methods and properties

So far so good? Great, let's move on. Click on the Add Method button. The Add Method dialog appears, as shown in Figure 11-6.

Figure 11-6: Adding a new method

In this window you define the properties of your method. The *External Name* value determines the name that other programs use to call your method. For the sake of this example, please enter a value of **Hello**.

The *Internal Name* value determines what your method will be named inside your class. This means that, for example, another program could call a function named *Hello* that would really execute an internal method named *Goodbye*. In this example, we are not going to play such games, so you can safely leave this property as is.

Next, you need to choose what kind of data your method will return. At first blush, you may think that this is an important decision. Actually, it's not. VBScript only supports one kind of variable—a variant. If you return any type other than that, ASP is only going to convert it to a variant. Therefore, you should always set your return type to *VARIANT*.

An Exception to Every Rule

There is one exception to the rule about always returning a VARIANT. When your method returns an OLE object (like a Recordset), you need to set your return type to LPDISPATCH. Other than that, use VARIANT.

Finally, you need to decide what (if any) parameters your method is going to take. For this example, you should leave that section empty.

When you finish, click on OK. You notice that the ClassWizard dialog has changed (see Figure 11-7).

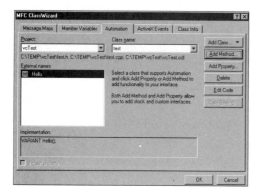

Figure 11-7: Your new class listing

The new Hello() method appears in the *External names* list (the *M* stands for *Method*).

EDIT THE METHOD'S CODE

Because an empty method isn't any good, click on the Edit Code button. Your method code should look like this:

```
VARIANT Test::Hello()
{
  VARIANT vaResult;
  VariantInit(&vaResult);
  // TODO: Add your dispatch handler code here

  return vaResult;
}
```

The ClassWizard has created a method named **Hello()** that returns a VARIANT. It has even gone so far as to create the return variable, initialize it, and return it. All you have to do is put in whatever custom code is needed to return the right type.

Unfortunately, the ClassWizard was a little overanxious in its decisions. Much simpler and more useful code should be used, such as the following:

```
VARIANT Test::Hello()
{
 COleVariant vRval;
 return vRval;
}
```

The COleVariant class is an MFC class that hides much of the ugliness of the VARIANT data type. (The VARIANT data type is actually a *struct*. See the online help for more details.)

For the time being, place the following code in your method:

```
VARIANT Test::Hello()
{
 COleVariant vRval = "<h1><center>Hello World!</center></h1>";
 return vRval;
}
```

All this code does is create a variant that holds some HTML and returns it. Actually, if you really want to be efficient, you can write:

```
VARIANT Test::Hello()
{
 return (COleVariant) "<h1><center>Hello World!</center></h1>";
}
```

Step 3: Compile and Test

When you are done editing your code, it's time to compile and test it. To create your new .dll, select the Build⇨Build vcTest.dll menu item. (You can also use the F7 key.)

When you are done compiling your component, you need to register it. Do this with the *regsvr32.exe* utility we have been using. Assuming, for example, that your project directory is *c:\temp\vcTest*, your .dll is in *c:\temp\vcTest\debug* or *c:\temp\vcTest\release* – depending on which build mode you chose.

Finally, it's time to test your code. You can use the following ASP:

```
<html>
<body>

<%
 set vcTest = Server.CreateObject("VCTEST.TEST")
 sTest = vcTest.Hello()
 Response.Write( sTest )
%>

</body>
</html>
```

An Interesting Bug

You may expect to also use the following ASP code:

```
<%
  set vcTest = Server.CreateObject("VCTEST.TEST")
  Response.Write( vcTest.Hello() )
%>
```

After all, this code should yield the following HTML:

```
<html>
<body>

<h1><center>Hello World!</center></h1>

</body>
```

Interestingly enough, however, ASP sometimes spits out the following:

```
</html>
<html>
<body>

—

</body>
</html>
```

Our guess is that sometimes ASP has a hard time figuring out what to do with the variant and is, in fact, displaying the ASCII character that is equivalent to the value of the variant pointer. Fortunately, you can circumvent this by either assigning the return value to a variable or using the **CStr()** VBScript function to tell ASP that the return value should be treated as a string.

Accessing ASP Internals from Your Component

In the last chapter, we discussed the way in which ASP allows your components to use the server's internal objects. In this section, we show you how to implement that in VC++. If you skipped the last chapter because you aren't interested in Visual Basic, then go back and read the section titled "Interfacing with the ASP Server."

As before, you have to define an **OnStartPage()** method into which ASP passes the scripting context of the page. What you do in the function is a matter of some debate. The examples from Microsoft tell you to do it one way, but we recommend another. We cover both.

The Microsoft Way

ASP ships with a header file named *asptlb.h*. This file defines the OLE type library information for the internal ASP components. In order to proceed with the following method, you need to copy this file to your project directory and add the following to the top of your *Test.cpp* file:

```
#include "asptlb.h"
```

After you have included the type library information, you need to define your **OnStartPage()** method. Once again, it's best to use the ClassWizard. Before doing so, you need to figure out the parameters and the return value. You can do this by looking at the sample code that Microsoft provides in the online ASP documents. They implement their method as the following:

```
STDMETHODIMP CHowtos1::OnStartPage (IUnknown* pUnk)
{
 HRESULT hr;
 IScriptingContext *piContext;

 //Get IScriptingContext Interface
 hr = pUnk->QueryInterface(IID_IScriptingContext,
 (void**)&piContext);

 // Get Response Object Pointer
 IResponse* piResponse = NULL;
 hr = piContext->get_Response(&piResponse);

 //Build a String for Output
 VARIANT vtMessage;
 VariantInit(&vtMessage);
 V_VT(&vtMessage) = VT_BSTR;

 V_BSTR(&vtMessage) = SysAllocString(L"<CENTER><H1>Inside
 Component!</H1></CENTER>");

 //Write the String to the HTML Page
 piResponse->Write(vtMessage);

 VariantClear(&vtMessage);

 //Release interfaces
 piResponse->Release();
 piContext->Release();

 return S_OK;
}
```

Fits and Starts

If ASP has already used your component, then the .dll will be locked and you will not be able to compile successfully. The only way around this is to stop and restart your Web server. This doesn't mean that you have to reboot your machine. Just stop and restart the service.

You should notice two important things in this code. First, it is returning an enumerated type named S_OK. This type belongs to the SCODE family of variables. So now you know the first thing—what the function returns. The next thing to notice is that this method takes one parameter of type *IUnknown* *. In other words, this parameter is a pointer to an *IUnknown*. This is also known as an LPUNKNOWN.

Now you know the two things you need to define your method: the return type and the parameter types. Go ahead and create your **OnStartPage()** method with the ClassWizard so that it returns an SCODE and takes one LPUNKNOWN parameter named *pUnk*. While you're at it, paste the previous code into your method. All it does (in a *very* circuitous fashion) is print some HTML to the client browser. When you are done, re-compile your component.

Did the component compile okay? What! You got a linker error? Say it ain't so! Okay, all kidding aside, you should have received the following error:

```
Test.obj : error LNK2001: unresolved external symbol
_IID_IscriptingContext
```

The following text comes straight from the Visual C++ knowledge-base files:

```
A GUID must be initialized exactly once. For this reason, there are
two different versions of the DEFINE_GUID macro. One version just
declares an external reference to the symbol name. The other
version actually initializes the symbol name to the value of the
GUID. If you receive an LNK2001 error for the symbol name of the
GUID, the GUID was not initialized.

You can make sure your GUID gets initialized in one of two ways:

-If you are using precompiled header files, include the INITGUID.H
header file before defining the GUID in the implementation file
where it should be initialized. (AppWizard-generated MFC projects
use precompiled headers by default.)

-If you are not using precompiled headers, define INITGUID before
including OBJBASE.H. (OBJBASE.H is included by OLE2.H.)
```

Because this particular project *is* using precompiled headers, the top of *Test.cpp* needs to say the following:

```
#include <initguid.h>
#include "asptlb.h"
```

Once you make this change, your component should compile cleanly. To test it, use the following ASP:

```
<html>
<body>

<%
 set vcTest = Server.CreateObject("VCTEST.TEST")
%>

</body>
</html>
```

Even though you now have a working component, it still suffers from some problems. First, the code for **OnStartPage()** is entirely too complicated. A greatly simplified version follows:

```
HRESULT hr;
IScriptingContext *piContext;

//Get IScriptingContext Interface
hr = pUnk->QueryInterface(IID_IScriptingContext,
(void**)&piContext);

// Get Response Object Pointer
IResponse* piResponse = NULL;
hr = piContext->get_Response(&piResponse);

//Build a String for Output
COleVariant vtMessage = "<CENTER><H1>Inside
Component!</H1></CENTER>";

//Write the String to the HTML Page
piResponse->Write(vtMessage);

//Release interfaces
piResponse->Release();
piContext->Release();

return S_OK;
```

Using a COleVariant object instead of the unwieldy VARIANT type has saved a bunch of lines here. You should also note that the function names are different than in the last chapter. For example, in the last chapter we used the **Response()** method to get the **Response** object. Now, however, we are using the **get_Response()** method. For a complete list of all the C++ methods supported in these interfaces, please refer to the online ASP documentation.

Unless you are already an experienced OLE programmer, the previous code may be confusing. In our opinion, this particular implementation is not the best way to go. In the next section, we outline an alternate and simpler way of interfacing with the ASP internal objects.

A Much Simpler Way

The *asptlb.h* file that comes with ASP is nice insofar as it defines all the ASP object interfaces for you, but it is still too complicated. In fact, Visual C++ itself provides the tools to do a much cleaner job using these objects.

Before we begin, however, you need to clean up a little. First, remove the following lines from the *Test.cpp* file:

```
#include <initguid.h>
#include "asptlb.h"
```

Next, delete the contents of the entire **OnStartPage()** method from *Test.cpp*. Don't delete the method itself—just the contents. After you have removed all vestiges of this code, you can begin.

STEP 1: CLASSWIZARD TO THE RESCUE!

If you have type library information for a given object (either in a .tlb, .olb, .exe, or .dll format), then ClassWizard can construct C++ classes that hide all the OLE programming from you. This is exactly what we are going to do here.

Click on the Add Class button in the ClassWizard, but this time choose **From an OLE TypeLib**. Next, navigate to your ASP directory and choose the file *asp.dll*. This is the main control file for all of ASP, and it contains type library information for all the ASP objects. The window shown in Figure 11-8 appears.

Figure 11-8: Adding from a type library

This list contains all the classes that can be created from this .dll. The only ones we are interested in right now are the *IScriptingContext* and *IResponse* classes. Select only those and click on OK.

ClassWizard has now created two files: *asp.h* and *asp.cpp*. These files contain definitions for the IScriptingContext and IResponse classes. To use them, add the following line of code to the top of *Test.cpp*:

```
#include "asp.h"
```

STEP 2: RECODE YOUR ONSTARTPAGE() METHOD

Before you do this, take a moment to peruse the newly created classes. Specifically, take a look at the IScriptingContext class. You should notice two things.

First, the method names are different than in the last section. For example, get_Response() has been replaced with **GetResponse()**.

Second, this class has three constructors. The first takes no arguments, the second takes an LPDISPATCH, and the third takes a reference to another **IScriptingContext** object. Of the three, the one that takes an LPDISPATCH as a parameter is the most important, and it is the one we use in our new **OnStartPage()** method.

Okay, it's time to create the code. Copy the following code into the method:

```
SCODE test::OnStartPage(LPUNKNOWN pUnk)
{

    LPDISPATCH pdisp;
    pUnk->QueryInterface(IID_IDispatch, (void **)&pdisp);

    IscriptingContext isc( pdisp );

    IResponse ir = isc.GetResponse();

    ir.Write( (ColeVariant) "<h1>Hello World!</h1>" );

    return S_OK;
}
```

Wow, this code is a lot shorter and easier than the last example! Let's take a quick look at what's happening here.

First, we know that we can create a new **IScriptingContext** object if we can just manage to get the appropriate LPDISPATCH. The problem is that the parameter passed to the **OnStartPage()** method is an LPUNKNOWN, not an LPDISPATCH. If you are already an experienced OLE programmer, then you know how to get around this apparent problem. For those of you who are not, here's the scoop.

Every OLE object must support at least two interfaces: *IUnknown* and *IDispatch*. An object must also support a method named **QueryInterface()**. This method allows a calling program to ask the object about the things it supports. The following lines ask the unknown object (which we know to be an IScriptingContext) to provide its IDispatch to us:

```
LPDISPATCH pdisp;
pUnk->QueryInterface(IID_IDispatch, (void **)&pdisp);
```

Why Not Use LPDISPATCH Instead of LPUNKNOWN?

Just for a lark, we tried the following code:

```
IscriptingContext isc( (LPDISPATCH) pdisp );
IResponse ir = isc.GetResponse();
ir.Write( (ColeVariant) "<h1>Hello World!</h1>" );
return S_OK;
```

Notice that instead of using **QueryInterface()** to get a copy of the object's IDispatch, we simply cast the LPUNKNOWN as an LPDISPATCH and used it directly in the constructor. The odd thing, though, is that it worked! We got exactly the output we intended. This confused us because IUnknowns and Idispatchs are not the same thing. In fact, after hours of experimenting, we could find no other objects for which this shortcut worked. In the end, we chalked it up to luck. This shortcut is dangerous and wrong! Most of our attempts to use it with other objects resulted in the Web server crashing. It's a curious little phenomenon, but nothing more. Don't use it! (If you think you know why this works, please e-mail us. No one we asked knew, and all the OLE documentation seemed to indicate that it shouldn't.)

Once we have a pointer to the object's **IDispatch** object, the rest is easy. We simply use that pointer to create our own **IScriptingContext** object and use it, in turn, to get a copy of the current **IResponse** object. In other words, once you understand the role of **QueryInterface()**, the rest is easy.

WHY BOTHER?

There are some good reasons why you should consider using this method over the one used in the examples provided by Microsoft. First, it's simpler. Second, you don't have to worry about linking errors because of uninitialized GUIDs. Finally, the resulting code hides all the difficult OLE things from you and makes your methods easy to read and maintain.

Passing Objects to and from ASP

You already learned that objects are passed into an ASP component as LPUNKNOWNs. How, though, do you pass objects out of a component to ASP? At first glance, you may think that they have to be passed back as LPUNKNOWNs. Fortunately, this is not the case. In fact, you want to pass back the LPDISPATCH of an object. For example, the prototype of a function that accepts an object of one type and passes back an object of another is

```
LPDISPATCH MyFunction( LPUNKNOWN pUnk )
```

The other thing you need to know is that only OLE objects can be passed out of components. This means that if your component is going to pass back a custom-built object, then that object must be inherited from CCmdTarget (or some other OLE-capable class) and must have OLE automation enabled. The easiest way to create such a thing is with ClassWizard. Simply select the Add Class⇨New option, make your base class CCmdTarget, and be sure to select either the *Automation* or *Creatable by type ID* options.

The Data2HTML Example

In this section, we are going to show you how to implement the same Data2HTML example in C++ that you did in the last chapter in Visual Basic. If you skipped the last chapter because you aren't interested in VB, please go back and skim it so that you know what this component is supposed to do.

The first challenge to implementing this component lies in the fact that we are going to pass a **Recordset** object from ASP into this component. This means that we have to set up our environment to understand that class.

Remember in the last section how we added the ASP objects to our project by choosing to read them from an OLE type library file? Well, we are going to do the same thing here. The Recordset class is part of Microsoft's ADO component. That component exists on your system as

```
C:\Program Files\Common Files\System\ADO\msado10.dll
```

If you choose to add a new class from a type library and choose that file, you are presented with a familiar list of ADO classes. The ones you want are the *Recordset*, *Fields*, and *Field* classes. ClassWizard automatically creates two files—*msado10.h* and *msado10.cpp*. Add the .cpp file to your project and be sure to include the .h file at the top of your implementation file.

Use ClassWizard to create your TableFromData class and add the **Transform()** method. Remember, it returns a VARIANT and takes an LPUNKNOWN as a parameter.

The Transform() Method

Now that you have set up everything, it's time to look at the code for **Transform()**:

```
VARIANT TableFromData::Transform(LPUNKNOWN pUnk)
{

  CString strResult;

  // Get a pointer to the Recordset's IDispatch interface.

LPDISPATCH pdisp;
  pUnk->QueryInterface(IID_IDispatch, (void **)&pdisp);
```

```
// Create a _Recordset object with the IDispatch pointer.

_Recordset rs( pdisp );

// Get the fields for the Recordset.

Fields flds = rs.GetFields();

// Store the number of fields in each row.

long lCnt = flds.GetCount(),
 i = 0;

// Begin the table definition.

strResult = "<table border=1>\r\n<tr>";

// Iterate over each field and construct the header portion of the
table.

for (i = 0; i < lCnt; i++ ) {

    Fields fsTmp = rs.GetFields();
    Field fTmp = fsTmp.GetItem( (COleVariant) i );

    strResult += "<th>" + fTmp.GetName() + "</th>";
}

// Close the header row.

strResult += "</tr>\r\n";

// Iterate over each row and construct the rows of the table.

while ( !rs.GetEof() ) {

    strResult += "<tr>";

    for (i = 0; i < lCnt; i++ ) {

        Fields fsTmp = rs.GetFields();
        Field fTmp = fsTmp.GetItem( (COleVariant) i );

        COleVariant vTmp = fTmp.GetValue();
        vTmp.ChangeType(VT_BSTR);

        CString sTmp = ((VARIANT) vTmp).bstrVal;

        strResult += "<td>" + sTmp + "</td>";
    }

    strResult += "</tr>\r\n";
```

```
        rs.MoveNext();
}

// Close the table and return the data.

strResult += "</table>\r\n";

return (COleVariant) strResult;
}
```

This code really doesn't differ much from the code we did in Visual Basic. There are, however, a few notable differences.

First, we don't have the luxury of using the object in a collection syntax. That is to say, the construction rs(1) isn't going to return the value of the first column for the current row. For that, we are going to have to ask more precisely.

The other interesting construction comes from the following code:

```
COleVariant vTmp = fTmp.GetValue();
vTmp.ChangeType(VT_BSTR);

CString sTmp = ((VARIANT) vTmp).bstrVal;

strResult += "<td>" + sTmp + "</td>";
```

The **GetValue()** method of the Field class returns a VARIANT that represents the value in the field. The problem is that we don't know what type that is. All we know is that we need to convert it to a string. Fortunately for us, the COleVariant class provides a method named **ChangeType()** that converts the internal value of the variant to whatever you want. In this case, we convert it to a string.

A VARIANT type is really a structure. Which of its members is filled in depends on the type of data it holds. One of its members is named *bstVal*. As you might guess, this element holds the value of the structure if that value is a BSTR. (We cover BSTRs more in the next chapter.) Therefore, the line

```
CString sTmp = ((VARIANT) vTmp).bstrVal;
```

is simply converting the BSTR value of the VARIANT structure into a CString.

TESTING THE COMPONENT

After you have compiled and registered your component, you need to test it. To do so, use the following ASP:

```
<html>
<body>

<%
  set conn = Server.CreateObject("ADODB.CONNECTION")
```

```
conn.Open("AdvWorks")

set rs = conn.Execute("SELECT ShipName as Name FROM orders")

set data2html = Server.CreateObject("Data2HTML.TableFromData")
sHTML = data2html.Transform( rs )
%>

<%= sHTML %>

</body>
</html>
```

Summary

Creating an ASP component in Visual C++ isn't as hard as you may think. Only a couple steps are extra from Visual Basic. The main thing to remember is to plan your component's interfaces well. Make sure you know how it interacts with its environment *before* you start writing code. Above all, make good use of both the ClassWizard and the MFC. They make your life a whole lot easier!

Chapter 12

The NETUTILS Component

IN THIS CHAPTER

Congratulations! If you've made it this far in this book, then you have come a long way. Rémember all the way back in Chapter 4 when we showed you how to create TCP/IP connections from ASP? Well, in this chapter we explain the internals of that particular component.

To be perfectly honest, you don't have to read this chapter to use ASP effectively. In fact, you never have to understand the contents of this chapter to use ASP to its fullest potential. So why bother?

This chapter is really for those of you who are curious as to how a real-world component is implemented. You can think of this as a case study. In this chapter, we cover the following points:

◆ The architecture of the TCPCLIENT class

◆ The private attributes of the class

◆ The public methods of the class

◆ How the EMAIL class was built using the TCPCLIENT class

◆ How the EMAIL class extends the TCPCLIENT class

◆ Some valuable lessons learned about building ASP components

Before we begin, however, we should get a few things straight. First, we assume that you are an experienced C++ programmer. If you aren't, you will be lost. Second, we assume that, if need be, you can find your way around the MFC. We make heavy use of the MFC in this object and won't stop to explain a lot of it. Finally, we assume that you have the ambition to read the supporting documentation for the third party classes we use here.

So if you're sure you're hearty enough for this, let's go!

The TCPCLIENT Class

The TCPCLIENT class encapsulates basic TCP/IP client functionality into one easy class. Using it is simple. (That is, after all, the point!) The component, however, has some interesting nuances.

A Quick Overview

The TCPCLIENT class exposes OLE automation interfaces. This means that it has to be inherited from something that contains a message pump. In this case, we inherited from the CWnd class. This class is the basic MFC window class. The declaration is as follows:

```
class tcpclient : public CWnd
{
```

For example, the basic message pump for this class is

```
//}}AFX_MSG
DECLARE_MESSAGE_MAP()
DECLARE_OLECREATE(tcpclient)
// Generated OLE dispatch map functions
//{{AFX_DISPATCH(tcpclient)
afx_msg void ConnectWith(LPCTSTR sServer, long lPort);
afx_msg BSTR Get();
afx_msg long IsConnected();
afx_msg void Send(LPCTSTR sData);
//}}AFX_DISPATCH
```

As you can see, all the public methods of the class are accounted for in this map. Each time you add or delete methods using ClassWizard, it automatically edits this area of code.

Private Properties

The TCPCLIENT class has a few internal properties that are hidden from the calling program:

- ◆ **CSocket sockClient.** CSocket is an MFC class that encapsulates the synchronous socket capabilities of the Winsock API. The sockClient variable is the main socket that the client uses for communication.

- ◆ **CSocketFile *sFile.** In Winsock, all data is transferred between clients and servers via a shared file. The CSocketFile class wraps up all this functionality.

- ◆ **CArchive *arIn.** Once you have a shared file through which to transfer data, you have to declare specific input and output archives. The arIn variable is an archive that collects data.

- ◆ **CArchive *arOut.** Any guess as to what this variable does? Of course, it is for writing data out from the client.

◆ **int isConnected.** This variable stores whether or not the client is currently connected. This is important so that the program doesn't try to read data from a closed connection, which will throw an exception.

Methods

Most of the methods in the TCPCLIENT class are public. Not only that, most of them are also accessible from OLE. (Just because something is public doesn't mean that your OLE clients can see it.) In this section, we discuss the methods and why they are constructed the way they are.

TCPCLIENT()

This is the constructor for this class. Although it is public, it cannot be called directly from OLE. We added the first two lines. Here, we're simply initializing some internal state variables. The important code comes in the last two lines. (Coincidentally, these lines are also automatically added by ClassWizard.)

```
tcpclient::tcpclient()
{

  isConnected = 0;
  hasBeenCreated = 0;

  EnableAutomation();

  // To keep the application running as long as an OLE automation
  //   object is active, the constructor calls AfxOleLockApp.

  AfxOleLockApp();
}
```

The last two lines enable OLE automation and make sure that the application is running as long as OLE automation is active. This makes perfect sense. Say you are accessing the OLE automation features of MS Word. If Word were to terminate in the middle of one of your commands, your program would be in big trouble.

~TCPCLIENT()

The destructor for this class simply unlocks the automation application:

```
tcpclient::~tcpclient()
{
  // To terminate the application when all objects created with
  //   with OLE automation, the destructor calls AfxOleUnlockApp.

  AfxOleUnlockApp();
}
```

ONFINALRELEASE()

Each time you create an instance of an automation object, the object keeps count of how many programs are accessing it. This is called the *reference count.* When the client closes its connection to the object, the object decrements the reference count. When the reference count drops to zero, the object destroys itself. When this occurs, the **OnFinalRelease()** method is called. In this particular object, we take the opportunity to clean up all the goo we had to create in order to make the code work. The code is as follows:

```
void tcpclient::OnFinalRelease()
{
  // When the last reference for an automation object is released
  // OnFinalRelease is called. The base class will automatically
  // delete the object. Add additional cleanup required for your
  // object before calling the base class.

  delete arOut;
  delete arIn;
  delete sFile;

  sockClient.Close();

  CWnd::OnFinalRelease();
}
```

CONNECTWITH()

The **ConnectWith()** method represents the first non-administrative method discussed here. As you know from Chapter 4, this method connects your client to a server. The code here is straightforward enough.

First, we construct the socket client. Next, we try to establish a TCP/IP connection to the server on a given port. If that works, then we construct the socket file and input and output archives. Here's the code:

```
void tcpclient::ConnectWith(LPCTSTR sServer, long lPort)
{

  sockClient.Create();

  if ( !sockClient.Connect(sServer, lPort) ) {
      isConnected = 0;
      return;
  }

  isConnected = 1;

  sFile = new CSocketFile(&sockClient);

  arIn = new CArchive(sFile, CArchive::load);
  arOut = new CArchive(sFile, CArchive::store);
```

```
hasBeenCreated = 1;
}
```

GET()

The **Get()** method returns a line of text from the server as a string. Notice that the return type of the function is a BSTR. This type is a Unicode string and is used to pass all string information in OLE.

BSTR's aren't easy to work with without the help of the MFC. In this case, we used the CString class. This is Microsoft's string class. The CString class has the virtue of being able to return a BSTR representation of its contents via the **AllocsysString()** method. This makes the coding of the **Get()** method a heck of a lot easier! Here's the code:

```
BSTR tcpclient::Get()
{
  CString ioStr;

  if ( !arIn->ReadString(ioStr) ){
      isConnected = 0;
  }

  return (ioStr.AllocSysString());
}
```

ISCONNECTED()

The rules governing encapsulation mandate that a class should never allow its data members to be directly manipulated. This tenet says that the class instead should make methods available to perform these functions. The **IsConnected()** method is just such a creature. All it does is return the value of the isConnected data member. Here it is in its entirety:

```
long tcpclient::IsConnected()
{
  return (isConnected);
}
```

Uni-Who?

Strings of data can be fairly tricky for computer programmers. The standard ASCII character set does not support all the characters in all the world's languages. This makes writing international applications difficult. To alleviate this problem, the Unicode standard was implemented. Unicode is a 16-bit character set capable of encoding all known characters and is used as a worldwide character-encoding standard.

SEND()

The last method supported in the TCPCLIENT class is the **Send()** function. It is very simple. All it does is send a string of data to the server using the output archive variable *arOut*:

```
void tcpclient::Send(LPCTSTR sData)
{
  arOut->WriteString( sData );
  arOut->Flush();
}
```

TCPCLIENT.H

Normally, we aren't big on code listings. However, we are making an exception here. Listing 12-1 shows the TCPCLIENT.H header file. Take a moment to read it. Pay particular attention to all the detail automatically added by ClassWizard.

Listing 12-1: TCPCLIENT.H Header File

```
#include <afxsock.h>
#include <afx.h>

// tcpclient.h : header file
//

/////////////////////////////////////////////////////////////////////////////
/////////
// tcpclient window

class tcpclient : public CWnd
{
  DECLARE_DYNCREATE(tcpclient)

// Construction
protected:

  CSocket sockClient;
  CSocketFile *sFile;
  CArchive *arIn;
  CArchive *arOut;
  int isConnected;
  int hasBeenCreated;


public:
  tcpclient();

// Attributes
public:

// Operations
```

```
public:

// Overrides
  // ClassWizard generated virtual function overrides
  //{{AFX_VIRTUAL(tcpclient)
  public:
  virtual void OnFinalRelease();
  //}}AFX_VIRTUAL

// Implementation
public:
  virtual ~tcpclient();

  // Generated message map functions
protected:
  //{{AFX_MSG(tcpclient)
        // NOTE - the ClassWizard will add and remove member
  functions here.
  //}}AFX_MSG
  DECLARE_MESSAGE_MAP()
  DECLARE_OLECREATE(tcpclient)
  // Generated OLE dispatch map functions
  //{{AFX_DISPATCH(tcpclient)
  afx_msg void ConnectWith(LPCTSTR sServer, long lPort);
  afx_msg BSTR Get();
  afx_msg long IsConnected();
  afx_msg void Send(LPCTSTR sData);
  //}}AFX_DISPATCH
  DECLARE_DISPATCH_MAP()
  DECLARE_INTERFACE_MAP()
};
```

As you can see, Visual C++ has done most of the declaration work for us. All we needed to do was define the specific methods and attributes of our class.

TCPCLIENT.CPP

Listing 12-2 is the complete TCPCLIENT.CPP file. Again, notice how many of the OLE details are taken care of for you by ClassWizard.

Listing 12-2: TCPCLIENT.CPP

```
// tcpclient.cpp : implementation file
//

#include "stdafx.h"
#include "netutils.h"
#include "tcpclient.h"

#ifdef _DEBUG
#define new DEBUG_NEW
#undef THIS_FILE
```

```
static char THIS_FILE[] = __FILE__;
#endif

/////////////////////////////////////////////////////////////////
/////////
// tcpclient

IMPLEMENT_DYNCREATE(tcpclient, CWnd)

tcpclient::tcpclient()
{

 isConnected = 0;
 hasBeenCreated = 0;

 EnableAutomation();

 // To keep the application running as long as an OLE automation
 //   object is active, the constructor calls AfxOleLockApp.

 AfxOleLockApp();
}

tcpclient::~tcpclient()
{
 // To terminate the application when all objects created with
 //   OLE automation, the destructor calls AfxOleUnlockApp.

 AfxOleUnlockApp();
}

void tcpclient::OnFinalRelease()
{
 // When the last reference for an automation object is released
 // OnFinalRelease is called. The base class will automatically
 // delete the object. Add additional cleanup required for your
 // object before calling the base class.

 delete arOut;
 delete arIn;
 delete sFile;

 sockClient.Close();

 CWnd::OnFinalRelease();
}


BEGIN_MESSAGE_MAP(tcpclient, CWnd)
 //{{AFX_MSG_MAP(tcpclient)
        // NOTE - the ClassWizard will add and remove mapping macros
 here.
 //}}AFX_MSG_MAP
END_MESSAGE_MAP()
```

```
BEGIN_DISPATCH_MAP(tcpclient, CWnd)
 //{{AFX_DISPATCH_MAP(tcpclient)
 DISP_FUNCTION(tcpclient, "ConnectWith", ConnectWith, VT_EMPTY,
 VTS_BSTR VTS_I4)
 DISP_FUNCTION(tcpclient, "Get", Get, VT_BSTR, VTS_NONE)
 DISP_FUNCTION(tcpclient, "IsConnected", IsConnected, VT_I4,
 VTS_NONE)
 DISP_FUNCTION(tcpclient, "Send", Send, VT_EMPTY, VTS_BSTR)
 //}}AFX_DISPATCH_MAP
END_DISPATCH_MAP()

// Note: we add support for IID_Itcpclient to support typesafe
 binding
// from VBA. This IID must match the GUID that is attached to the
// dispinterface in the .ODL file.

// {16883DA4-6CCC-11D0-83D2-0080C765AB10}
static const IID IID_Itcpclient =
{ 0x16883da4, 0x6ccc, 0x11d0, { 0x83, 0xd2, 0x0, 0x80, 0xc7, 0x65,
 0xab, 0x10 } };

BEGIN_INTERFACE_MAP(tcpclient, CWnd)
 INTERFACE_PART(tcpclient, IID_Itcpclient, Dispatch)
END_INTERFACE_MAP()

// {16883DA5-6CCC-11D0-83D2-0080C765AB10}
IMPLEMENT_OLECREATE(tcpclient, "NETUTILS.TCPCLIENT", 0x16883da5,
 0x6ccc, 0x11d0, 0x83, 0xd2, 0x0, 0x80, 0xc7, 0x65, 0xab, 0x10)

/////////////////////////////////////////////////////////////////
/////////
// tcpclient message handlers

void tcpclient::ConnectWith(LPCTSTR sServer, long lPort)
{

 sockClient.Create();

 if ( !sockClient.Connect(sServer, lPort) ) {
      isConnected = 0;
      return;
 }

 isConnected = 1;

 sFile = new CSocketFile(&sockClient);

 arIn = new CArchive(sFile, CArchive::load);
 arOut = new CArchive(sFile, CArchive::store);

 hasBeenCreated = 1;
}
```

```
BSTR tcpclient::Get()
{
 CString ioStr;

 if ( !arIn->ReadString(ioStr) ){
      isConnected = 0;
 }

 return (ioStr.AllocSysString());
}

long tcpclient::IsConnected()
{
 return (isConnected);
}

void tcpclient::Send(LPCTSTR sData)
{
 arOut->WriteString( sData );
 arOut->Flush();

}
```

Again, all of the ugly OLE goo has been handled for us. All we had to do was worry about writing the code.

The EMAIL Class

The other class in the NETUTILS object is the EMAIL class. This class lets you manipulate e-mail via Post Office Protocol Version 3 (POP3) and send mail via the Simple Mail Transfer Protocol (SMTP). Besides being extremely useful, this class also has the virtue of using the TCPCLIENT class.

Properties

There are only a few basic properties in this class:

- **Assoc<SPString> spHeaders.** spHeaders is an associative array. This kind of array is like a regular array, except that it is indexed by a string rather than a number.

- **int iMsgCount.** This variable holds the number of messages in the user's account.

- **tcpclient tcp.** This variable is the actual client object used to connect to the mail server.

A PERL Of Wisdom

A long time ago . . .

In a galaxy not so far away . . .

A man had an epiphany. His name is Larry Wall, and he invented a language named PERL. PERL stands for Practical Extraction and Reporting Language and is a tremendous tool for parsing text and quickly prototyping applications. Recently, another man named Jim Morris (morris@netcom.com) created a C++ library named Simple Perl-like Array and String Handler (SPLASH). This useful library gives C++ programmers many of the wonderful features of PERL. We make extensive use of these classes in this particular OLE object. You can get the latest version of SPLASH at ftp.netcom.com/pub/mo/morris/splash190.zip.

Methods

The methods in this class aren't terribly complex. Some of them will seem familiar to you, while others will require some explanation.

EMAIL()

There's nothing particularly special about this constructor. In fact, it's nothing more than the stock code generated by ClassWizard:

```
email::email()
{
  EnableAutomation();

  // To keep the application running as long as an OLE automation
  //    object is active, the constructor calls AfxOleLockApp.

  AfxOleLockApp();
}
```

~EMAIL()

The destructor is as simple as the constructor. Once again, it's just the stock code generated by ClassWizard:

```
email::~email()
{
  // To terminate the application when all objects created with
  //    OLE automation, the destructor calls AfxOleUnlockApp.

  AfxOleUnlockApp();
}
```

ONFINALRELEASE()

Our **OnFinalRelease()** method is also simple. In fact, we have added nothing to it. ClassWizard does it all. (Have we mentioned yet how great this feature of VC++ is?) The code is as follows:

```
void email::OnFinalRelease()
{
  // When the last reference for an automation object is released
  // OnFinalRelease is called. The base class will automatically
  // delete the object. Add additional cleanup required for your
  // object before calling the base class.

  tcp.OnFinalRelease();

  CWnd::OnFinalRelease();
}
```

CONNECT()

The **Connect()** method simply connects your client to a specific POP3 server and logs you on. In order for this code to make perfect sense, you have to know that POP3 says that all messages are sent as a request/response pair. This means that any time you send a command to a POP3 server, you get a response, which is why we are reading from the server after each command. The code is as follows:

```
void email::Connect(LPCTSTR sServer, LPCTSTR userID, LPCTSTR
password)
{

  tcp.ConnectWith( sServer, 110 );

  CString ioStr;

  ioStr = tcp.Get();

  tcp.Send("user " + (CString) userID + "\n");
  ioStr = tcp.Get();

  tcp.Send("pass " + (CString) password + "\n");
  ioStr = tcp.Get();

}
```

MSGCOUNT()

The **MsgCount()** method returns the number of messages in the user's account. To get this information, the client must send a *stat* command to the server. In response, the server sends back the number of messages in the account. For example, this transaction would look similar to the following:

```
stat
OK 13 messages
```

The only confusing part about this code is the way in which we extract the number of messages from the above string. We use a pattern matching tool called *Regular Expressions*. A regexp is a pattern that you can apply to a string to check for matches. In the next example, we are asking to extract one or more numbers following the string "OK:"

```
long email::MsgCount()
{

  CString ioStr;

  tcp.Send("stat\n");
  ioStr = tcp.Get();

  SPString foo = ioStr;
  SPStringList spMatches;

  foo.m("OK ([0-9]+) ", spMatches);
  iMsgCount = atoi((LPCTSTR) spMatches[1]);

  return (iMsgCount);
}
```

HEADER()

An e-mail message has a certain defined form under POP3. Namely, it consists of a bunch of headers, followed by a blank line, followed by the e-mail note, and ending with a line that has only a period (.) on it. For example:

```
FROM: drensin@noblestar.com
TO: afedorchek@noblestar.com
SUBJECT: This is a test

This is my email note.. How do you like it?

We skipped a line here, but it doesn't matter!
```

The **Header()** method retrieves a specific header from a specific message. For example, say that the above message is message number one. The following code:

```
MyObject.Header(1, "SUBJECT")
```

would return the string drensin@noblestar.com

The logic here is actually quite simple. Follow these basic steps:

1. Convert the message number parameter to a string.

2. Tell the server to send the specific message by sending the POP3 *retr* command.

3. Read each line until you hit a blank line (this signifies the end of the headers). If the line begins with some characters that are not colons (:) and then continues immediately with a colon, we have a valid header line. For example:

```
SUBJECT: This is a test
```

4. When you find a header line, push its contents into an associative array.

5. When the headers are done, read until the end of the message, and then return the appropriate header value.

Here's the code:

```
BSTR email::Header(long iMsg, LPCTSTR sHeader)
{
 CString strResult;
 CString ioStr;
 SPString spMatch;
 SPStringList spMatches;

 char *currentMsg = " ";

 currentMsg = itoa( iMsg, currentMsg, 10 );

 tcp.Send("retr " + (CString) currentMsg + "\n");
 ioStr = tcp.Get();

 while (!ioStr.IsEmpty()) {

        spMatch = ioStr;
        CString foo;

        if ( spMatch.m( "^([^:]+): (.*)", spMatches )) {
                foo = spMatches[1];
                foo.MakeUpper();
                spHeaders( (LPCTSTR) foo ) = spMatches[2];
        }

        ioStr = tcp.Get();

 }

 while (ioStr != ".") {
        ioStr = tcp.Get();
 }

 strResult = spHeaders( sHeader );

 return strResult.AllocSysString();
}
```

BODY()

The process of reading the body of a message is similar to reading the header. In this case, we blow right past the header information and store everything after the first blank line:

```
BSTR email::Body(long iMsg)
{
 CString strResult, ioStr;
 char *currentMsg = " ";

 currentMsg = itoa( iMsg, currentMsg, 10 );

 tcp.Send("retr " + (CString) currentMsg + "\n");
 ioStr = tcp.Get();

 while (!ioStr.IsEmpty()) {
       ioStr = tcp.Get();
 }

 ioStr = "";

 do {

       strResult += ioStr;
       ioStr = tcp.Get();
       ioStr += "\n";

 } while (ioStr.Left(1) != ".");

 return strResult.AllocSysString();
}
```

DELETE()

Deleting a POP3 message is also easy. All you need to do is send the server the *dele* command followed by the intended message:

```
void email::Delete(long iMsg)
{
 CString ioStr;
 char *currentMsg = " ";

 currentMsg = itoa( iMsg, currentMsg, 10 );

 tcp.Send("dele " + (CString) currentMsg + "\n");
 ioStr = tcp.Get();

}
```

QUIT()

Quitting a POP3 session is easiest of all. Just send the *quit* command:

```
void email::Quit()
{
  CString ioStr;

  tcp.Send("quit\n");
  ioStr = tcp.Get();
}
```

SENDMAIL()

POP3 was designed to retrieve and manage e-mail messages. It has no facilities to send an e-mail note. For that, you have to use the Simple Mail Transfer Protocol (SMTP). This means connecting to an SMTP server – often the same machine as your POP3 server – and following a different set of transmission rules.

The basic SMTP session looks like this:

```
MAIL FROM:<whomever you are>
RCP TO:<the person to whom you are sending the note>
DATA
<your email text here>
.
QUIT
```

The **SendMail()** method takes all of that information, formats an SMTP-compliant message, and sends it. Here's the code:

```
void email::SendMail(LPCTSTR server, LPCTSTR sender, LPCTSTR
  recipient, LPCTSTR data)
{

  tcpclient tcpSMTP;
CString ioStr;

tcpSMTP.ConnectWith( server, 25 );
  ioStr = tcpSMTP.Get();

  tcpSMTP.Send("MAIL FROM:" + (CString) sender + "\n");
  ioStr = tcpSMTP.Get();

  tcpSMTP.Send("RCPT TO:" + (CString) recipient + "\n");
  ioStr = tcpSMTP.Get();

  tcpSMTP.Send("DATA\n");
  ioStr = tcpSMTP.Get();

  tcpSMTP.Send( (CString) data + "\n.\n");
  ioStr = tcpSMTP.Get();
```

```
tcpSMTP.Send("QUIT\n");

}
```

EMAIL.H

Now that you understand all the constituent parts, it's time to look at the whole.
Listing 12-3 shows the header file.

Listing 12-3: EMAIL.H

```
///////////////////////////////////////////////////////////////
/////////

// email.h : header file
//

///////////////////////////////////////////////////////////////
/////////
// email window

#include "tcpclient.h"
#include <splash\splash.h>
#include <splash\assoc.h>

class email : public CWnd
{
  DECLARE_DYNCREATE(email)

private:
  Assoc<SPString> spHeaders;
  int iMsgCount;
  tcpclient tcp;

// Construction
public:
  email();

// Attributes
public:

// Operations
public:

// Overrides
  // ClassWizard generated virtual function overrides
  //{{AFX_VIRTUAL(email)
  public:
  virtual void OnFinalRelease();
  //}}AFX_VIRTUAL

// Implementation
```

```
public:
 virtual ~email();

 // Generated message map functions
protected:
 //{{AFX_MSG(email)
      // NOTE - the ClassWizard will add and remove member
 functions here.
 //}}AFX_MSG
 DECLARE_MESSAGE_MAP()
 DECLARE_OLECREATE(email)
 // Generated OLE dispatch map functions
 //{{AFX_DISPATCH(email)
 afx_msg long MsgCount();
 afx_msg void Connect(LPCTSTR sServer, LPCTSTR userID, LPCTSTR
 password);
 afx_msg BSTR Header(long iMsg, LPCTSTR sHeader);
 afx_msg BSTR Body(long iMsg);
 afx_msg void Delete(long iMsg);
 afx_msg void Quit();
 afx_msg void SendMail(LPCTSTR server, LPCTSTR sender, LPCTSTR
 recipient, LPCTSTR data);
 //}}AFX_DISPATCH
 DECLARE_DISPATCH_MAP()
 DECLARE_INTERFACE_MAP()
};
```

EMAIL.CPP

Listing 12-4 shows the implementation file. Notice how all the pieces fit together.

Listing 12-4: EMAIL.CPP

```
/////////////////////////////////////////////////////////////////
/////////

// email.cpp : implementation file
//

#include "stdafx.h"
#include "netutils.h"
#include "email.h"
#include <stdlib.h>

#ifdef _DEBUG
#define new DEBUG_NEW
#undef THIS_FILE
static char THIS_FILE[] = __FILE__;
#endif

/////////////////////////////////////////////////////////////////
/////////
// email
```

```
IMPLEMENT_DYNCREATE(email, CWnd)

email::email()
{
 EnableAutomation();

 // To keep the application running as long as an OLE automation
 //    object is active, the constructor calls AfxOleLockApp.

 AfxOleLockApp();
}

email::~email()
{
 // To terminate the application when all objects created with
 //    OLE automation, the destructor calls AfxOleUnlockApp.

 AfxOleUnlockApp();
}

void email::OnFinalRelease()
{
 // When the last reference for an automation object is released
 // OnFinalRelease is called. The base class will automatically
 // delete the object. Add additional cleanup required for your
 // object before calling the base class.

 tcp.OnFinalRelease();

 CWnd::OnFinalRelease();
}


BEGIN_MESSAGE_MAP(email, CWnd)
 //{{AFX_MSG_MAP(email)
      // NOTE - the ClassWizard will add and remove mapping macros
 here.
 //}}AFX_MSG_MAP
END_MESSAGE_MAP()


BEGIN_DISPATCH_MAP(email, CWnd)
 //{{AFX_DISPATCH_MAP(email)
 DISP_FUNCTION(email, "MsgCount", MsgCount, VT_I4, VTS_NONE)
 DISP_FUNCTION(email, "Connect", Connect, VT_EMPTY, VTS_BSTR
 VTS_BSTR VTS_BSTR)
 DISP_FUNCTION(email, "Header", Header, VT_BSTR, VTS_I4 VTS_BSTR)
 DISP_FUNCTION(email, "Body", Body, VT_BSTR, VTS_I4)
 DISP_FUNCTION(email, "Delete", Delete, VT_EMPTY, VTS_I4)
 DISP_FUNCTION(email, "Quit", Quit, VT_EMPTY, VTS_NONE)
 DISP_FUNCTION(email, "SendMail", SendMail, VT_EMPTY, VTS_BSTR
 VTS_BSTR VTS_BSTR VTS_BSTR)
 //}}AFX_DISPATCH_MAP
END_DISPATCH_MAP()
```

```
// Note: We add support for IID_Iemail to support typesafe binding
// from VBA. This IID must match the GUID that is attached to the
// dispinterface in the .ODL file.

// {6DDF0160-70B4-11D0-83D2-0080C765AB10}
static const IID IID_Iemail =
{ 0x6ddf0160, 0x70b4, 0x11d0, { 0x83, 0xd2, 0x0, 0x80, 0xc7, 0x65,
  0xab, 0x10 } };

BEGIN_INTERFACE_MAP(email, CWnd)
  INTERFACE_PART(email, IID_Iemail, Dispatch)
END_INTERFACE_MAP()

// {6DDF0161-70B4-11D0-83D2-0080C765AB10}
IMPLEMENT_OLECREATE(email, "NETUTILS.EMAIL", 0x6ddf0161, 0x70b4,
  0x11d0, 0x83, 0xd2, 0x0, 0x80, 0xc7, 0x65, 0xab, 0x10)

/////////////////////////////////////////////////////////////////
/////////
// email message handlers

long email::MsgCount()
{

  CString ioStr;

  tcp.Send("stat\n");
  ioStr = tcp.Get();

  SPString foo = ioStr;
  SPStringList spMatches;

  foo.m( "OK ([0-9]+) ", spMatches );
  iMsgCount = atoi((LPCTSTR) spMatches[1]);

  return (iMsgCount);
}

void email::Connect(LPCTSTR sServer, LPCTSTR userID, LPCTSTR
  password)
{

  tcp.ConnectWith( sServer, 110 );

  CString ioStr;

  ioStr = tcp.Get();

  tcp.Send("user " + (CString) userID + "\n");
  ioStr = tcp.Get();

  tcp.Send("pass " + (CString) password + "\n");
  ioStr = tcp.Get();
```

```
}

BSTR email::Header(long iMsg, LPCTSTR sHeader)
{
 CString strResult;
 CString ioStr;
 SPString spMatch;
 SPStringList spMatches;

 char *currentMsg = " ";

 currentMsg = itoa( iMsg, currentMsg, 10 );

 tcp.Send("retr " + (CString) currentMsg + "\n");
 ioStr = tcp.Get();

 while (!ioStr.IsEmpty()) {

        spMatch = ioStr;
        CString foo;

        if ( spMatch.m( "^([^:]+): (.*)", spMatches )) {
                foo = spMatches[1];
                foo.MakeUpper();
                spHeaders( (LPCTSTR) foo ) = spMatches[2];
        }

        ioStr = tcp.Get();

 }

 while (ioStr != ".") {
        ioStr = tcp.Get();
 }

 strResult = spHeaders( sHeader );

 return strResult.AllocSysString();
}

BSTR email::Body(long iMsg)
{
 CString strResult, ioStr;
 char *currentMsg = " ";

 currentMsg = itoa( iMsg, currentMsg, 10 );

 tcp.Send("retr " + (CString) currentMsg + "\n");
 ioStr = tcp.Get();

 while (!ioStr.IsEmpty()) {
        ioStr = tcp.Get();
 }
```

```
  ioStr = "";

  do {

        strResult += ioStr;
        ioStr = tcp.Get();
        ioStr += "\n";

  } while (ioStr.Left(1) != ".");

  return strResult.AllocSysString();
}

void email::Delete(long iMsg)
{
 CString ioStr;
 char *currentMsg = " ";

 currentMsg = itoa( iMsg, currentMsg, 10 );

 tcp.Send("dele " + (CString) currentMsg + "\n");
 ioStr = tcp.Get();

}

void email::Quit()
{
 CString ioStr;

 tcp.Send("quit\n");
 ioStr = tcp.Get();
}

void email::SendMail(LPCTSTR server, LPCTSTR sender, LPCTSTR
 recipient, LPCTSTR data)
{

 tcpclient tcpSMTP;
 tcpSMTP.ConnectWith( server, 25 );

 CString ioStr;

 ioStr = tcpSMTP.Get();

 tcpSMTP.Send("MAIL FROM:" + (CString) sender + "\n");
 ioStr = tcpSMTP.Get();

 tcpSMTP.Send("RCPT TO:" + (CString) recipient + "\n");
 ioStr = tcpSMTP.Get();

 tcpSMTP.Send("DATA\n");
 ioStr = tcpSMTP.Get();

 tcpSMTP.Send( (CString) data + "\n.\n");
```

```
ioStr = tcpSMTP.Get();

tcpSMTP.Send("QUIT\n");

}
```

Summary

We think that writing OLE Automation components is fun. It gives you the opportunity to write code that you can reuse — unchanged — in just about any application development environment. We hope that after reading this chapter you realize that the NETUTILS component is not anywhere near as magical as it may have first seemed. In fact, it's downright simple!

Part V

Appendixes

Appendix A

About the CD-ROM

Possibly one of the hardest things about writing a book is figuring out what goes on the companion CD-ROM. Sure, the source code is a no-brainer. It's the rest of the material that's hard. In this book, we tried to a assemble CD-ROM that gives you everything you could possibly need to start using ASP, including the following:

♦ **The custom components.** Throughout the book, we have written a number of custom components. You can find them in the \cmpnts directory of the CD-ROM.

♦ **Complete source code.** The \src directory on the CD-ROM has the complete source code for all the ASP in all the chapters. This also includes the source code for the custom components.

♦ **Internet Explorer.** ASP isn't much good without a Web browser, so we've included Microsoft's latest offering. Enjoy.

Appendix B

Using JScript

JScript is Microsoft's version of Netscape's JavaScript and – for the purposes of ASP scripting – is almost exactly like JavaScript 1.1. This of course begs the question: What is JavaScript? Netscape describes JavaScript as its "cross-platform, object-based scripting language for client and server applications." We focus solely on the server-side portion of JScript. There is a plethora of JScript client-side objects that you can't use in ASP, so we don't cover them here.

Entire books have been written on JavaScript, so there is a limit to how much we can accomplish in one appendix. Our focus is on giving an experienced programmer the essentials of JScript required to begin scripting immediately. We pay special attention to the differences between JScript and other languages and to those features of JScript particularly relevant to ASP.

JScript is part of the family of languages that borrow syntax from C. If you already know C, C++, Perl, or Java, you will pick up JScript syntax quickly. We cover this syntax rapidly so that we can take some time to delve into the more exciting features of JScript.

One important point before we start: JavaScript is *not* Java. It is true that VBScript is essentially Visual Basic for Applications (VBA) tweaked for scripting, and PerlScript is essentially the same as Perl. However, JavaScript is in no way the Java language modified for scripting. Sun Microsystems owns Java; Netscape independently created a language called LiveScript and – in a regrettable marketing ploy – changed the name to JavaScript at the last minute.

This appendix is an overview of JScript, including the following:

◆ The lexical structure of JScript

◆ Variable names

◆ Literals

◆ Comments

◆ Data types

◆ Operators

◆ Functions

◆ References

◆ Control of Flow commands

◆ Arrays

- ◆ Wrapper objects
- ◆ User objects

Lexical Structure

JScript code consists of one or more statements. In VBScript, a statement is terminated by a new line. In PerlScript, you terminate a statement with a ; (semicolon). What would you guess JScript uses? Both a new line and a semicolon, as it turns out. You can (and should, in our opinion) explicitly terminate a JScript statement with a semicolon. However, a new line also terminates a JScript statement, but only when it makes sense. For example, you can write code such as the following:

```
<%@ language = JScript %>
<%
 foo
      =
            "JScript says 'Hello World!'"
 Response
      .
            write
                 ( "<H1>" + foo + "</H1>" )
%>
```

We encourage you not to do this, but you can. Alternatively, you can put multiple statements on one line, in which case semicolons are required to separate them, such as the following:

```
<%@ language = JScript %>
<%
 foo = "Hello World!"; Response.write( "<H1>" + foo + "</H1>" )
%>
```

Generally, we try to put one statement per line and terminate each statement with a semicolon.

Variable Names

JScript variable names are similar to those of most major languages. They must begin with a letter or underscore, and subsequent characters can be letters, numbers, or underscores. JScript is case-sensitive and, therefore, so are its variable names. Variable names must not duplicate reserved words. The following variable names are legal (and distinct) names:

```
Foo
foo
you_can_use_underscores
thisHas19Characters
```

Each of these names is illegal:

```
12eggs // Starts with a number;
My Favorite Color // Includes spaces;
for // Reserved word;
```

You may declare variables with the keyword var, but it seems rather silly when you can't specify a type:

```
var foo = 555
var bar
```

However, var plays an important role in variable scoping within functions, which we discuss later in this appendix. Note that you can initialize a variable as you declare it.

Literals

A JScript literal is a data value that appears directly in your program, such as:

```
3.14159
"Hello World"
42
```

There are a number of points to keep in mind about JScript literals. Let's explore how JScript expects you to write octal, hexadecimal, string, and Boolean literals.

Octal and Hexadecimal Literals

A leading 0 designates an octal (base 8) number. For example:

```
0105
```

This isn't 105, it's 69. A literal beginning with 0x or 0X is a hexadecmial, so 69 in hex would be:

```
0x45
```

String Literals

JScript lets you use either double or single quotes to delimit your strings. Whichever you start with, you can embed the other inside. For example:

```
mother = "Don't forget your hat, it's cold outside.";
foo = '<IMG SRC="/the_graphic.gif">';
```

For the cases in which you need both single and double quotes in your literal, JScript lets you escape quotes with \' and \". We therefore can write

```
bar = "\"Don't forget your hat,\" she said.";
```

Because the backslash is the escape character, you must write a double backslash to get a backslash in a string. For example, the following command doesn't do what you want it to do:

```
Response.write( "Install this in \usr\local" );
```

Your output is

```
Install this in usrlocal
```

Instead, you must write

```
Response.write( "Install this in \\usr\\local" );
```

Boolean Literals

In JScript, true and false are literals. This means you can write code such as the following:

```
foo = 1;
if ( foo == true ) Response.write( "It's true" );
```

Happily, you can also write

```
if ( foo ) Response.write( "It's true" );
```

JScript evaluates any expression and interprets it as a Boolean when necessary. This capability is sorely lacking in VBScript.

Comments

JScript has the standard C++ comments, where // comments out everything to the end of a line, and /* */ denotes a multi-line comment. One of the subtle differences between JScript and JavaScript is that JavaScript also treats the HTML comment <!– the same way it treats //. JScript doesn't do that.

JScript Data Types

As a scripting language, JScript doesn't have strict typing the way that C++ and Java do. You don't declare a variable to be an integer, a float, a char, or a string. You just use variables as what you want them to be. This means you can do things that would never fly in Java, such as the following:

```
<%@ language = JScript %>
<%
 foo = "some bunch of characters";
 foo = "555";
 Response.write( foo / 5 );
%>
```

Clearly, foo starts out as a string, but the output of this code is 111, so JScript is changing foo to number for us automatically.

Traps with Loosely Typed Variables

Continuing the previous example, watch out if you instead write the following:

```
Response.write( foo + 5 );
```

The output isn't 560, it's 5555. This is the kind of problem you face with scripting languages. You also have to worry about comparisons like this:

```
foo = "2";
bar = 10;

if (foo < bar) {
      Response.write("Numeric comparison");
} else {
      Response.write("String comparison");
}
```

If JScript converts foo to number, then (foo < bar) is true; if JScript converts bar to string, then (foo < bar) is false. In this case, JScript happens to convert foo to a number. There are rules for this conversion, but we discourage you from relying on them. It's better to change explicitly your arguments to the correct type when in doubt. JScript doesn't have a cast command, but it does provide functions: parseInt() and parseFloat() convert strings to numbers, and toString() converts numbers to strings. For example:

```
if ( parseInt(foo) < parseInt(bar) ) { ...
if ( foo.toString() < bar.toString() ) { ...
```

We discuss the differences in syntax in "User Objects in JScript," later in this chapter, but the short version is this: parseInt() and parseFloat() are functions, but toString() is a method of the **String** object. JScript automatically converts foo and bars to strings so that you can use this method.

If you want to rely on the rules, here they are:

♦ In concatenation, JScript interprets both arguments as strings if one argument is a string.

♦ In comparison, JScript interprets both arguments as numbers if one argument is a number.

It sounds simple enough, but when you write a + b < c + d, you have to remember that the + is going to be concatenation if either a or b is string. Use explicit conversions when in doubt.

Variable Scope

If you have used languages such as C, you are accustomed to seeing variables scoped by blocks. Variables declared within a block exist only within that block. This doesn't work in JScript. For example, consider the following code:

```
<%@ language = JScript %>
<%
foo = "main"; // line 3
  Response.write(foo + "<BR>");
  {
      foo = "block one"; /* This is the same variable we used on
  lane 3 */
      Response.write(foo + "<BR>");
      {
          foo = "block two";// Again, the same variable
          bar = "block two only";
          Response.write(foo + "<BR>");
      };
      Response.write(foo + "<BR>");
      Response.write("bar = bar" + "<BR>");
// We can still see bar
  };
  Response.write(foo + "<BR>");
%>
```

This doesn't produce the output that a C programmer would expect. Instead, we get the following:

```
main
block one
block two
block two
bar = bar
block two
```

Notice that foo simply retains the last value assigned to it. Although two blocks exist in this program, they did not create local copies of foo. Additionally, the variable bar created in the innermost block continues to exist outside the block.

What JScript does support by way of variable scoping is function level scoping. Any variable declared within a function with **var** is local to the function. For example:

```
<%@ language = JScript %>
<%
 function foo () {
      var a = "a inside foo";
      b = "b inside foo";
      Response.write(a + "; " + b + "<BR>");
 };
 a = "a main script";
 b = "b main script";
 foo();
 Response.write(a + "; " + b + "<BR>");
%>
```

The output of this script is

```
a inside foo; b inside foo
a main script; b inside foo
```

Notice that *a* is a local variable for the function foo. However, *b* is not, because we did not declare it using **var**. This differs slightly from VBScript's implementation of scoping. In VBScript, *b* would be local to foo() unless *b* had been explicitly declared outside of foo().

The lack of variable scoping by block is one of the most annoying flaws in JScript, in our opinion. You should at least have the option of scoping a variable within a block, as with the **my** command in Perl.

Operators

This is one area in which we assume that you have some programming experience. You hardly need us to tell you that < means *less than* or that multiplication takes precedence over addition. If you are not familiar with the fundamentals of operators, you can look in any number of places, starting with the ASP documentation. Instead, we want to call your attention to a few high points.

Shortcut Operators

VBScript programmers not privy to the C heritage find that, once again, C is relentless in its pursuit of conciseness, leading to the following shortcuts. Many scripts contain code such as the following:

```
foo = foo + something_else;
```

The += operator shortens this code:

```
foo += something_else
```

The += operator is simply shorthand for the longer version. There are any number of these shortcuts, such as -=, *=, /=, and more.

In the special case of incrementing by one, which happens often in loops, even foo += 1 was deemed too verbose. In its place you usually see the autoincrement operator ++. Thus foo++ is equivalent to foo += 1, which is equivalent to foo = foo + 1. The trouble with autoincrements is that they are generally used as side effects, which is to say that you see code such as

```
bar = 2 * foo++.
```

This code gets a bit tricky because it is not equivalent to

```
bar = 2 * (foo = foo + 1);
```

Rather, it is the same as this code:

```
bar = 2 * foo; foo = foo + 1 ;
```

The difference is that when you write foo++ in an expression, the expression is evaluated *first*, and then foo is incremented. To force foo to be incremented first, you must write ++foo. Clear as mud? Great. What does the following code do?

```
foo = 1; bar = ++foo + ++foo * 5;
```

Because multiplication takes precedence over addition, should we first increment foo to 2, then multiply by five, and then increment foo again to 3 so that 3 + (2 * 5) = 13? The short answer is: Don't write code like this. Even if you know exactly what the rules are, you can be sure the poor sap stuck with maintaining your code doesn't. In any case, the result here is 2 + (3 * 5) = 17, so we see that

JScript incremented foo left to right.

The companion to the autoincrement operator is the autodecrement operator −, which behaves the same way but subtracts 1 instead of adds 1.

Comparison

The JScript comparison operator to test equality is ==. This leads many people to write the following classic bug:

```
while (foo = bar) {/* do some stuff */};
```

Unfortunately, this is *not* a comparison. You have set foo equal to bar, and the truth of the expression depends on whether or not bar is 0 or "". The code is correctly written as

```
while (foo == bar) {/* do some stuff */};
```

When you compare two objects with ==, JScript checks to see that they are the same object. For example:

```
foo = new Array(1009, 1013, 1019);
bar = new Array(1009, 1013, 1019);
if (foo!=bar) Response.write("Not the same object");
```

This script reports that foo and bar are not the same, even though we know they are identical arrays. In order for foo == bar to be true, we would have to write the following:

```
foo = new Array(1009, 1013, 1019);
bar = foo;
if (foo == bar) Response.write("They're the same!");
```

This code can create some real gotchas. Suppose you want to exclude everyone but yourself from your Web site as you write new code. You innocently write

```
if (Request.ServerVariables("REMOTE_ADDR") != "127.0.0.1")
  Response.End;
```

You find that this locks you out, too! The problem is that Request.ServerVariables("REMOTE_ADDR") is an object, not a string as you expected. One solution is to write

```
if (String(Request.ServerVariables("REMOTE_ADDR")) != "127.0.0.1")
  Response.End;
```

Note in this case that String() is a constructor creating a new **String** object for us.

Short Circuit Evaluation

JScript supports short circuit evaluation, which means that JScript stops evaluating an expression as soon as the truth is known. For example:

```
bar = foo = -1;
if (foo < 0 || ++bar == 0) {//...
```

Since foo is negative, there is no reason for JScript to test whether ++bar == 0, and so JScript never increments bar. It is still -1. Perl programmers are famous for their use of short circuits, writing code such as this:

```
(String(Request.ServerVariables("REMOTE_ADDR")) == "127.0.0.1") ||
Response.End;
```

Here we are using the short circuit as a poor man's if . . . else statement. If the IP address is 127.0.0.1, there is no need to evaluate the second half of the expression, so the Response.End doesn't execute. When the IP address isn't 127.0.0.1, JScript has to evaluate the truth of "Response.End." Of course, it hardly matters what that method returns, because it immediately ends the execution of the script.

Functions

The declaration of a function in JScript follows this syntax:

```
function name (arguments) {
  // code here
}
```

You notice that there's no mention of whether or not the function returns a value, nor what type of return value. Because JScript is untyped, there's no point. You may return whatever you like, or you may return nothing, if that's your preference. Just be aware that one of the main reasons why languages such as C++ or Java use type checking is to let the compiler catch bugs related to using the wrong datatype. You are now assuming the responsibility for making sure that your return values make sense to the calling code.

You've also lost the benefit of type checking on the arguments, too, so your argument list only gives names to the function's parameters. JScript won't even check the number of arguments passed to your function. The calling code may pass more or fewer parameters than you want. The arguments are stored in an array named arguments, so you can access them as you need to. For example:

```
function argument_count(foo, bar) {
  Response.write(argument_count.arguments.length+"-");
};
```

```
argument_count(0);
argument_count(0, 1);
argument_count(0, 1, 2);
argument_count(0, 1, 2, 3);
```

The output of this script is 1-2-3-4. In this case, foo == arguments[0] and bar == arguments[1].

To return a value from your function, use the return command. For example:

```
function factorial_approx(x) {
 with Math {
        // Use Stirling's formula
        return exp(-x)*pow(x,x)*sqrt(2*PI*x);
 };
};
```

JScript allows a function to retrieve the name of its calling function with the **Caller** property:

```
function who_called_me () {
 Response.write("I was called by ");
Response.write(who_called_me.caller+"<BR>");
}
function f1 () {who_called_me()};
function f2 () {who_called_me()};
f1();
f2();
```

The **Caller** property prints the following:

```
I was called by function f1() {[native code]}
I was called by function f2() {[native code]}
```

What is fascinating about functions in JScript is that they behave like ordinary datatypes. What do we mean by this? Here are a few examples:

```
<%@ language = JScript %>
<%
 function foo () {
        Response.write("You called foo<BR>")
 }

 bar = foo
 bar()

 function foobar(x) {
        x()
 }
 foobar(foo)
%>
```

The output of this script is

```
You called foo
You called foo
```

As you can see, you are getting much of the functionality that requires pointers in other languages, such as C and C++. Speaking of which, we now discuss just what JScript does about pointers.

JScript and Pointers

C sparked a religious debate among programmers that rages to this day: Are pointers good or bad? We do not intend to comment on this debate, because we (Dave and Andrew) don't even agree. However, we will tell you what JScript does about pointers.

JScript joins Java in removing pointers from the programmer's tool set. However, this means that JScript needs to provide a method of passing data by reference so that large objects aren't copied to a new location in memory every time they are passed to a function. This is exactly what JScript does: Objects and arrays (which are objects of a sort) are always passed by reference. However, it is transparent to you as the programmer. You don't have to use any operators that denote taking or passing a reference. All you have to do is understand what you are manipulating.

Here's an example:

```
<%@ language = JScript %>
<%
 foo = "Original";
 bar = foo;
 bar = "Copy";
 Response.write("foo = " + foo + "; bar = " + bar);
%>
```

The output of this script shows that foo equals "Original" and bar = "Copy." But if we write the following:

```
<%@ language = JScript %>
<%
 foo = new Array("Original");
 bar = foo;
 bar[0] = "Same Array";
 Response.write("foo = " + foo + "; bar = " + bar);
%>
```

then we find that both foo[0] and bar[0] equal "Same Array." Later in the chapter, we take a more detailed look at arrays in JScript.

Control of Flow

Control of flow commands allow you to dictate the order in which statements are executed. These are traditionally divided into conditional statements and loop statements.

Conditional Statements

JScript provides the **if...else** statement to branch script execution. The syntax is

```
if (condition) {
 statements1
[ } else {
 statements2 ]
}
```

JScript employs blocks to control execution. You could write this syntax as

```
if (condition) statement1
[else statement2]
```

In this formulation, statement1 and statement2 can each be a single statement or a compound statement enclosed in braces. The use of blocks avoids the "end if," "next," "wend," and "loop" commands used to close groups of statements in VBScript.

If the condition is true, then the first block of statements executes; otherwise, the second block executes. This second block, starting with "else," is optional. The condition is anything that JScript can evaluate in a Boolean context. VBScript programmers should note that this is a more flexible and powerful definition of a condition. Here are some examples of JScript conditions:

```
if (a == b ) { /* ... */};
if (a = b = 1) {/* ... */};
foo = "Hello World"; if (foo) {/* ... */};
```

Note that the second and third conditions would not be valid in VBScript.

JScript provides no explicit else if construct. You simply write your code like this:

```
if (condition) {
 statements1
} else if {
 statements2
} else if { ...
```

The Conditional Operator

The C programming language, famous for economy of expression, popularized the conditional operator:

```
test ? expression1 : expression2
```

This looks similar to an **if...else** statement, but we have expressions following the test, not statements as the ASP documentation would have you believe. Because **?:** manipulates expressions, it is properly categorized as a trinary operator, not a Control of Flow statement. However, you typically use it instead of a control of flow command. Instead of writing

```
if (a == b) {foo = "true block"}
else {foo = "false block"};
Response.write(foo);
```

you can write

```
Response.write((a == b) ? "true block" : "false block");
```

This is particularly helpful when using the compact form of response.write:

```
<%= (a == b) ? "true block" : "false block"%>
```

or when assigning a value to a variable:

```
c = (a == b) ? true_c_value : false_c_value
```

Loop Statements

Executing a set of commands repeated is called looping. JScript has a C style loop:

```
for (initialization; test ; increment) {statements};
```

The first statement is the initialization. It is executed only once, at the start of the for loop execution. The second statement is the conditional test. It is evaluated before the execution of each loop iteration. If the test is true, then the loop block is executed; otherwise, the loop terminates. The increment is executed at the completion of each loop. The standard for loop looks something like this:

```
for (i = 1; i < 10; i++) {
 //    do something
};
```

However, you can be much more creative, but creativity can be powerful and dangerous. For example, what type of error would you expect the following code to generate?

```
for (i = 1; i++; i < 10) {
 //   do something
};
```

The answer is that this code generates no errors, aside from the fact that it runs forever. (Presumably, *i* will eventually exceed the size of the largest floating point number and generate an error, terminating execution.) This is a valid for loop. The variable *i* is initialized to 1 at the beginning of the loop. Then the *condition* i++ is evaluated; *i* is incremented to 2, and 2 is true, so the loop executes. At the end of the loop, the *increment* i < 10 is evaluated. This doesn't actually change *i*, but JScript doesn't worry about it. Then the condition i++ is evaluated again and is still true, and so on.

You may omit any or all of the loop statements. A lazy (and hard to read) way to write the first for loop is

```
for ( ; i++ < 10; ) {
 //   do something
};
```

Here we are assuming that i is uninitialized, so it starts off as 0 and is incremented to 1 before the loop starts. Mind you, we are not advocating writing code like this; we are just telling you that it works.

FOR...IN
Recognizing that one often needs to iterate over the elements of an array or object, JScript offers the for...in command. The syntax is

```
for (variable in [object | array]) {
 statement
}
```

For an array, this is a convenience; for an object or associative array, this is an absolute necessity. For example:

```
foo = new Array(10007, 10009, 10037, 10039);
foo.prime1 = 20021;
foo["prime2"] = 20023;
function boring() {Response.write( "boring")};
foo.func = boring;
for (bar in foo) {
Response.write("foo["+bar+"] = "+foo[bar]+"<BR>")
};
```

The output of this script is

```
foo[0] = 10007
foo[1] = 10009
foo[2] = 10037
foo[3] = 10039
foo[prime1] = 20021
foo[func] = function boring() {[native code]}
foo[prime2] = 20023
```

Unfortunately, some of the system-defined properties of objects are not listed by for...in. For example, all arrays have the methods **sort**, **join**, and **reverse**, yet these were not listed above.

BREAK
The condition of the for loop terminates the loop when it becomes false; typically, this is a test on the increment variable. However, there may be other reasons why you want to break out of the loop that are at best tangentially related to the increment variable. To test for these conditions, you can write a long and complicated test expression, but the clearest way is to use the **break** statement. The **break** statement causes the loop to end immediately. For example:

```
for (col_name in rs.fields) {
  total_length += length(col_name);
  if total_length > 200 break;
  // other stuff
};
```

CONTINUE
For the occasions when you simply want to skip the rest of the loop statements and proceed to the next iteration of the loop, JScript provides the **continue** statement. Both **break** and **continue** are necessary so that JScript can provide rich flow control and still not have the dreaded goto statement.

WHILE
The foo loop explicitly declares a loop variable. When you don't need a loop variable, you can write

```
for (; condition;) {
  // code here
};
```

However, this is bit inelegant, so JScript provides a while loop:

```
while (condition) {
  statements
};
```

The statements are executed only if the condition is true, and the condition is evaluated before each loop. You often see this while loop in ASP code:

```
while (! rs.EOF) {// rs is a Recordset object
 statements
};
```

The break and continue statements work with while statements as well.

Arrays

Arrays in JScript are essentially objects. You can argue that arrays are part of the built-in data types, but arrays require constructors, and arrays have methods. If it walks like a duck and talks like a duck . . .

Handling arrays in a scripting language is one of the areas in which you see the richest variation between languages. In Java, all variables must be declared, so when you need an array, you declare a variable to be an array. What should a scripting language do? VBScript requires you to declare arrays explicitly. (Confusingly, VBScript has **Array** objects as well as **Variants** that are arrays, and the two are not the same.) PerlScript lets arrays spring into existence as you need them, so if you write

```
$foo[9] = "I just made a 10 element array";
```

then PerlScript creates the array @foo, even if you have never used @foo before.

JScript has you create arrays as if they were objects – with a constructor. For example:

```
my_array = new Object;
my_array[0] = "First element";
```

If you try to assign a value to my_array[0] without creating the variable first, you get an error.

A variable can't be both an array and a scalar, but JScript doesn't catch attempts to treat a variable this way. The following code runs:

```
<%@ language = JScript %>
<%
 foo = 1;
 foo[0] = 2;
 Response.write("foo=" + foo + "; foo[0]=" + foo[0]);
%>
```

However, the value of foo[0] is null, not 2. Notice that we did not declare foo as an array. We used foo as an ordinary variable. JScript created an array for us with a wrapper object, which we discuss later, but the net effect is that foo is still an ordinary variable.

Arrays have a length property that returns the index of their highest element. There are also join, reverse, and sort methods that do exactly what their names imply. The following code:

```
<%@ language = JScript %>
<%
 a = new Array(4, 2, 3, 1);
 Response.write("length = " + a.length + "<BR>");
 Response.write("join() " + a.join(':') + "<BR>");
 Response.write("reverse() " + a.reverse() + "<BR>");
 Response.write("sort() " + a.sort() + "<BR>");
%>
```

produces this result:

```
length = 4
join() 4:2:3:1
reverse() 1,3,2,4
sort() 1,2,3,4
```

Finally, you notice that JScript provides an Array constructor, which allows you to initialize an array as you create it. There are three forms to this constructor. Array() simply creates an array object. Array(number) creates an array of length number. Finally, Array (list) creates an array whose elements are the list you supply.

Multidimensional Arrays

Multidimensional JScript arrays are just arrays of arrays. For example:

```
a = new Array(2);
a[0] = new Array(3, 4);
a[1] = new Array(1, 2);
Response.write('a[1][1] = ' + a[1][1]);
```

Notice that we first declare a to be a one dimensional array. We then define each element of *a* to an array. You can access individual members with the array_name[][] notation. This scales to any number of dimensions.

In summary, JScript supports arrays as objects. However, there are actually objects for all variables, which we discuss next.

Wrapper Objects

In addition to the **Array** object, JScript includes **Boolean, Date, Function, Math, Number,** and **String** objects. As with arrays, you need these objects in your daily use of data more so than in other languages, such as VBScript. For example, earlier we used the rather cryptic syntax foo.toString() to convert a number to a string. Why didn't we just write toString(foo)? The answer is that JScript doesn't have a free floating toString() function. However, the **Number** object has a toString() method, so we can invoke that method to convert foo to a string.

Wait a minute, you cry! We never declared foo as an object. (Actually, we haven't even discussed how to do this.) How can we use a method of foo when it's not an object? JScript is kind enough to create the object for us on the fly. When you attempt to invoke a method, JScript creates a temporary object for you. Look at the following example using a date:

```
the_start = "1/1/97";
the_end = the_start.setMonth(the_start.getMonth() + 6);
```

JScript has objects for any of the data types you might use. Again, we use the term data type loosely, because in reality you create variables without worrying about their type. Yet JScript allows you to do things such as:

```
my_string = "Rensin and Fedorchek"
Response.write("Your string is "+my_string.length+" characters")
```

JScript has changed my_string on the fly to an object and allowed you to access the length property of that string object.

Default Objects

JScript's heavy reliance on objects means that you write lots of code with

```
object_name.[property | method].
```

When you use the same object over and over again, this gets a bit tedious. JScript allows you to declare a default object using the **with** command. The syntax is

```
with (object_name){
 statements
}
```

Inside the block, any properties or methods not explicitly qualified with an object name refer to object_naee. For example, in our approximation of factorials we wrote

```
with Math {
     // Use Stirling's formula
     return exp(-x)*pow(x,x)*sqrt(2*PI*x);
};
```

This is equivalent to, but much more readable than

```
Math.exp(-x) * Math.pow(x,x) * Math.sqrt(2 * Math.PI * x)
```

User Objects in JScript

JScript is Microsoft's JavaScript, and JavaScript is a name Netscape made up, presumably to exploit the popularity of Java. Because Java is object-oriented from the start, you hope that JavaScript holds up to this namesake. Let's investigate whether it does. JScript has a proliferation of built-in objects, but in an OO programming environment, you expect to be able to create your own objects that are the true peers of the built-in objects.

To test things, we want to create a simple class that provides a vector data type. In Java, the code may be something like this:

```
class Vector {
  int size;
  double[] elements = new double[3];

  Vector( double x, double y, double z ) {
        size = 3;
        elements[0] = x;
        elements[1] = y;
        elements[2] = z;
  }

  double length() {
        int i;
        double temp = 0;
        for (i = 0; i < size; i++) {
                temp += elements[i] * elements[i];
        }
        return Math.sqrt(temp);
  };
};
```

In JScript, we don't have the benefit of a **class** command. Instead, we have to tie everything to the constructor, like so:

```
<%@ language = JScript %>
<%
  function Vector_length() {
        var i;
        var temp = 0;
        for (i = 0; i < this.size; i++) {
                temp += this.elements[i] * this.elements[i];
        };
        return Math.sqrt(temp);
  };
  function Vector(x, y, z) {
        this.size = 3;
        this.elements = new Array (x,y,z);
        this.length = Vector_length;
  }
```

```
v = new Vector(1, 2, 3);
Response.write(v.length());
%>
```

Now we can create and use vector objects:

```
v = new Vector(1,2,3);
v_length = v.length();
```

There are no such keywords as *public* or *private* in JScript objects. Every property and method of your objects is available to all users of the object, which seriously violates encapsulation. Why the JavaScript designers chose this implementation eludes us.

Notice that we had to create the methods first, using the keyword **this** to refer to the instance of the object. We then make the methods attributes of the object in the constructor function. This makes perfect sense when you consider that functions are data types in JScript.

The New Function Constructor

This is slightly inelegant, however, because we were forced to invent the name Vector_length for nothing. Why should we have to name a function that we immediately use as a method for an object? We don't, but the cure isn't much better than the disease. In JScript, you can create function objects with a new constructor:

```
foo = new Function(arguments, function_string)
```

The final argument to the Function constructor is a string that is the function definition. However, you would have to write the previous class as:

```
function Vector(x, y, z) {
    this.size = 3;
    this.elements = new Array (x,y,z);
    this.length = new Function( "var i;var
temp=0;for(i=0;i<this.size;i++)
temp+=this.elements[i]*this.elements[i];return Math.sqrt(temp)");
}
```

In this book, the new Function constructor argument wraps onto several lines, but in the source code file, it is one long string, extending some 144 characters. This method of defining functions is readable only for one or two line functions.

Adding Data to Objects

JScript allows you to add data to objects at any time. For example:

```
a = new Vector;
a.owner = "Fedorchek";
```

```
function Vector_max() {
      // Definition here
  };
a.max_element = Vector_max;
```

Because functions are data types, we can add both properties and methods to an object. You can add data to both JScript built-in objects and user objects.

Let's repeat that, because this is truly an unusual feature of JScript. You can add both properties and methods to any object on the fly. JScript is giving you a lot of rope to swing with – or hang yourself.

The **Math** built-in object includes a max() function that accepts only two arguments. Perhaps we want to create a function that accepts n arguments:

```
function Math_maxn () {
      var temp = arguments[0];
      for (var i = 1; i < arguments.length; i++)
            if ( arguments[i] > temp ) temp = arguments[i]
      return temp
}
Math.maxn = Math_maxn;
Response.write( Math.maxn( 2, 10, 15, 5, 25, 0, -1 ) );
```

We have now added a new method to the **Math** object that we can use for the rest of our script.

Associative Arrays

An array is a set of values indexed by a set of consecutive integers starting at zero. Why should the indexing set be so restrictive? Why can't we index on a general set of numbers or even a set of strings? A set of values indexed by a set of strings is an extremely useful data type called an *associative array*.

Recall that in VBScript there is a special **Dictionary** object created to handle associative arrays. Perl has a more robust implementation; the hash is one of the fundamental data types. However, JScript tops them all! In JScript, you can dynamically name object methods and properties, so you can treat virtually anything as an associative array. A few examples shed some light on this. First, a *normal* associative array:

```
preferences = new Object;
preferences.browser = "Netscape 4.0";
preferences["operating system"] = "Windows NT 4.0";
for (x in preferences)
 Response.write("<BR>" + x + "=" + preferences[x]);
preferences["home page"] = "www.microsoft.com";
```

This lists the elements of our new associative array:

```
browser=Netscape 4.0
operating system=Windows NT 4.0
home page=www.microsoft.com
```

You should notice several things, including:

◆ There is no explicit *associative array* data type. We just created an object and began using it as an associative array.

◆ We use the same [] notation that we use with normal arrays.

◆ When the index is a legal variable name, we can use it as a normal property with the dot syntax. Later, we can treat it as part of the associative array.

If we combine associative arrays and the with command, we get something that looks like VBA code:

```
with preferences {
  ["browser"] = "Netscape 4.0";
  ["operating system"] = "Windows NT 4.0";
  ["home page"] = "www.microsoft.com";
}
```

This defines the same associative array as before. The [] property definition works with all objects, so we can have code like this:

```
function f1 () {/* definition here */};
f1["Author"] = "Andrew Fedorchek";
f1["Creation Date"] = new Date("April 13, 1997");
f1["Other details"] = new Array("foo", "bar", "glarch");
```

This is the **function** object, but it has properties that are indexed by strings. Notice that the properties themselves are also objects.

Important JScript Functions

The online documentation for ASP provides a complete list of JScript functions and their syntax. We want to highlight a few of the most important functions.

Eval

The capability to evaluate a string as script code is extremely useful. The **eval** function does exactly that. For example:

```
<%@ language = JScript %>
<%
```

```
foo = "Response.write(\"This string provided to you by eval\")";
eval(foo);
%>
```

Variables in eval act as if the code were part of your main script:

```
<%@ language = JScript %>
<%
foo = "main script variable"
eval("foo += ', modified by eval'");
Response.write(foo);
%>
```

indexOf

Netscape is including regular expressions in JavaScript 1.2. Hopefully, Microsoft will release an update to JScript that implements the JavaScript 1.2 specification, including regular expressions. Until that happens, your best bet for heavy-duty text manipulation is to create an ASP component out of a regular expression library. For simplistic string replacement, you can combine the substring and indexOf methods. Suppose you want to replace all occurrences of "/virtual_path1" with "/virtual_path2." You can handle it this way:

```
foo = "Some long string.";
fromIndex = 0;
findString = "/virtual_path1";
replaceString = "/virtual_path2";
while (foo.indexOf("AMF", fromIndex) > 0) {
 bar = foo.indexOf("AMF", fromIndex)
 foo = foo.substring(0, bar)
       + replaceString
       + foo.substring(bar + findString.length, foo.length);
};
```

Summary

JScript is Microsoft's implementation of Netscape's JavaScript. In the context of ASP, it is an object-based language for writing scripts. JScript borrows heavily from the C heritage for its syntax but also has substantial differences. In this chapter, we touched upon the following issues:

♦ JScript statements may be terminated with either a semicolon or a new line.

♦ JScript variable names must start with a letter or underscore; subsequent characters may be letters, numbers, or underscores.

◆ JScript is an untyped language, and variable declaration is optional.

◆ JScript variables have only two kinds of scope: local to a function or global.

◆ Strings in JScript may be delimited with either double or single quotes; the backslash functions as an escape character.

◆ Single-line comments in JScript start with // and end with a new line.

◆ Multi-line comments are contained in /* */ pairs.

◆ JScript has the standard compliment of numeric and string operators, including autoincrement and autodecrement operators.

◆ When JScript compares objects with ==, objects are equal only if they are the same exact object, not merely two objects containing the same data.

◆ JScript expressions short circuit, which can be creatively used to control which expressions are evaluated.

◆ JScript functions take a variable number of arguments and can optionally return any kind of variable or object.

◆ The arguments[] array gives access to unnamed function parameters. Functions are JScript data types, which effectively eliminates the need for function pointers found in languages such as C++.

◆ JScript provides if...else statements, for loops, and while loops to control program flow. Each of these commands can be followed by a block to execute a group of statements.

◆ The for...in loop iterates over the data of an object.

◆ Arrays are objects in JScript, so they must be created with constructors, and they have helpful methods such as length().

◆ JScript converts a variable to a wrapper object as necessary to use methods such as string and date manipulation functions.

◆ The with command sets up a default object for a block.

◆ User objects in JScript are defined by writing the constructor. You may add other properties and methods to objects on the fly.

◆ Associate arrays in JScript are implemented as properties of objects, a powerful way of generalizing the associative array concept.

Appendix C

VBScript

VBScript is Microsoft's adaptation of Visual Basic for active scripting. It is mostly a stripped-down version of Visual Basic for applications, but Microsoft did add one or two new features. If you have experience with Visual Basic (VB) or Visual Basic for Applications (VBA), then you don't need to read this appendix. For the rest of you, we wrote this chapter for programmers who want to pick up Visual Basic. If you are new to programming, all the information you need is here, in a condensed format.

In this appendix we cover all aspects of VBScript, including:

◆ Lexical structure

◆ Variable names

◆ Literals

◆ Comments

◆ Data types

◆ Operators

◆ Functions

◆ Control of Flow commands

◆ Arrays

Lexical Structure

VBScript code consists of one or more statements. In VBScript, a statement is terminated by a new line. At first, this may seem like a convenience, because you don't have to remember those pesky semicolons, but we find that new line terminators limit your flexibility when writing code. Although it's usually poor style, you may have a good reason to put several statements on one line. VBScript doesn't allow that, but you can kludge it using ASP delimiters because the %> delimiter terminates a VBScript statement:

```
<% temp = a %><% a = b %><% b = temp %>
```

When you want a statement to span multiple lines, you must use an underscore (_) as a line continuation character:

```
If a = b or _
a = c or _
a = d then
'Do Something
end if
```

Note that if you are continuing a string across multiple lines, you must break it up and concatenate the pieces:

```
sql = "SELECT c1, c2, c3, sum( c4 )" & _
  " FROM my_favorite_table" & _
  " WHERE c2 < c3" & _
  " GROUP BY c1, c2, c3" & _
  " ORDER BY c1, c2, c3"
```

Variable Names

VBScript variable names are similar to those of many major languages, with a few differences. Variable names must begin with a letter. Unlike JScript or C, a VBScript variable may not begin with an underscore. Subsequent characters can be letters, numbers, or underscores, and the complete variable name must be less than 256 characters. VBScript is case-insensitive, which means that Foo, foo, and fOO are the same variable. Variable names must not duplicate reserved words. The following variable names are legal names:

```
Foo
you_can_use_underscores
thisHas19Characters
```

Each of these names is illegal:

```
12eggs ' Starts with a number;
My Favorite Color ' Includes spaces;
for ' Reserved word;
```

VBScript has a rather unusual feature in that you can enclose variable names in square brackets and put whatever you want inside. Believe it or not, the following variable name is valid:

```
[!@#$%^&*(){}',.."<>;: ]
```

Give it a try! The practical use of square brackets in variable names is typical to embed spaces in a name or to use a reserved word:

```
<% [My Cat] = "Ashley"
Response.write("My cat's name is " & [My Cat])
[next] = "Andrew" %>
<%= [next] %> is next
```

You may optionally declare variables with the keyword **Dim** (more about **Dim** later in this appendix):

```
Dim foo, bar
```

Literals

A VBScript literal is a data value that appears directly in your program, such as

```
3.14159
"Hello World"
42
```

You need to keep a number of points in mind about VBScript literals. Next, we explore how VBScript expects you to write numeric, string, and Boolean literals.

Numeric Literals

A sequence of digits without quotes is a number. For example:

```
a = 52367
```

Unlike languages with C-syntax, a leading zero means nothing. For example, 0105 is not the octal representation of 69; it is just 105. You can convert numbers to hexadecimal with the hex() function.

String Literals

VBScript delimits strings with double quotes. You may embed a double quote with a string by using two double quotes in a row. For example:

```
bar = "He said ""It's not my fault."""
```

There is no support for such characters as tabs or carriage returns. Generally, this is not a problem for an ASP developer. Because a browser displays tabs and carriage returns in an HTML file as ordinary spaces, there is seldom a reason to use them. If you need to embed such a character in a string, use the chr() function. For example:

```
bar = "Here is a break:" & chr(13) & "."
```

Boolean Literals

In VBScript, true and false are literals. This means you can write code such as the following:

```
foo = -1
if (foo = true) then
 Response.write("It's true")
end if
```

Notice that -1 is true in VBScript, just as it is in Microsoft Access. Regrettably, you cannot also write

```
if (foo) Response.write("It's true");
```

VBScript does not evaluate arbitrary expressions as Booleans.

Comments

VBScript comments start with either the keyword REM or a single quote ('). All text from REM—or ' until the next new line character—is ignored. VBScript does not support multi-line comments.

VBScript Data Types

As a scripting language, VBScript doesn't have strict typing, as do C++ and Java. You don't declare a variable to be an integer, a float, a char, or a string. You simply use variables as what you want them to be. This means that you can do things that would never fly in Java, such as the following:

```
<%
foo = "some bunch of characters"
foo = "555"
Response.write(foo / 5)
%>
```

Clearly, foo starts out as a string, but the output of this code is 111, so VBScript is changing foo to number for us automatically.

Traps with Loosely-Typed Variables

You should be worried about comparisons such as the following:

```
foo = "2"
bar = 10
```

```
if (foo < bar) then
 Response.write("Numeric comparison")
else
 Response.write("String comparison")
end if
```

If VBScript converts foo to number, then (foo < bar) is true; if VBScript converts bar to string, then (foo < bar) is false. In this case, VBScript happens to convert bar to a number. If you were using JScript, the opposite would happen. We recommend explicitly changing your arguments to the correct type in situations like these. The commands Cint() and CStr() convert their arguments to integers and strings, respectively.

Variable Scope

In VBScript, a variable has either *procedure-level* scope or *script-level* scope. Variables declared with a procedure are visible only within that procedure; all other variables are visible to the entire script.

Operators

This is one area in which we assume that you have some programming experience. You hardly need us to tell you that < means *less than* or that multiplication takes precedence over addition. If you are not familiar with the fundamentals of operators, you can look in any number of places, starting with the ASP documentation. Instead, we want to call your attention to a few high points.

Shortcut Operators

If you're looking for the autoincrement operators ++ and − or for the shortcut operators such as +=, *=, and so on, then you are out of luck. VBScript doesn't offer such constructs.

Comparison

The VBScript comparison operator to test equality is simply =. Therefore, the following code, which looks wrong to a C programmer, is correct:

```
do while (foo = bar)
'do some stuff
loop
```

If you have a C background, then you will find this construct ambiguous. Are we comparing foo and bar, or are we setting the contents of foo to be the same as the contents of bar? The answer is that VBScript doesn't allow assignments as a side effect, so this can only be a comparison test. If you want to change foo to be equal to bar, then you must do that in a separate statement in VBScript.

Functions

The declaration of a function in VBScript follows this syntax:

```
Function name [(arglist)]
 [statements]
 [name = expression]
 [Exit Function]
 [statements]
 [name = expression]
End Function
```

The argument list is optional, but in VBScript you can't send arguments to a variable number. When you invoke a function, you must supply the correct number of arguments. To return an argument from a function, simply assign the return value to the function name within the definition of the function body.

VBScript also has a **Sub** command. The syntax is the same, except that **Sub** commands can return a value.

VBScript and Pointers

C sparked a religious debate among programmers that rages to this day: Are pointers good or bad? We do not intend to comment on this debate, because we (Dave and Andrew) don't even agree. However, we will tell you what VBScript does about pointers.

VBScript joins Java in removing pointers from the programmer's tool set. However, this means that VBScript needs to provide a method of passing data by reference so that large objects aren't copied to a new location in memory every time they are passed to a function. This is exactly what VBScript does: Objects and arrays (which are objects of a sort) are always passed by reference. However, it is transparent to you as the programmer. You don't have to use any operators that denote taking or passing a reference. All you have to do is understand what you are manipulating.

Here's an example:

```
<%@ language = VBScript %>
<%
foo = "Original"
bar = foo
bar = "Copy"
Response.write("foo = " + foo + " bar = " + bar)
%>
```

The output of this script shows that foo equals "Original" and bar = "Copy." But if we write

```
<%@ language = VBScript %>
<%
foo = new Array("Original")
bar = foo
bar[0] = "Same Array"
Response.write("foo = " + foo + " bar = " + bar)
%>
```

then we find that both foo[0] and bar[0] equal "Same Array."

Control of Flow

Control of flow commands enable you to dictate the order in which statements are executed. These are traditionally divided into conditional statements and loop statements.

Conditional Statements

VBScript provides the **If...Then...Else** statement to branch script execution. The syntax is

```
If condition Then
 [statements]
[ElseIf condition-n Then
 [elseifstatements]]...
[Else
 [elsestatements]]
End If
```

Note that VBScript does not use blocks to control execution, so you must close the **If...Then...Else** with the **End If** command.

If the condition is true, then the first block of statements executes; otherwise, the second block executes. This second block, starting with **ElseIf**, is optional.

When you are testing a single variable against several possible values, the **Select Case** statement may be more appropriate:

```
Select Case testexpression
 [Case expressionlist-n
 [statements-n]] . . .
 [Case Else expressionlist-n
 [elsestatements-n]]
End Select
```

Loop Statements

Executing a repeated set of commands is called *looping*. When you want a variable that will increment or decrement by a fixed amount at each pass, you use a For...Next loop:

```
For counter = start To end [Step step]
  [statements]
  [Exit For]
  [statements]
Next
```

When the code begins, counter is set to start. At each pass, counter is incremented by step, until counter is equal to end. The standard for loop would look something like this:

```
For i = 1 To 10
'do something
Next
```

Here we have left out the Step command, so *i* is incremented by 1 by default.

FOR EACH...NEXT

Recognizing that one often needs to iterate over the elements of an array or object, VBScript offers the For Each...Next command. The syntax is

```
For Each element In group
  [statements]
  [Exit For]
  [statements]
Next [element]
```

For an array, this is a convenience; for an object or associative array, this is an absolute necessity. For Each...Next is most commonly used in collections, such as the Request.QueryString collection:

```
For Each x In Request.QueryString
  Response.write( x & "=" & _
  Request.QueryString(x) & "<BR>" )
Next
```

DO...LOOP

When you do not need a loop variable, use the Do...Loop:

```
Do [{While | Until} condition]
  [statements]
  [Exit Do]
```

```
[statements]
Loop
```

The **Do...Loop** executes as long as (**While**) or (**Until**) *condition* is true. For example, when you are accessing a **Recordset** object:

```
Set rs = My_Connection.Execute( "my_stored_procedure" )
Do Until rs.EOF
' Code for displaying rs data on the HTML page
 rs.MoveNext
Loop
rs.Close()
```

There is also a **While...Wend** loop construct, but **Do...Loop** provides the same functionality and is the preferred method for looping.

Arrays

For...Next loops are often used to manipulate array variables. An array is a collection of variables indexed by sequential non-negative integers. Individual array elements are accessed with parentheses.

In VBScript, you can create an array one of two ways. You can declare it with **Dim**, or you can create it with the **Array** Function. The syntax of **Dim** is

```
Dim varname[([subscripts])][, varname[([subscripts])]]...
```

Dim is so named as a shorthand for **Dim**ension. Eons ago, before VBScript and Visual Basic, when only BASIC existed, DIM was a BASIC command that specified the DIMension of your BASIC arrays. Today **Dim** functions as a general variable declaration statement. For example:

```
Dim foo(100)
```

Arrays are always indexed starting with zero, so in the previous example, foo has 101 elements. When you know what elements you want to initialize an array with, use **Array**:

```
Array(arglist)
```

For example:

```
a = Array("Red", "Green", "Blue")
```

In this case, a(0) = "Red."

Associative Arrays

An array is a set of values indexed by a set of consecutive integers starting at zero. Why should the indexing set be so restrictive? Why can't we index on a general set of numbers or even a set of strings? A set of values indexed by a set of strings is an extremely useful data type called an *associative array.*

In VBScript, Microsoft has created a special **Dictionary** object created to handle associative arrays. This is kludge on Microsoft's part. Both Perl and JavaScript have built-in, robust support for associate arrays. Nonetheless, the **Dictionary** object is better than nothing.

Because it is an object, the syntax for creating a **Dictionary** is

```
Set variable_name = CreateObject("Scripting.Dictionary")
```

Thereafter, you may access elements with string indexes:

```
d("name") = "Andrew"
```

Important VBScript Functions

The online documentation for ASP provides a complete list of VBScript functions and their syntax. We want to highlight a few of the most important functions.

Eval

The capability to evaluate a string as script code is extremely useful. The **eval** function does exactly that. For example:

```
<%@ language = VBScript %>
<%
foo = "Response.write( \"This string provided to you by eval\" )"
eval( foo )
%>
```

Variables in eval act as if the code were part of your main script:

```
<%@ language = VBScript %>
<%
foo = "main script variable"
eval( "foo += ', modified by eval'" )
Response.write( foo )
%>
```

indexOf

Netscape is including regular expressions in JavaScript 1.2. Hopefully, Microsoft will release an update to VBScript that implements the JavaScript 1.2 specification, including regular expressions. Until that happens, your best bet for heavy-duty text manipulation is to create an ASP component out of a regular expression library. For simplistic string replacement, you can combine the substring and indexOf methods. Suppose you want to replace all occurrences of "/virtual_path1" with "/virtual_path2." You can handle it this way:

```
foo = "Some long string."
fromIndex = 0
findString = "/virtual_path1"
replaceString = "/virtual_path2"
while (foo.indexOf("AMF", fromIndex) > 0) {
bar = foo.indexOf("AMF", fromIndex)
foo = foo.substring(0, bar)
• replaceString
• foo.substring(bar + findString.length, foo.length)
}
```

Summary

VBScript is Microsoft's adaptation of Visual Basic for active scripting. In this chapter, we touched upon the following issues:

◆ VBScript statements end with a new line unless explicitly continued with an underscore.

◆ VBScript variable names must start with a letter; subsequent characters may be letters, numbers, or underscores. Other characters may be used if you enclose the variable name in square brackets.

◆ VBScript is an untyped language, and variable declaration is optional.

◆ VBScript variables have only two kinds of scope: local to a function or global.

◆ Strings in VBScript are delimited with double quotes; two double quotes in a row is an escape sequence for putting a double quote into a string.

◆ All VBScript comments are single-line comments; they start with either a single quote or **Rem**.

◆ VBScript has the standard compliment of numeric and string operators but does not offer autoincrement, autodecrement, or shortcut operators.

♦ VBScript functions take a fixed number of arguments.

♦ VBScript provides if...else statements, for loops, and do loops to control program flow.

♦ The for...in loop iterates over the data of an object.

♦ Arrays in VBScript are created with Dim or Array.

♦ Associate arrays in VBScript are implemented as a scripting dictionary object.

Appendix D

Post Office Protocol – Version 3

Status of This Memo

This document specifies an Internet standards track protocol for the Internet community and requests discussion and suggestions for improvements. Please refer to the current edition of the *Internet Official Protocol Standards (STD 1)* for the standardization state and status of this protocol. Distribution of this memo is unlimited.

Table of Contents

Overview

This memo is a revision to RFC 1460, a Draft Standard. It makes the following changes from that document:

♦ removed text regarding "split-UA model," which didn't add anything to the understanding of POP

♦ clarified syntax of commands, keywords, and arguments

♦ clarified behavior on broken connection

♦ explicitly permitted an inactivity autologout timer

♦ clarified the requirements of the "exclusive-access lock"

♦ removed implementation-specific wording regarding the parsing of the maildrop

♦ allowed servers to close the connection after a failed authentication command

♦ removed the LAST command

♦ fixed typo in example of TOP command

♦ clarified that the second argument to the TOP command is non-negative

♦ added the optional UIDL command

♦ added warning regarding length of shared secrets with APOP

♦ added additional warnings to the security considerations section

1. Introduction

On certain types of smaller nodes in the Internet it is often impractical to maintain a message transport system (MTS). For example, a workstation may not have sufficient resources (cycles, disk space) in order to permit a SMTP server [RFC821] and associated local mail delivery system to be kept resident and continuously running. Similarly, it may be expensive (or impossible) to keep a personal computer interconnected to an IP-style network for long amounts of time (the node is lacking the resource known as "connectivity").

Despite this, it is often very useful to be able to manage mail on these smaller nodes, and they often support a user agent (UA) to aid the tasks of mail handling. To solve this problem, a node which can support an MTS entity offers a maildrop service to these less endowed nodes. The Post Office Protocol – Version 3 (POP3) is intended to permit a workstation to dynamically access a maildrop on a server host in a useful fashion. Usually, this means that the POP3 is used to allow a workstation to retrieve mail that the server is holding for it.

For the remainder of this memo, the term "client host" refers to a host making use of the POP3 service, while the term "server host" refers to a host which offers the POP3 service.

2. A Short Digression

This memo does not specify how a client host enters mail into the transport system, although a method consistent with the philosophy of this memo is presented here:

```
When the user agent on a client host wishes to enter a message into
   the transport system, it establishes an SMTP connection to its
   relay host (this relay host could be, but need not be, the POP3
   server host for the client host).
```

3. Basic Operation

Initially, the server host starts the POP3 service by listening on TCP port 110. When a client host wishes to make use of the service, it establishes a TCP connection with the server host. When the connection is established, the POP3 server sends a greeting. The client and POP3 server then exchange commands and responses (respectively) until the connection is closed or aborted.

Commands in the POP3 consist of a keyword, possibly followed by one or more arguments. All commands are terminated by a CRLF pair. Keywords and arguments consist of printable ASCII characters. Keywords and arguments are each separated by a single SPACE character. Keywords are three or four characters long. Each argument may be up to 40 characters long.

Responses in the POP3 consist of a status indicator and a keyword possibly followed by additional information. All responses are terminated by a CRLF pair. There are currently two status indicators: positive ("+OK") and negative ("-ERR").

Responses to certain commands are multi-line. In these cases, which are clearly indicated below, after sending the first line of the response and a CRLF, any additional lines are sent, each terminated by a CRLF pair. When all lines of the response have been sent, a final line is sent, consisting of a termination octet (decimal code 046, ".") and a CRLF pair. If any line of the multi-line response begins with the termination octet, the line is "byte-stuffed" by pre-pending the termination octet to that line of the response. Hence a multi-line response is terminated with the five octets "CRLF.CRLF". When examining a multi-line response, the client checks to see if the line begins with the termination octet. If so and if octets other than CRLF follow, the first octet of the line (the termination octet) is stripped away. If so and if

CRLF immediately follows the termination character, then the response from the POP server is ended and the line containing ".CRLF" is not considered part of the multi-line response.

A POP3 session progresses through a number of states during its lifetime. Once the TCP connection has been opened and the POP3 server has sent the greeting, the session enters the AUTHORIZATION state. In this state, the client must identify itself to the POP3 server. Once the client has successfully done this, the server acquires resources associated with the client's maildrop, and the session enters the TRANSACTION state. In this state, the client requests actions on the part of the POP3 server. When the client has issued the QUIT command, the session enters the UPDATE state. In this state, the POP3 server releases any resources acquired during the TRANSACTION state and says goodbye. The TCP connection is then closed.

A POP3 server MAY have an inactivity autologout timer. Such a timer MUST be of at least 10 minutes' duration. The receipt of any command from the client during that interval should suffice to reset the autologout timer. When the timer expires, the session does NOT enter the UPDATE state—the server should close the TCP connection without removing any messages or sending any response to the client.

4. The AUTHORIZATION State

Once the TCP connection has been opened by a POP3 client, the POP3 server issues a one-line greeting. This can be any string terminated by CRLF. An example might be:

```
S:   +OK POP3 server ready
```

Note that this greeting is a POP3 reply. The POP3 server should always give a positive response as the greeting.

The POP3 session is now in the AUTHORIZATION state. The client must now identify and authenticate itself to the POP3 server. Two possible mechanisms for doing this are described in this document, the USER and PASS command combination and the APOP command. The APOP command is described later in this document.

To authenticate using the USER and PASS command combination, the client must first issue the USER command. If the POP3 server responds with a positive status indicator ("+OK"), then the client may issue either the PASS command to complete the authentication, or the QUIT command to terminate the POP3 session. If the POP3 server responds with a negative status indicator ("-ERR") to the USER command, then the client may either issue a new authentication command or may issue the QUIT command.

When the client issues the PASS command, the POP3 server uses the argument pair from the USER and PASS commands to determine if the client should be given access to the appropriate maildrop.

Once the POP3 server has determined through the use of any authentication command that the client should be given access to the appropriate maildrop, the POP3 server then acquires an exclusive- access lock on the maildrop, as necessary to prevent messages from being modified or removed before the session enters the UPDATE state. If the lock is successfully acquired, the POP3 server responds with a positive status indicator. The POP3 session now enters the TRANSACTION state, with no messages marked as deleted. If the maildrop cannot be opened for some reason (for example, a lock can not be acquired, the client is denied access to the appropriate maildrop, or the maildrop cannot be parsed), the POP3 server responds with a negative status indicator. (If a lock was acquired but the POP3 server intends to respond with a negative status indicator, the POP3 server must release the lock prior to rejecting the command.) After returning a negative status indicator, the server may close the connection. If the server does not close the connection, the client may either issue a new authentication command and start again, or the client may issue the QUIT command.

After the POP3 server has opened the maildrop, it assigns a message- number to each message, and notes the size of each message in octets. The first message in the maildrop is assigned a message-number of "1", the second is assigned "2", and so on, so that the nth message in a maildrop is assigned a message-number of "n". In POP3 commands and responses, all message-number's and message sizes are expressed in base-10 (i.e., decimal).

Here are summaries for the three POP3 commands discussed thus far:

```
USER name

Arguments:
a string identifying a mailbox (required), which is of significance
 ONLY to the server

Restrictions:
may only be given in the AUTHORIZATION state after the POP3 greeting
 or after an unsuccessful USER or PASS command

Possible Responses:
+OK name is a valid mailbox
-ERR never heard of mailbox name

Examples:
C: USER mrose
S: +OK mrose is a real hoopy frood
 ...
C: USER frated
S: -ERR sorry, no mailbox for frated here

PASS string

Arguments:
a server/mailbox-specific password (required)
```

Restrictions:
may only be given in the AUTHORIZATION state after a successful USER
  command

Discussion:
Since the PASS command has exactly one argument, a POP3 server may
  treat spaces in the argument as part of the password, instead of as
  argument separators.

Possible Responses:
+OK maildrop locked and ready
-ERR invalid password
-ERR unable to lock maildrop

Examples:
C: USER mrose
S: +OK mrose is a real hoopy frood
C: PASS secret
S: +OK mrose's maildrop has 2 messages (320 octets)
...
C: USER mrose
S: +OK mrose is a real hoopy frood
C: PASS secret
S: -ERR maildrop already locked

QUIT

Arguments: none

Restrictions: none

Possible Responses:
+OK

Examples:
C: QUIT
S: +OK dewey POP3 server signing off

5. The TRANSACTION State

Once the client has successfully identified itself to the POP3 server and the POP3
server has locked and opened the appropriate maildrop, the POP3 session is now in
the TRANSACTION state. The client may now issue any of the following POP3 commands repeatedly. After each command, the POP3 server issues a response.
Eventually, the client issues the QUIT command and the POP3 session enters the
UPDATE state.

Here are the POP3 commands valid in the TRANSACTION state:

STAT

Arguments: none

Restrictions:
may only be given in the TRANSACTION state

Discussion:
The POP3 server issues a positive response with a line containing
  information for the maildrop. This line is called a "drop listing"
  for that maildrop.

In order to simplify parsing, all POP3 servers required to use a
  certain format for drop listings. The positive response consists
  of "+OK" followed by a single space, the number of messages in the
  maildrop, a single space, and the size of the maildrop in octets.
  This memo makes no requirement on what follows the maildrop size.
  Minimal implementations should just end that line of the response
  with a CRLF pair. More advanced implementations may include other
  information.

NOTE: This memo STRONGLY discourages implementations from supplying
  additional information in the drop listing. Other, optional,
  facilities are discussed later on which permit the client to parse
  the messages in the maildrop.

Note that messages marked as deleted are not counted in either
  total.

Possible Responses:
+OK nn mm

Examples:
C: STAT
S: +OK 2 320

LIST [msg]

Arguments:
a message-number (optional), which, if present, may NOT refer to a
  message marked as deleted

Restrictions:
may only be given in the TRANSACTION state

Discussion:
If an argument was given and the POP3 server issues a positive
  response with a line containing information for that message. This
  line is called a "scan listing" for that message.

If no argument was given and the POP3 server issues a positive
response, then the response given is multi-line. After the initial
+OK, for each message in the maildrop, the POP3 server responds
with a line containing information for that message. This line is
also called a "scan listing" for that message.

In order to simplify parsing, all POP3 servers are required to use a
certain format for scan listings. A scan listing consists of the
message-number of the message, followed by a single space and the
exact size of the message in octets. This memo makes no requirement
on what follows the message size in the scan listing. Minimal
implementations should just end that line of the response with a
CRLF pair. More advanced implementations may include other
information, as parsed from the message.

NOTE: This memo STRONGLY discourages implementations from supplying
additional information in the scan listing. Other, optional,
facilities are discussed later on which permit the client to parse
the messages in the maildrop.

Note that messages marked as deleted are not listed.

Possible Responses:
+OK scan listing follows
-ERR no such message

Examples:
C: LIST
S: +OK 2 messages (320 octets)
S: 1 120
S: 2 200
S: .
...
C: LIST 2
S: +OK 2 200
...
C: LIST 3
S: -ERR no such message, only 2 messages in maildrop

RETR msg

Arguments:
a message-number (required) which may not refer to a message marked
as deleted

Restrictions:
may only be given in the TRANSACTION state

Discussion:

If the POP3 server issues a positive response, then the response
given is multi-line. After the initial +OK, the POP3 server sends
the message corresponding to the given message-number, being
careful to byte-stuff the termination character (as with all multi-
line responses).

Possible Responses:
+OK message follows
-ERR no such message

Examples:
C: RETR 1
S: +OK 120 octets
S: <the POP3 server sends the entire message here>
S: .

DELE msg

Arguments:
a message-number (required) which may not refer to a message marked
 as deleted

Restrictions:
may only be given in the TRANSACTION state

Discussion:
The POP3 server marks the message as deleted. Any future reference
 to the message-number associated with the message in a POP3 command
 generates an error. The POP3 server does not actually delete the
 message until the POP3 session enters the UPDATE state.

Possible Responses:
+OK message deleted
-ERR no such message

Examples:
C: DELE 1
S: +OK message 1 deleted
   ...
C: DELE 2
S: -ERR message 2 already deleted

NOOP

Arguments: none

Restrictions:
may only be given in the TRANSACTION state

Discussion:
The POP3 server does nothing, it merely replies with a positive
 response.

```
Possible Responses:
+OK

Examples:
C: NOOP
S: +OK

RSET

Arguments: none

Restrictions:
may only be given in the TRANSACTION state

Discussion:
If any messages have been marked as deleted by the POP3 server, they
  are unmarked.  The POP3 server then replies with a positive
  response.

Possible Responses:
+OK

Examples:
C: RSET
S: +OK maildrop has 2 messages (320 octets)
```

6. The UPDATE State

When the client issues the QUIT command from the TRANSACTION state, the POP3 session enters the UPDATE state. (Note that if the client issues the QUIT command from the AUTHORIZATION state, the POP3 session terminates but does NOT enter the UPDATE state.)

If a session terminates for some reason other than a client-issued QUIT command, the POP3 session does NOT enter the UPDATE state and MUST not remove any messages from the maildrop.

```
QUIT

Arguments: none

Restrictions: none

Discussion:
The POP3 server removes all messages marked as deleted from the
  maildrop.  It then releases any exclusive-access lock on the
  maildrop and replies as to the status of these operations.  The TCP
  connection is then closed.
```

```
Possible Responses:
+OK

Examples:
C: QUIT
S: +OK dewey POP3 server signing off (maildrop empty)
   ...
C: QUIT
S: +OK dewey POP3 server signing off (2 messages left)
   ...
```

7. Optional POP3 Commands

The POP3 commands discussed above must be supported by all minimal implementations of POP3 servers.

The optional POP3 commands described below permit a POP3 client greater freedom in message handling, while preserving a simple POP3 server implementation.

```
NOTE: This memo STRONGLY encourages implementations to support these
  commands in lieu of developing augmented drop and scan listings.
  In short, the philosophy of this memo is to put intelligence in the
  part of the POP3 client and not the POP3 server.

TOP msg n

Arguments:
a message-number (required) which may NOT refer to a message marked
  as deleted, and a non-negative number  (required)

Restrictions:
may only be given in the TRANSACTION state

Discussion:
If the POP3 server issues a positive response, then the response
  given is multi-line.  After the initial +OK, the POP3 server sends
  the headers of the message, the blank line separating the headers
  from the body, and then the number of lines indicated message's
  body, being careful to byte-stuff the termination character (as
  with all multi-line responses).

Note that if the number of lines requested by the POP3 client is
  greater than the number of lines in the body, then the POP3 server
  sends the entire message.

Possible Responses:
+OK top of message follows
-ERR no such message

Examples:
C: TOP 1 10
```

```
S: +OK
S: <the POP3 server sends the headers of the message, a blank line,
   and the first 10 lines of the body of the message>
S: .
   ...
C: TOP 100 3
S: -ERR no such message
```

UIDL [msg]

Arguments:
a message-number (optionally) If a message-number is given, it may
NOT refer to a message marked as deleted.

Restrictions:
may only be given in the TRANSACTION state.

Discussion:
If an argument was given and the POP3 server issues a positive
response with a line containing information for that message. This
line is called a "unique-id listing" for that message.

If no argument was given and the POP3 server issues a positive
response, then the response given is multi-line. After the initial
+OK, for each message in the maildrop, the POP3 server responds
with a line containing information for that message. This line is
called a "unique-id listing" for that message.

In order to simplify parsing, all POP3 servers are required to use a
certain format for unique-id listings. A unique-id listing
consists of the message-number of the message, followed by a single
space and the unique-id of the message. No information follows the
unique-id in the unique-id listing.

The unique-id of a message is an arbitrary server-determined string,
consisting of characters in the range 0x21 to 0x7E, which uniquely
identifies a message within a maildrop and which persists across
sessions. The server should never reuse an unique-id in a given
maildrop, for as long as the entity using the unique-id exists.

Note that messages marked as deleted are not listed.

Possible Responses:
+OK unique-id listing follows
-ERR no such message

Examples:
C: UIDL
S: +OK
S: 1 whqtswO00WBw418f9t5JxYwZ
S: 2 QhdPYR:00WBw1Ph7x7
S: .
   ...
C: UIDL 2
```
```

```
S: +OK 2 QhdPYR:00WBw1Ph7x7
   ...
C: UIDL 3
S: -ERR no such message, only 2 messages in maildrop
```

APOP name digest

Arguments:
a string identifying a mailbox and a MD5 digest string (both
 required)

Restrictions: may only be given in the AUTHORIZATION state after the
 POP3 greeting

Discussion:
Normally, each POP3 session starts with a USER/PASS exchange.
 This results in a server/user-id specific password being sent
 in the clear on the network. For intermittent use of POP3, this
 may not introduce a sizable risk. However, many POP3 client
 implementations connect to the POP3 server on a regular basis — to
 check for new mail. Further the interval of session initiation may
 be on the order of five minutes. Hence, the risk of password
 capture is greatly enhanced. An alternate method of authentication
 is required which provides for both origin authentication and
 replay protection, but which does not involve sending a password in
 the clear over the network. The APOP command provides this
 functionality.

A POP3 server which implements the APOP command will include a
 timestamp in its banner greeting. The syntax of the timestamp
 corresponds to the `msg-id' in [RFC822], and MUST be different each
 time the POP3 server issues a banner greeting. For example, on a
 UNIX implementation in which a separate UNIX process is used for
 each instance of a POP3 server, the syntax of the timestamp might
 be:

<process-ID.clock@hostname>

where `process-ID' is the decimal value of the process's PID, clock
 is the decimal value of the system clock, and hostname is the
 fully-qualified domain-name corresponding to the host where the
 POP3 server is running.

The POP3 client makes note of this timestamp, and then issues the
 APOP command. The `name' parameter has identical semantics to the
 `name' parameter of the USER command. The `digest' parameter is
 calculated by applying the MD5 algorithm [RFC1321] to a string
 consisting of the timestamp (including angle-brackets) followed by
 a shared secret. This shared secret is a string known only to the
 POP3 client and server. Great care should be taken to prevent
 unauthorized disclosure of the secret, as knowledge of the secret
 will allow any entity to successfully masquerade as the named user.
 The `digest' parameter itself is a 16-octet value which is sent in
 hexadecimal format, using lower-case ASCII characters.

When the POP3 server receives the APOP command, it verifies
the digest provided. If the digest is correct, the POP3 server
issues a positive response, and the POP3 session enters the
TRANSACTION state. Otherwise, a negative response is issued and
the POP3 session remains in the AUTHORIZATION state.

Note that as the length of the shared secret increases, so does the
difficulty of deriving it. As such, shared secrets should be long
strings (considerably longer than the 8-character example shown
below).

Possible Responses:
+OK maildrop locked and ready
-ERR permission denied

Examples:
S: +OK POP3 server ready <1896.697170952@dbc.mtview.ca.us>
C: APOP mrose c4c9334bac560ecc979e58001b3e22fb
S: +OK maildrop has 1 message (369 octets)

In this example, the shared secret is the string `tan- staaf'.
 Hence, the MD5 algorithm is applied to the string

<1896.697170952@dbc.mtview.ca.us>tanstaaf

which produces a digest value of

c4c9334bac560ecc979e58001b3e22fb

8. POP3 Command Summary

Minimal POP3 Commands:

- ◆ USER name – valid in the AUTHORIZATION state

- ◆ PASS string

- ◆ QUIT

- ◆ STAT – valid in the TRANSACTION state

- ◆ LIST [msg]

- ◆ RETR msg

- ◆ DELE msg

- ◆ NOOP

- ◆ RSET

- ◆ QUIT – valid in the UPDATE state

Optional POP3 Commands:

◆ APOP name digest — valid in the AUTHORIZATION state

◆ TOP msg n — valid in the TRANSACTION state

◆ UIDL [msg]

POP3 Replies:

◆ +OK

◆ -ERR

Note that with the exception of the STAT, LIST, and UIDL commands, the reply given by the POP3 server to any command is significant only to "+OK" and "-ERR". Any text occurring after this reply may be ignored by the client.

9. Example POP3 Session

```
S: <wait for connection on TCP port 110>
C: <open connection>
S:    +OK POP3 server ready <1896.697170952@dbc.mtview.ca.us>
C:    APOP mrose c4c9334bac560ecc979e58001b3e22fb
S:    +OK mrose's maildrop has 2 messages (320 octets)
C:    STAT
S:    +OK 2 320
C:    LIST
S:    +OK 2 messages (320 octets)
S:    1 120
S:    2 200
S:    .
C:    RETR 1
S:    +OK 120 octets
S:    <the POP3 server sends message 1>
S:    .
C:    DELE 1
S:    +OK message 1 deleted
C:    RETR 2
S:    +OK 200 octets
S:    <the POP3 server sends message 2>
S:    .
C:    DELE 2
S:    +OK message 2 deleted
C:    QUIT
S:    +OK dewey POP3 server signing off (maildrop empty)
C: <close connection>
S: <wait for next connection>
```

10. Message Format

All messages transmitted during a POP3 session are assumed to conform to the standard for the format of Internet text messages [RFC822].

It is important to note that the octet count for a message on the server host may differ from the octet count assigned to that message due to local conventions for designating end-of-line. Usually, during the AUTHORIZATION state of the POP3 session, the POP3 server can calculate the size of each message in octets when it opens the maildrop. For example, if the POP3 server host internally represents end-of-line as a single character, then the POP3 server simply counts each occurrence of this character in a message as two octets. Note that lines in the message which start with the termination octet need not be counted twice, since the POP3 client will remove all byte-stuffed termination characters when it receives a multi-line response.

11. References

[RFC821] Postel, J., "Simple Mail Transfer Protocol", STD 10, RFC 821, USC/Information Sciences Institute, August 1982.

[RFC822] Crocker, D., "Standard for the Format of ARPA-Internet Text Messages", STD 11, RFC 822, University of Delaware, August 1982.

[RFC1321] Rivest, R. "The MD5 Message-Digest Algorithm", RFC 1321, MIT Laboratory for Computer Science, April, 1992.

12. Security Considerations

It is conjectured that use of the APOP command provides origin identification and replay protection for a POP3 session. Accordingly, a POP3 server which implements both the PASS and APOP commands must not allow both methods of access for a given user; that is, for a given "USER name" either the PASS or APOP command is allowed, but not both.

Further, note that as the length of the shared secret increases, so does the difficulty of deriving it.

Servers that answer -ERR to the USER command are giving potential attackers clues about which names are valid.

Use of the PASS command sends passwords in the clear over the network.

Use of the RETR and TOP commands sends mail in the clear over the network.

Otherwise, security issues are not discussed in this memo.

13. Acknowledgments

The POP family has a long and checkered history. Although primarily a minor revision to RFC 1460, POP3 is based on the ideas presented in RFCs 918, 937, and 1081.

In addition, Alfred Grimstad, Keith McCloghrie, and Neil Ostroff provided significant comments on the APOP command.

14. Authors' Addresses

John G. Myers
Carnegie-Mellon University
5000 Forbes Ave
Pittsburgh, PA 15213
EMail: jgm+@cmu.edu

Marshall T. Rose
Dover Beach Consulting, Inc.
420 Whisman Court
Mountain View, CA 94043-2186
EMail: mrose@dbc.mtview.ca.us

Appendix E

Review Questions

Introduction

Okay, so you've read the entire book and now think you are an ASP expert. Here's your chance to prove it. In this appendix, we present a series of review questions – and answers – for each chapter. If you can answer them, congratulations!

Chapter 1

Why bother with ASP when CGI and ISAPI solutions will do?   ASP offers a number of features that these approaches do not. For example, you do not need to recompile an ASP script to test it. You can also put your program code right in with your HTML, which makes debugging much easier. ASP also prints useful error messages when you make a programming mistake. Basically, ASP has all the advantages of both CGI and ISAPI without all the headaches.

What advantages does OLE automation bring to ASP?   The most important one is that this capability allows you to use the features of hundreds of other programs in your Web application. This is a real time saver!

What do you need to be aware of when using the StartConnectionPool key?   Connection pooling does not work well with Microsoft Access data sources.

Chapter 2

Why won't you see "mandatory" HTML tags, such as <HTML> or <HEAD>, in many of the examples in this book?   These tags are no longer necessary in the HTML 3.2 standard.

What does ASP do with code in <SCRIPT> tags without the RUNAT=Server attribute?   ASP simply passes this code along to the browser with the rest of the HTML.

What happens if you "run" an ASP Script that contains no scripting commands, just HTML?   This is still a valid ASP script, and it simply outputs the HTML to the browser.

In both VBScript and JavaScript, what syntax is used to access methods and properties of objects?   The dot operator (.) indicates methods or attributes of objects.

What is the shortcut for response.write?   The <%= %> tag pair.

Can you switch scripting languages in the middle of a page, and if so, what is the command to do so?   No, you can't arbitrarily switch scripting languages. What you can do is write functions in another scripting language and call them.

With which Web servers can you use ASP?   Basically, anything Microsoft owns.

Chapter 3

What's the point of using the request.querystring object when you have access to the request.servervariables("QUERY_STRING") environment variable?   Technically speaking, you can get all the information from the environment variable. If you are porting some CGI code, you may want to do just that, for convenience. However, the request.querystring collection gives a consistent interface to information and should make your code easier to read and maintain.

What happens if a parameter is passed in the URL with encoding, such as %20 for a space? What will be the value retrieved by the Request object?   The Request object performs the decoding for you.

Does the request.querystring(variable).count property exist for variables of which there is only a single instance?   Yes, and their count is 1.

What are the differences between how request.querystring and request.form behave?   There are none.

How can you see a list of all the variables in the request.servervariables collection?   Because it's a collection, you can use a for each loop iterator to see them all.

Chapter 4

How do you keep HTML-unfriendly text from getting on your page?   Use the HTMLEncode() method.

What value does CreateObject() provide?   Not much. It just opens up the features of hundreds of other applications to you!

What is the NETUTILS component?   The NETUTILS component is a custom ASP component that we wrote for you. It lets you open TCP/IP client connections and read POP3 e-mail.

Why did the authors write this component?   We're just geeky that way!

Chapter 5

Why do you need to use the AddHeader method of the Response object?   This method is helpful when you have no other way, either through ASP or your Web server, to put the information in the header. You shouldn't use it when you have alternatives, such as the response.cookies collection.

Why must calls to the response.cookies collection be completed before you write any HTML output?   Because the cookies must go in the HTTP header. If you have begun to write to the *body* of the HTML document, the header must by definition be completed.

Is there any way around this problem?   Yes. Buffer your output.

How can you make separate calls to response.write appear on separate lines in your HTML source?   In VBScript, this is a pain. You must response.write the carriage return character, chr(13). In JScript, you at least have the \n escape for the new line. In PerlScript, you are on easy street because PerlScript interpolates strings.

Why doesn't response.write accept a variable number of arguments, like most print commands in programming languages do?   Good question. Wish we knew. It doesn't, so you have to concatenate multiple arguments with the & character. This is no big deal in an untyped scripting language, because all arguments automagically convert to strings for concatenation and output.

Chapter 6

What is an ASP application?   An ASP application is defined as all the .asp files in a given virtual directory and its subdirectories.

Why would you want to store variables in the Application object?   You store information there that you want to be available to all the users of the current application. It's a great way, for example, to pass messages back and forth.

What is a session?   A session, in ASP, is defined as the time a particular user is using a specific application.

Why bother storing items in the Session object?   Sometimes, it is the only way to pass information, such as objects, from page to page. It also makes your HTML much easier to read because you don't need a bunch of hidden fields.

What's the value of the Application and Session level events?   They are a great place in which to put code to initialize and clean up your objects and data when you enter and exit an application or session.

Chapter 7

When you call the open method of a connection, what is the first parameter that you pass?   The name of the ODBC data source.

If you want to connect to an RDBMS using TCP/IP, can you simply use the IP address as your data source parameter?   No. How would ADO know what you want? Are you looking for SQL Server at that IP address? Oracle? Sybase? You must create an ODBC data source and specify all this information.

What is connection pooling, and why is it better than storing connection objects in session variables?   Connection pooling is a feature of ODBC 3.0 that allows a pool of connection to be kept open to the RDBMS. Clients requesting connections are assigned one from the pool, thus minimizing the amount of connecting and disconnecting to the RDBMS. With a session variable, you create a connection that will last for 20 minutes for each and every visitor to your site. You can rapidly exceed the upper limit on connections to your RDBMS that way.

How do you access fields in a Recordset object, by column name or by column number?   The Recordset object supports both.

When your Recordset holds more than one row, what method(s) can you use to see other rows?   With forward-only cursor, which we recommend you use, you must call the MoveNext method.

Is there a simple way to dump all the rows of a Recordset into an array?   Yes, with the GetRows method.

Chapter 8

Who cares about the Ad Rotator? Isn't it just some afterthought Microsoft threw in? You should care, that's who! Advertising is the preferred way of funding commercial Web sites. Even if you are working on an internal Web site, you can still use this object to advertise important announcements to your users.

What is the value in creating a custom redirection file? Using a custom redirection file is the only way to track the effectiveness of a given advertisement. You can do many useful things with a redirection file. Be creative!

How do you indicate that a particular ad does not have pages to which the user should be redirected? Put a hyphen (-) in the **adHomePageURL** section of the schedule file for that particular ad.

Chapter 9

Why is a special File Access component needed? Can't we just use the I/O facilities of the scripting languages? First of all, some scripting languages, such as JScript, don't have access to the file system for security reasons. Second, it's good OO design to use the **File Access** component.

Which method of the File Access component returns a directory listing? Trick question. No method returns a directory listing.

How does the Read method treat new lines? Just like any other character.

What's the difference between WriteLine and WriteBlankLines? WriteLine writes a string to a TextStream object, followed by a new line. WriteBlankLines writes a specific number of new line characters only.

What is the name of the property that becomes true at the end of the file (EOF)? AtEndOfStream.

Can you get all the Browser Capability information from the HTTP header? Not directly. The HTTP Header includes the User Agent, which is what the **Browser Capability** component is reading. From the User Agent, you can determine a browser's properties, if you take the time to make a list of what each browser can and can't do. However, this is a classic case of reinventing the wheel.

New versions of browsers come out all the time. What information will the Browser Capability component report for a browser version that it doesn't know about?   All properties default to Unknown, except for properties for which you have supplied your own faults.

What might you do to make a new browser match the browscap.ini file, even though the browser's exact version number isn't in the file?   Use wildcards in the file. Specifying Version 4* matches all future interations of Version 4.

What character separates items in the Content Linking List file?   The tab character.

What kinds of URLs may be used in the Content Linking List file?   Only relative and absolute URLs local to the server. You can't use http:// URLs, nor can you use real path names. They must be virtual paths.

What happens when an ASP file not on the Content Linking List uses GetNext or GetPrevious methods?   Information for the first and last files, respectively, is returned.

You have a bunch of plain old HTML files that you want to juice up with the Content Linker. What can you do?   You have to convert them to ASP files and create a Content Linking List file. Get the source code for this chapter off the disc, and you should be up and running in minutes.

Chapter 10

What is an ASP component?   It's actually an OLE Automation component.

What's an OLE Automation component?   An application that allows an external program to control its actions or access its data via a standard set of language-independent commands.

What's the difference between an in-process server and an out-process server?   An in-process server runs in the same memory space as the calling application. An out-process server runs in its own memory space.

Why do your OLE classes have to be declared as Public in Visual Basic.   If they are not, then they will not be visible to outside programs.

How do custom ASP components access the internal structures and functions of a particular ASP instance?   Each component is passed a ScriptingContext object in its OnStartPage() method. The component can then use that object to get a reference to the current ASP internal objects.

How are objects passed to a custom ASP component?   In Visual Basic, they are passed as Variants. This means that you need to take extra care to recast them as OLE objects.

Chapter 11

If Visual Basic is so easy, why would anyone write an ASP component in Visual C++? No matter how many features Visual Basic gets, there will still be things for which VC++ is better suited. For example, Visual Basic doesn't allow you to create individual threads. As an experienced programmer, you know that correctly using threads greatly helps the performance of complicated applications.

Which Visual C++ tool makes OLE automation easy?   ClassWizard!

Why do we recommend that you have your methods take and return Variants? Doing so avoids nasty ASP messages about incorrect parameter types. Remember, in ASP, the Variant is the only data type.

If Microsoft's own MFC makes accessing the ASP internals so easy, why don't their examples use it?   They wrote their code to be portable to other C++ compilers, too. Many of those packages don't support the MFC.

Why do we go to all the trouble of passing the ScriptingContext object as an LPU-KNOWN when passing it as an LPDISPATCH seems to work?   Generally speaking, treating objects passed into your methods as LPDISPATCHs is dangerous. If you are not absolutely sure that you are getting the right thing, you will crash your Web server. The safest approach is treat the object as an LPUNKNOWN and query its interface for its IDispatch interface.

Chapter 12

The NETUTILS component isn't really all that magical, is it?   Nope.

Appendix A

How do you create a class in JScript?   Write the constructor function and instantiate objects with the keyword **new**.

What are the JScript rules for variable scoping?   Variables are global unless you localize them to a function with the keyword **var**.

What does JScript do if you pass too many or too few arguments to a function? JScript attempts to execute the function anyway. It's up to you to code defensively and plan for a variable number of arguments.

How can you determine how many arguments were passed to a function? Every function has an arguments[] Array Object containing all the arguments to the function, so function_name.arguments.length returns the number of arguments passed.

What does the with command do? *with* object_name {block} establishes a default object in a block so that you don't have to keep writing object_name.property_name.

What does it mean to say that functions are a data type in JScript? It literally means that you can use a function anywhere you would use a "normal" variable. You can pass functions as arguments to other functions, make functions attributes of other objects, or give attributes to functions.

JScript doesn't have a C–style switch statement. How might you implement one? The most likely bet is to use an if...else if...else if... construct.

Which character delimits JScript string literals? You can use either double or single quotes.

If foo contains a floating point number, how do you convert it to a string? foo.toString()

What is a wrapper object? JScript provides objects that model the behavior of strings, numbers, Booleans, and Dates. When you attempt to invoke a method of these objects on an ordinary variable, JScript converts the variable to one of these objects, called a wrapper object, for you.

How are associative arrays implemented in JScript? Associative arrays are implemented as properties of objects. You can name an object property with the object_name[property] syntax.

What character(s) terminate a JScript statement? Either a semicolon or a newline character.

When is it mandatory to use a semicolon to terminate a statement? When is it mandatory to use a newline? If you intend to put two JScript statements on a line, you must use a semicolon. If you terminate every statement with a semicolon, you never need a newline.

Illustrate three different reasons why a variable name would be illegal.   The variable name *foo bar* is illegal because it contains a space. The name *1way* is illegal because it starts with a number (numbers may be used in the rest of the name). The name *function* is illegal because it is a reserved word.

What is the difference between break and continue?   Break terminates loop execution. Continue skips the remainder of the block and starts the next iteration of the loop.

Which command would you use to loop over the attributes of an object?   for...in

What object properties or methods will be omitted by the for...in loop?   Built-in methods such as toString(), join(), and sort().

Construct an array and intialize it with the numbers 11113, 22229, 33331.   foo = new Array(11113, 22229, 33331)

Can you take a string and evaluate it as JScript code?   Yes, use the eval command.

What are the two kinds of comments used in JScript?   // and /* */

What's the best way to handle ambiguous expressions in which operators are manipulating or comparing both strings and numbers?   Use the parseInt() and parseFloat() functions and the toString() method to disambiguate the expression.

How do you know whether a function parameter is passed by value or reference? How do you specify in the parameter list which method you want JScript to use?   Objects are passed by reference, and remember that Arrays are objects. Ordinary values are passed by value. You can't control this in the parameter list.

Under what circumstances can you add attributes to objects after you have created them? Can you add both properties and methods? Can you make additions to built-in objects?   You can add whatever you want to any object you want. There are no restrictions.

Appendix F

Glossary

AdRotator   An ASP component that encapsulates the functions of rotating ads based on a frequency that you provide, including creating the <A HREF> tags for the ad.

array   A variable which is actually just a list of variables indexed by integers starting at 0.

ASP (Active Server Pages)   A new technology from Microsoft for dynamically creating Web pages with the scripting language of your choice.

attribute   A variable that is tied to an object and specifies some information about whatever the object models.

Boolean   Something that can be only true or false.

CGI (Common Gateway Interface)   A specification for communication between a Web server and an application.

class   A specification for an object.

ClassID   A globally unique string that identifies a given OLE class.

Collection   A VBScript object that serves as a container for other objects.

comment   Text that is ignored by the interpreter or compiler.

comparison operator   A binary operator that returns true or false. Examples include equal to, not equal to, greater than, less than, greater than or equal to, and less than or equal to.

component   An ActiveX control (OLE automation server).

condition   A test that can be evaluated to true or false, typically used with Control of Flow commands.

ConnectionString   The string that tells an ADO Connection or Recordset object to which server to connect. Typically, this string includes a username and password, as well.

constant   A variable whose value cannot change.

constructor   A function that returns an object. Typically, constructors allocate memory and initialize objects.

ContentType   A string that tells a browser how to display the text stream it is receiving. Typical content types are HTML and plain text.

cookie   A small, sweet cake, usually flat and often crisp. Best made with chocolate. What? Oh, sorry. A cookie is a small file that your browser writes to your hard drive at the request of a Web server. The server can request information from this file in the future, thus retaining information about you.

cursor   A pointer to a database record. Cursors also record, by record, access to sets of rows in a database.

CursorType   A name for the properties of your database cursor. Some cursors types sacrifice the capability to change data or the capability to scroll backwards in exchange for better performance.

Data Source   The place from which you intend to get your data, generally tied to an RDBMS. Typically, you create an ODBC Data Source, because objects such as ADO use ODBC.

Date   An object that encapsulates the manipulation of calendar dates, such as resolving an arbitrary date into a day of the week.

debugging   The art of determining why a program behaves unexpectedly and modifying the program so that it works properly.

default   A value to be used when no value is supplied.

delimiter   The characters that specify where a set of commands begin and end. The HTML delimiters are <,>, and the ASP delimiters are <%,%>.

Elseif statements   A continuation of an if... Control of Flow command that continues the branching.

expression   A group of variables and operators that can be resolved into a single value.

FieldName   The name of a column in a database; a vertical slice of a database table.

fields   The columns of a database table.

flag   A parameter that turns some behavior on or off.

frame   An HTML tag that divides a browser window into scrollable subwindows.

HTTP   HyperText Transfer Protocol.

HTTPUserAgentHeader   A string that your browser sends to a Web server identifying exactly which browser you are using.

identifier   A variable name.

include   To take another file and interpret the host file as if it contained the text of this file.

initialization   Giving a variable its first value in a program.

in-process application   An application that shares a memory space with its host application.

JavaScript   Netscape's "cross-platform, object-based scripting language for client and server applications."

JScript   Microsoft's adaptation of Netscape's JavaScript 1.1.

method   A function attached to an object.

object   A bundling of data and functions into a reusable package.

operator   A special function that manipulates numbers or strings and returns a single value. Operators have a syntax all their own that models how mathematicians write equations.

parameter   A value passed to a function.

password   A string that you memorize (hopefully) to prove to a system that you are who you claim to be.

path   A string that tells the operating system where to find a file.

Perl (Practical Extraction and Reporting Language)   A UNIX system administration language with extremely powerful text manipulation features. Perl has become the language of choice for many Web developers.

pointer   The address of a variable. Pointers are used extensively in some languages because they provide the only way to pass data by reference.

property   See *attribute*.

Recordset   An object that represents a database table, query, or stored procedure.

rows   Horizontal slice of a database table.

scalar   Single value, in contrast to an array.

scope   The range during which a variable exists in a program.

scripting language   A programming language that is best suited to writing small programs quickly and easily. Scripting languages typically don't enforce type checking.

separator   A character that separates tokens.

statements   A complete sentence or command in a programming language.

stored procedure   Code that is compiled with the database of an RDBMS. Stored procedures often return result set(s) to their callers.

string   A sequence of characters, such as *abcedfg*.

Unicode   A format for stored characters using two bytes, thus allocating enough room for all foreign language characters.

URL (Uniform Resource Locator)   The standard for naming locations of resources across the Internet. For example: `http://www.microsoft.com`.

UserID   Name that identifies a person within a computer system.

value   The contents of a variable.

variable   Name for a memory location. Variable allows programs to manipulate data.

VBA (Visual Basic for Applications)   A relatively easy-to-learn but limited programming language.

VBScript   Microsoft's adaptation of Visual Basic for Applications for Internet scripting. It is mostly a subset of VBA without interactive elements such as messages boxes. There are a few additions to VBScript not found in VBA, such as the Dictionary object.

Quick Reference

The ASP Objects and Components

As you know, ASP comes with a number of built-in objects and pre-made components. For your convenience, we have included this Quick Reference to help you remember the important items about each.

Application Object–Chapter 6

An application is defined as all the ASP pages in a given virtual directory hierarchy. The **Application** object, therefore, governs certain actions and properties of a specific application.

Methods	Properties	Collections
Lock()		
Unlock()		

APPLICATION METHODS

Lock: Locks the **Application** object and all of its variables until you specifically unlock them or the lock expires.

Unlock: Unlocks the **Application** object and all of its variables.

Request Object–Chapter 3

The **Request** object is used to parse out requests from the client to the server.

Methods	Properties	Collections
		ClientCertificate
		Cookies
		QueryString
		ServerVariables

REQUEST COLLECTIONS

ClientCertificate: Retrieves the certification fields from the request issued by the Web browser.

Cookies: Retrieves the values of the cookies sent from the Web server.

Form: Retrieves any values passed from the Web browser via the POST method.

QueryString: Retrieves any values passed from the Web browser via the GET method.

ServerVariables: Retrieves the values in the HTTP header. The following table lists the variables.

AUTH_TYPE	The authentication method that the server uses to validate users when they attempt to access a protected script.
CONTENT_LENGTH	The length of the content as given by the client.
CONTENT_TYPE	The data type of the content. Used with queries that have attached information, such as the HTTP queries POST and PUT.
GATEWAY_INTERFACE	The revision of the CGI specification used by the server. Format: CGI/revision
HTTP_<HeaderName>	The value stored in the header HeaderName. Any header other than those listed in this table must be prefixed by "HTTP" in order for the ServerVariables collection to retrieve its value. Note: The server interprets any underscore (_) characters in HeaderName as dashes in the actual header. For example, if you specify HTTP_MY_HEADER, then the server searches for a header sent as MY-HEADER.

LOGON_USER	The Windows NT account that the user is logged into.
PATH_INFO	Extra path information as given by the client. You can access scripts by using their virtual path and the PATH_INFO server variable. If this information comes from a URL, it is decoded by the server before it is passed to the CGI script.
PATH_TRANSLATED	A translated version of PATH_INFO that takes the path and performs any necessary virtual-to-physical mapping.
QUERY_STRING	Query information stored in the string following the question mark (?) in the HTTP request.
REMOTE_ADDR	The IP address of the remote host making the request.
REMOTE_HOST	The name of the host making the request. If the server does not have this information, it sets REMOTE_ADDR and leaves this empty.
REQUEST_METHOD	The method used to make the request. For HTTP, this is GET, HEAD, POST, and so on.
SCRIPT_MAP	Gives the base portion of the URL.
SCRIPT_NAME	A virtual path to the script being executed. This is used for self-referencing URLs.
SERVER_NAME	The server's host name, DNS alias, or IP address as it would appear in self-referencing URLs.
SERVER_PORT	The port number to which the request was sent.
SERVER_PORT_SECURE	A string that contains either 0 or 1. If the request is being handled on the secure port, then this will be 1. Otherwise, it will be 0.
SERVER_PROTOCOL	The name and revision of the request information protocol. Format: protocol/revision
SERVER_SOFTWARE	The name and version of the server software answering the request (and running the gateway). Format: name/version
URL	Gives the base portion of the URL.

Response Object—Chapter 5

The **Response** object is responsible for sending data back to your client from your server.

Methods	Properties	Collections
AddHeader(name, value)	Buffer	Cookies
AppendToLog(string)	ExpiresContentType	
BinaryWrite(data)	ExpiresAbsolute	
Clear()	Status	
End()		
Flush()		
Redirect(URL)		
Write(variant)		

RESPONSE COLLECTIONS
Cookies: Allows you to set the client cookies to be stored on the browser.

RESPONSE PROPERTIES
Buffer: Determines whether ASP waits until you explicitly tell it before it sends your output.

ContentType: Holds the HTTP Content-Type header for your output.

Expires: Specifies how long (in minutes) the browser should hold the page in cache.

ExpiresAbsolute: Specifies an absolute date after which the browser should flush the page from the cache.

Status: Sets the HTTP status code.

RESPONSE METHODS
AddHeader: Adds a new HTTP header to the response.

AppendToLog: Writes an entry to the IIS system log.

BinaryWrite: Writes binary data to the browser.

Clear: Erases the HTML buffer. This only works if the Buffer property is set to 1.

End: Terminates the execution of the current ASP script.

Flush: Sends the contents of the HTTP buffer to the client immediately.

Redirect: Sends the client browser to another URL.

Write: Writes a line of text to the HTML buffer.

Server Object—Chapter 4

The Server object gives you a glimpse into the internal workings of ASP. It also allows you to extend ASP by instantiating OLE components.

Methods	Properties	Collections
CreateObject(progID)	ScriptTimeout	
HTMLEncode(string)		
MapPath(path)		
URLEncode(string)		

SERVER PROPERTIES

ScriptTimeout: Specifies, in seconds, how long a script can run before the system terminates it.

SERVER METHODS

CreateObject: Instantiates an OLE object within your ASP script.

HTMLEncode: Takes a given string and makes sure that it is properly encoded for display in an HTML page.

MapPath: Returns the physical directory to which a given virtual directory is mapped.

URLEncode: Takes a given string and makes sure that it is properly encoded for display as a URL.

Session Object—Chapter 6

The **Session** object controls each user session. In ASP, a Session is defined as the time a particular user is using a given application.

Methods	Properties	Collections
Abandon()	SessionID	
	Timeout	

SESSION PROPERTIES

SessionID: Stores the unique value that differentiates one user session from another.

Timeout: The time, in minutes, after which an unattended session expires.

SESSION METHODS

Abandon: Immediately end the current session.

Global Elements—Chapter 6

ASP has a few things that qualify as global properties insofar as they affect all the sessions for a given application. Some of them are truly global, while others really don't fit anywhere else. The following list enumerates and discusses them a bit.

Global.asa

This file holds global information about your applications and sessions.

Application Events

APPLICATION_ONSTART

This event is called whenever the application starts. This code is called exactly once for any particular run of IIS.

APPLICATION_ONEND

This event is called when the current application ends.

Session Events

SESSION_ONSTART

This event is called whenever a particular session is started.

SESSION_ONEND

This event is called whenever a particular session ends.

<OBJECT> Declarations

This tag in the `global.asa` file allows you to declare objects when an application begins.

External Components

ASP also ships with a few useful add-on components. Here's a brief synopsis of the ones we find most useful.

Ad Rotator Component—Chapter 8

The Ad Rotator component is useful insofar as it allows you to put advertisements on your Web pages with a minimal amount of effort.

Methods	Properties	Collections
GetAdvertisement(Path)	Border	
	Clickable	
	TargetFrame	

ROTATOR SCHEDULE FILE

This file controls the frequency and placement of all the ads on your ASP pages.

REDIRECTION FILE

This file is invoked when a user clicks on an ad on your site.

AD ROTATOR PROPERTIES

Border: The width of the ad border.

Clickable: Determines whether a user can click on the ad.

TargetFrame: The HTML frame in which the ad displays.

AD ROTATOR METHODS

GetAdvertisement: Gets the HTML for a new ad from the *Rotator Schedule File*.

Browser Capabilities Component—Chapter 9

The **Browser Capabilities** component allows you to figure out what the current client browser supports. Because not all browsers support the same things, this component can be helpful in displaying pages that are palatable to a wide variety of clients.

BROWSCAP.INI FILE

This file specifies the capabilities of potential client browsers. ASP uses this file to determine which features of HTML to send to the client.

Index

Note: Page numbers in *italics* refer to illustrations or charts.

Special Characters

; (semicolons)
    editing browscap.ini, 147
    JScript, 220, 282
<> (angle brackets, per cent)
    delimiters, 18–19
    escape sequences, 67
    VBScript and, 245
<> (brackets), tags and, 42
= (equal sign)
    VBScript comparison operator, 249–250
    writing output, 21
== (equal sign, equal sign), JScript comparison operator, 227
_ (underscore), VBScript, 245
?: (question mark, colon) conditional operator, JScript, 232
@ language command, script languages, 20
@@identity, surrogate keys, 114

A

Abandon method, Session object, 77–78
accessing ASP internals from components (Visual C++), 180–186
    asptlb.h header, 181, 184
    ClassWizard, 184–185
    GetResponse() method, 183, 185
    GUID initialization, 182
    IScriptingContext object, 185
    IUnknown parameter, 182
    linker error, 182
    LPDISPATCH parameter, 185, 186, 281
    LPUNKNOWN parameter, 182, 185, 186, 281
    Microsoft way of, 181–184
    OnStartPage() method, 185–186
    QueryInterface() method, 185–186

recoding OnStartPage() method, 185–186
    simpler way of, 184–186
    test.cpp header, 182–183, 184
Active Server Pages. *See* ASP
Active Template Library (ATL), writing ASP components in Visual C++, 174
ActiveX components, writing in Visual C++, 173–190
ActiveX DLL, writing OLE servers in Visual Basic 5, 166–167
Ad Meter example (Ad Rotator component), 121–124
    adCounter table, 121
    example1.asp file, 122
    redirection file, 122–123
    schedule file, 122
    schedule file parameters, *121*
Ad Rotator component, 117–134
    Ad Meter example, 121–124
    adHomePageURL parameter, 119
    adURL parameter, 119
    BORDER numBorder parameter, 119
    Border property, 124
    Clickable property, 124
    defined, 285
    described, 9
    GetAdvertisement() method, 123
    HEIGHT numHeight parameter, 119
    image parameter, 120
    impressions parameter, 120
    overview, 117–118
    properties, 123–124
    Redirect() method, 118–119
    redirection file, 120–121
    schedule file, 118
    schedule file example, 120
    Schedule Maintenance example, 124–134
    summary, 134
    TargetFrame property, 124
    Text parameter, 120

(continued)

297

(continued)

The Fun & Easy Way™ to learn about computers and more!

Windows® 3.11 For Dummies, 3rd Edition
by Andy Rathbone

ISBN: 1-56884-370-4
$16.95 USA/
$22.95 Canada

SUPER STAR

Mutual Funds For Dummies™
by Eric Tyson

ISBN: 1-56884-226-0
$16.99 USA/
$22.99 Canada

SUPER STAR

DOS For Dummies, 2nd Edition
by Dan Gookin

ISBN: 1-878058-75-4
$16.95 USA/
$22.95 Canada

SUPER STAR

The Interne For Dumm 2nd Editior
by John Levin Carol Baroud

ISBN: 1-56884
$19.99 USA/
$26.99 Canada

Personal Finance For Dummies™
by Eric Tyson

ISBN: 1-56884-150-7
$16.95 USA/
$22.95 Canada

SUPER STAR

PCs For Dummies, 3rd Edition
by Dan Gookin & Andy Rathbone

ISBN: 1-56884-904-4
$16.99 USA/
$22.99 Canada

VIII
FINALIST

Macs® For Dummies, 3rd Edition
by David Pogue

ISBN: 1-56884-239-2
$19.99 USA/
$26.99 Canada

SUPER STAR

The SAT® I For Dummi
by Suzee Vlk

ISBN: 1-56884
$14.99 USA/
$20.99 Canada

Here's a complete listing of IDG Books' ...For Dummies® titles

Title	Author	ISBN	Price
DATABASE			
Access 2 For Dummies®	by Scott Palmer	ISBN: 1-56884-090-X	$19.95 USA/$26.95 Canad
Access Programming For Dummies®	by Rob Krumm	ISBN: 1-56884-091-8	$19.95 USA/$26.95 Canad
Approach 3 For Windows® For Dummies®	by Doug Lowe	ISBN: 1-56884-233-3	$19.99 USA/$26.99 Canad
dBASE For DOS For Dummies®	by Scott Palmer & Michael Stabler	ISBN: 1-56884-188-4	$19.95 USA/$26.95 Canad
dBASE For Windows® For Dummies®	by Scott Palmer	ISBN: 1-56884-179-5	$19.95 USA/$26.95 Canad
dBASE 5 For Windows® Programming For Dummies®	by Ted Coombs & Jason Coombs	ISBN: 1-56884-215-5	$19.99 USA/$26.99 Canad
FoxPro 2.6 For Windows® For Dummies®	by John Kaufeld	ISBN: 1-56884-187-6	$19.95 USA/$26.95 Canad
Paradox 5 For Windows® For Dummies®	by John Kaufeld	ISBN: 1-56884-185-X	$19.95 USA/$26.95 Canad
DESKTOP PUBLISHING/ILLUSTRATION/GRAPHICS			
CorelDRAW! 5 For Dummies®	by Deke McClelland	ISBN: 1-56884-157-4	$19.95 USA/$26.95 Canad
CorelDRAW! For Dummies®	by Deke McClelland	ISBN: 1-56884-042-X	$19.95 USA/$26.95 Canad
Desktop Publishing & Design For Dummies®	by Roger C. Parker	ISBN: 1-56884-234-1	$19.99 USA/$26.99 Canad
Harvard Graphics 2 For Windows® For Dummies®	by Roger C. Parker	ISBN: 1-56884-092-6	$19.95 USA/$26.95 Canad
PageMaker 5 For Macs® For Dummies®	by Galen Gruman & Deke McClelland	ISBN: 1-56884-178-7	$19.95 USA/$26.95 Canad
PageMaker 5 For Windows® For Dummies®	by Deke McClelland & Galen Gruman	ISBN: 1-56884-160-4	$19.95 USA/$26.95 Canad
Photoshop 3 For Macs® For Dummies®	by Deke McClelland	ISBN: 1-56884-208-2	$19.99 USA/$26.99 Canad
QuarkXPress 3.3 For Dummies®	by Galen Gruman & Barbara Assadi	ISBN: 1-56884-217-1	$19.99 USA/$26.99 Canad
FINANCE/PERSONAL FINANCE/TEST TAKING REFERENCE			
Everyday Math For Dummies™	by Charles Seiter	ISBN: 1-56884-248-1	$14.99 USA/$22.99 Canad
Personal Finance For Dummies™ For Canadians	by Eric Tyson & Tony Martin	ISBN: 1-56884-378-X	$18.99 USA/$24.99 Canad
QuickBooks 3 For Dummies®	by Stephen L. Nelson	ISBN: 1-56884-227-9	$19.99 USA/$26.99 Canad
Quicken 8 For DOS For Dummies® 2nd Edition	by Stephen L. Nelson	ISBN: 1-56884-210-4	$19.95 USA/$26.95 Canad
Quicken 5 For Macs® For Dummies®	by Stephen L. Nelson	ISBN: 1-56884-211-2	$19.95 USA/$26.95 Canad
Quicken 4 For Windows® For Dummies® 2nd Edition	by Stephen L. Nelson	ISBN: 1-56884-209-0	$19.95 USA/$26.95 Canad
Taxes For Dummies,™ 1995 Edition	by Eric Tyson & David J. Silverman	ISBN: 1-56884-220-1	$14.99 USA/$20.99 Canad
The GMAT® For Dummies™	by Suzee Vlk, Series Editor	ISBN: 1-56884-376-3	$14.99 USA/$20.99 Canad
The GRE® For Dummies™	by Suzee Vlk, Series Editor	ISBN: 1-56884-375-5	$14.99 USA/$20.99 Canad
Time Management For Dummies™	by Jeffrey J. Mayer	ISBN: 1-56884-360-7	$16.99 USA/$22.99 Canad
TurboTax For Windows® For Dummies®	by Gail A. Helsel, CPA	ISBN: 1-56884-228-7	$19.99 USA/$26.99 Canad
GROUPWARE/INTEGRATED			
ClarisWorks For Macs® For Dummies®	by Frank Higgins	ISBN: 1-56884-363-1	$19.99 USA/$26.99 Canad
Lotus Notes For Dummies®	by Pat Freeland & Stephen Londergan	ISBN: 1-56884-212-0	$19.95 USA/$26.95 Canad
Microsoft® Office 4 For Windows® For Dummies®	by Roger C. Parker	ISBN: 1-56884-183-3	$19.95 USA/$26.95 Canad
Microsoft® Works 3 For Windows® For Dummies®	by David C. Kay	ISBN: 1-56884-214-7	$19.99 USA/$26.99 Canad
SmartSuite 3 For Dummies®	by Jan Weingarten & John Weingarten	ISBN: 1-56884-367-4	$19.99 USA/$26.99 Canad
INTERNET/COMMUNICATIONS/NETWORKING			
America Online® For Dummies® 2nd Edition	by John Kaufeld	ISBN: 1-56884-933-8	$19.99 USA/$26.99 Canad
CompuServe For Dummies® 2nd Edition	by Wallace Wang	ISBN: 1-56884-937-0	$19.99 USA/$26.99 Canad
Modems For Dummies® 2nd Edition	by Tina Rathbone	ISBN: 1-56884-223-6	$19.99 USA/$26.99 Canad
MORE Internet For Dummies®	by John R. Levine & Margaret Levine Young	ISBN: 1-56884-164-7	$19.95 USA/$26.95 Canad
MORE Modems & On-line Services For Dummies®	by Tina Rathbone	ISBN: 1-56884-365-8	$19.99 USA/$26.99 Canad
Mosaic For Dummies® Windows Edition	by David Angell & Brent Heslop	ISBN: 1-56884-242-2	$19.99 USA/$26.99 Canad
NetWare For Dummies® 2nd Edition	by Ed Tittel, Deni Connor & Earl Follis	ISBN: 1-56884-369-0	$19.99 USA/$26.99 Canad
Networking For Dummies®	by Doug Lowe	ISBN: 1-56884-079-9	$19.95 USA/$26.95 Canad
PROCOMM PLUS 2 For Windows® For Dummies®	by Wallace Wang	ISBN: 1-56884-219-8	$19.99 USA/$26.99 Canad
TCP/IP For Dummies®	by Marshall Wilensky & Candace Leiden	ISBN: 1-56884-241-4	$19.99 USA/$26.99 Canad

For scholastic requests & educational orders please call Educational Sales at 1. 800. 434. 2086

FOR MORE INFO OR TO ORDER, PLEASE CALL ▶ 800 762 2974

For volume discounts & special orders pleas Tony Real, Special Sales, at 415. 655. 3048

...e Internet For Macs® For Dummies,® 2nd Edition	by Charles Seiter	ISBN: 1-56884-371-2	$19.99 USA/$26.99 Canada
...e Internet For Macs® For Dummies® Starter Kit	by Charles Seiter	ISBN: 1-56884-244-9	$29.99 USA/$39.99 Canada
...e Internet For Macs® For Dummies® Starter Kit Bestseller Edition	by Charles Seiter	ISBN: 1-56884-245-7	$39.99 USA/$54.99 Canada
...e Internet For Windows® For Dummies® Starter Kit	by John R. Levine & Margaret Levine Young	ISBN: 1-56884-237-6	$34.99 USA/$44.99 Canada
...e Internet For Windows® For Dummies® Starter Kit, ...stseller Edition	by John R. Levine & Margaret Levine Young	ISBN: 1-56884-246-5	$39.99 USA/$54.99 Canada

...ACINTOSH

...ac® Programming For Dummies®	by Dan Parks Sydow	ISBN: 1-56884-173-6	$19.95 USA/$26.95 Canada
...acintosh® System 7.5 For Dummies®	by Bob LeVitus	ISBN: 1-56884-197-3	$19.95 USA/$26.95 Canada
...ORE Macs® For Dummies®	by David Pogue	ISBN: 1-56884-087-X	$19.95 USA/$26.95 Canada
...geMaker 5 For Macs® For Dummies®	by Galen Gruman & Deke McClelland	ISBN: 1-56884-178-7	$19.95 USA/$26.95 Canada
...uarkXPress 3.3 For Dummies®	by Galen Gruman & Barbara Assadi	ISBN: 1-56884-217-1	$19.99 USA/$26.99 Canada
...pgrading and Fixing Macs® For Dummies®	by Kearney Rietmann & Frank Higgins	ISBN: 1-56884-189-2	$19.95 USA/$26.95 Canada

...ULTIMEDIA

...ultimedia & CD-ROMs For Dummies,® 2nd Edition	by Andy Rathbone	ISBN: 1-56884-907-9	$19.99 USA/$26.99 Canada
...ultimedia & CD-ROMs For Dummies,® ...teractive Multimedia Value Pack, 2nd Edition	by Andy Rathbone	ISBN: 1-56884-909-5	$29.99 USA/$39.99 Canada

...ERATING SYSTEMS:

...S

...ORE DOS For Dummies®	by Dan Gookin	ISBN: 1-56884-046-2	$19.95 USA/$26.95 Canada
...S/2® Warp For Dummies,® 2nd Edition	by Andy Rathbone	ISBN: 1-56884-205-8	$19.99 USA/$26.99 Canada

...IX

...ORE UNIX® For Dummies®	by John R. Levine & Margaret Levine Young	ISBN: 1-56884-361-5	$19.99 USA/$26.99 Canada
...NIX® For Dummies®	by John R. Levine & Margaret Levine Young	ISBN: 1-878058-58-4	$19.95 USA/$26.95 Canada

...INDOWS

...ORE Windows® For Dummies,® 2nd Edition	by Andy Rathbone	ISBN: 1-56884-048-9	$19.95 USA/$26.95 Canada
...indows® 95 For Dummies®	by Andy Rathbone	ISBN: 1-56884-240-6	$19.99 USA/$26.99 Canada

...S/HARDWARE

...llustrated Computer Dictionary For Dummies,® 2nd Edition	by Dan Gookin & Wallace Wang	ISBN: 1-56884-218-X	$12.95 USA/$16.95 Canada
...pgrading and Fixing PCs For Dummies,® 2nd Edition	by Andy Rathbone	ISBN: 1-56884-903-6	$19.99 USA/$26.99 Canada

...RESENTATION/AUTOCAD

...utoCAD For Dummies®	by Bud Smith	ISBN: 1-56884-191-4	$19.95 USA/$26.95 Canada
...owerPoint 4 For Windows® For Dummies®	by Doug Lowe	ISBN: 1-56884-161-2	$16.99 USA/$22.99 Canada

...ROGRAMMING

...orland C++ For Dummies®	by Michael Hyman	ISBN: 1-56884-162-0	$19.95 USA/$26.95 Canada
...C For Dummies,® Volume 1	by Dan Gookin	ISBN: 1-878058-78-9	$19.95 USA/$26.95 Canada
...++ For Dummies®	by Stephen R. Davis	ISBN: 1-56884-163-9	$19.95 USA/$26.95 Canada
...elphi Programming For Dummies®	by Neil Rubenking	ISBN: 1-56884-200-7	$19.99 USA/$26.99 Canada
...ac® Programming For Dummies®	by Dan Parks Sydow	ISBN: 1-56884-173-6	$19.95 USA/$26.95 Canada
...owerBuilder 4 Programming For Dummies®	by Ted Coombs & Jason Coombs	ISBN: 1-56884-325-9	$19.99 USA/$26.99 Canada
...QBasic Programming For Dummies®	by Douglas Hergert	ISBN: 1-56884-093-4	$19.95 USA/$26.95 Canada
...isual Basic 3 For Dummies®	by Wallace Wang	ISBN: 1-56884-076-4	$19.95 USA/$26.95 Canada
...isual Basic "X" For Dummies®	by Wallace Wang	ISBN: 1-56884-230-9	$19.99 USA/$26.99 Canada
...isual C++ 2 For Dummies®	by Michael Hyman & Bob Arnson	ISBN: 1-56884-328-3	$19.99 USA/$26.99 Canada
...Windows® 95 Programming For Dummies®	by S. Randy Davis	ISBN: 1-56884-327-5	$19.99 USA/$26.99 Canada

...PREADSHEET

...-2-3 For Dummies®	by Greg Harvey	ISBN: 1-878058-60-6	$16.95 USA/$22.95 Canada
...-2-3 For Windows® 5 For Dummies,® 2nd Edition	by John Walkenbach	ISBN: 1-56884-216-3	$16.95 USA/$22.95 Canada
...xcel 5 For Macs® For Dummies®	by Greg Harvey	ISBN: 1-56884-186-8	$19.95 USA/$26.95 Canada
...xcel For Dummies,® 2nd Edition	by Greg Harvey	ISBN: 1-56884-050-0	$16.95 USA/$22.95 Canada
...MORE 1-2-3 For DOS For Dummies®	by John Weingarten	ISBN: 1-56884-224-4	$19.99 USA/$26.99 Canada
...MORE Excel 5 For Windows® For Dummies®	by Greg Harvey	ISBN: 1-56884-207-4	$19.95 USA/$26.95 Canada
...Quattro Pro 6 For Windows® For Dummies®	by John Walkenbach	ISBN: 1-56884-174-4	$19.95 USA/$26.95 Canada
...Quattro Pro For DOS For Dummies®	by John Walkenbach	ISBN: 1-56884-023-3	$16.95 USA/$22.95 Canada

...TILITIES

...Norton Utilities 8 For Dummies®	by Beth Slick	ISBN: 1-56884-166-3	$19.95 USA/$26.95 Canada

...CRS/CAMCORDERS

...VCRs & Camcorders For Dummies™	by Gordon McComb & Andy Rathbone	ISBN: 1-56884-229-5	$14.99 USA/$20.99 Canada

...ORD PROCESSING

...Ami Pro For Dummies®	by Jim Meade	ISBN: 1-56884-049-7	$19.95 USA/$26.95 Canada
...MORE Word For Windows® 6 For Dummies®	by Doug Lowe	ISBN: 1-56884-165-5	$19.95 USA/$26.95 Canada
...MORE WordPerfect® 6 For Windows® For Dummies®	by Margaret Levine Young & David C. Kay	ISBN: 1-56884-206-6	$19.95 USA/$26.95 Canada
...MORE WordPerfect® 6 For DOS For Dummies®	by Wallace Wang, edited by Dan Gookin	ISBN: 1-56884-047-0	$19.95 USA/$26.95 Canada
...Word 6 For Macs® For Dummies®	by Dan Gookin	ISBN: 1-56884-190-6	$19.95 USA/$26.95 Canada
...Word For Windows® 6 For Dummies®	by Dan Gookin	ISBN: 1-56884-075-0	$16.95 USA/$22.95 Canada
...Word For Windows® For Dummies®	by Dan Gookin & Ray Werner	ISBN: 1-878058-86-X	$16.95 USA/$22.95 Canada
...WordPerfect® 6 For DOS For Dummies®	by Dan Gookin	ISBN: 1-878058-77-0	$16.95 USA/$22.95 Canada
...WordPerfect® 6.1 For Windows® For Dummies,® 2nd Edition	by Margaret Levine Young & David Kay	ISBN: 1-56884-243-0	$16.95 USA/$22.95 Canada
...WordPerfect® For Dummies®	by Dan Gookin	ISBN: 1-878058-52-5	$16.95 USA/$22.95 Canada

Fun, Fast, & Cheap!™

NEW!

The Internet For Macs® For Dummies® Quick Reference
by Charles Seiter
ISBN:1-56884-967-2
$9.99 USA/$12.99 Canada

NEW!

Windows® 95 For Dummies® Quick Reference
by Greg Harvey
ISBN: 1-56884-964-8
$9.99 USA/$12.99 Canada

SUPER STAR

Photoshop 3 For Macs® For Dummies® Quick Reference
by Deke McClelland
ISBN: 1-56884-968-0
$9.99 USA/$12.99 Canada

SUPER ST

WordPerfect® For DOS For Dummies® Quick Reference
by Greg Harvey
ISBN: 1-56884-009-8
$8.95 USA/$12.95 Canada

Title	Author	ISBN	Price
DATABASE			
Access 2 For Dummies® Quick Reference	by Stuart J. Stuple	ISBN: 1-56884-167-1	$8.95 USA/$11.95 Canad
dBASE 5 For DOS For Dummies® Quick Reference	by Barrie Sosinsky	ISBN: 1-56884-954-0	$9.99 USA/$12.99 Canad
dBASE 5 For Windows® For Dummies® Quick Reference	by Stuart J. Stuple	ISBN: 1-56884-953-2	$9.99 USA/$12.99 Canad
Paradox 5 For Windows® For Dummies® Quick Reference	by Scott Palmer	ISBN: 1-56884-960-5	$9.99 USA/$12.99 Canad
DESKTOP PUBLISHING/ILLUSTRATION/GRAPHICS			
CorelDRAW! 5 For Dummies® Quick Reference	by Raymond E. Werner	ISBN: 1-56884-952-4	$9.99 USA/$12.99 Canad
Harvard Graphics For Windows® For Dummies® Quick Reference	by Raymond E. Werner	ISBN: 1-56884-962-1	$9.99 USA/$12.99 Canad
Photoshop 3 For Macs® For Dummies® Quick Reference	by Deke McClelland	ISBN: 1-56884-968-0	$9.99 USA/$12.99 Canad
FINANCE/PERSONAL FINANCE			
Quicken 4 For Windows® For Dummies® Quick Reference	by Stephen L. Nelson	ISBN: 1-56884-950-8	$9.95 USA/$12.95 Canad
GROUPWARE/INTEGRATED			
Microsoft® Office 4 For Windows® For Dummies® Quick Reference	by Doug Lowe	ISBN: 1-56884-958-3	$9.99 USA/$12.99 Canad
Microsoft® Works 3 For Windows® For Dummies® Quick Reference	by Michael Partington	ISBN: 1-56884-959-1	$9.99 USA/$12.99 Canad
INTERNET/COMMUNICATIONS/NETWORKING			
The Internet For Dummies® Quick Reference	by John R. Levine & Margaret Levine Young	ISBN: 1-56884-168-X	$8.95 USA/$11.95 Canad
MACINTOSH			
Macintosh® System 7.5 For Dummies® Quick Reference	by Stuart J. Stuple	ISBN: 1-56884-956-7	$9.99 USA/$12.99 Canad
OPERATING SYSTEMS:			
DOS			
DOS For Dummies® Quick Reference	by Greg Harvey	ISBN: 1-56884-007-1	$8.95 USA/$11.95 Canad
UNIX			
UNIX® For Dummies® Quick Reference	by John R. Levine & Margaret Levine Young	ISBN: 1-56884-094-2	$8.95 USA/$11.95 Canad
WINDOWS			
Windows® 3.1 For Dummies® Quick Reference, 2nd Edition	by Greg Harvey	ISBN: 1-56884-951-6	$8.95 USA/$11.95 Canad
PCs/HARDWARE			
Memory Management For Dummies® Quick Reference	by Doug Lowe	ISBN: 1-56884-362-3	$9.99 USA/$12.99 Canad
PRESENTATION/AUTOCAD			
AutoCAD For Dummies® Quick Reference	by Ellen Finkelstein	ISBN: 1-56884-198-1	$9.95 USA/$12.95 Canad
SPREADSHEET			
1-2-3 For Dummies® Quick Reference	by John Walkenbach	ISBN: 1-56884-027-6	$8.95 USA/$11.95 Canad
1-2-3 For Windows® 5 For Dummies® Quick Reference	by John Walkenbach	ISBN: 1-56884-957-5	$9.95 USA/$12.95 Canad
Excel For Windows® For Dummies® Quick Reference, 2nd Edition	by John Walkenbach	ISBN: 1-56884-096-9	$8.95 USA/$11.95 Canad
Quattro Pro 6 For Windows® For Dummies® Quick Reference	by Stuart J. Stuple	ISBN: 1-56884-172-8	$9.95 USA/$12.95 Canad
WORD PROCESSING			
Word For Windows® 6 For Dummies® Quick Reference	by George Lynch	ISBN: 1-56884-095-0	$8.95 USA/$11.95 Canad
Word For Windows® For Dummies® Quick Reference	by George Lynch	ISBN: 1-56884-029-2	$8.95 USA/$11.95 Canad
WordPerfect® 6.1 For Windows® For Dummies® Quick Reference, 2nd Edition	by Greg Harvey	ISBN: 1-56884-966-4	$9.99 USA/$12.99/Canad

For scholastic requests & educational orders please call Educational Sales at 1. 800. 434. 2086

FOR MORE INFO OR TO ORDER, PLEASE CALL ▶ 800. 762. 2974

For volume discounts & special orders plea Tony Real, Special Sales, at 415. 655. 3048

Windows® 3.1 SECRETS™
by Brian Livingston

ISBN: 1-878058-43-6
$39.95 USA/$52.95 Canada
Includes software.

MORE Windows® 3.1 SECRETS™
by Brian Livingston

ISBN: 1-56884-019-5
$39.95 USA/$52.95 Canada
Includes software.

Windows® GIZMOS™
by Brian Livingston & Margie Livingston

ISBN: 1-878058-66-5
$39.95 USA/$52.95 Canada
Includes software.

Windows® 3.1 Connectivity SECRETS™
by Runnoe Connally, David Rorabaugh, & Sheldon Hall

ISBN: 1-56884-030-6
$49.95 USA/$64.95 Canada
Includes software.

Windows® 3.1 Configuration SECRETS™
by Valda Hilley & James Blakely

ISBN: 1-56884-026-8
$49.95 USA/$64.95 Canada
Includes software.

Internet SECRETS™
by John Levine & Carol Baroudi

ISBN: 1-56884-452-2
$39.99 USA/$54.99 Canada
Includes software.

Internet GIZMOS™ For Windows®
by Joel Diamond, Howard Sobel, & Valda Hilley

ISBN: 1-56884-451-4
$39.99 USA/$54.99 Canada
Includes software.

Network Security SECRETS™
by David Stang & Sylvia Moon

ISBN: 1-56884-021-7
Int'l. ISBN: 1-56884-151-5
$49.95 USA/$64.95 Canada
Includes software.

PC SECRETS™
by Caroline M. Halliday

ISBN: 1-878058-49-5
$39.95 USA/$52.95 Canada
Includes software.

WordPerfect® 6 SECRETS™
by Roger C. Parker & David A. Holzgang

ISBN: 1-56884-040-3
$39.95 USA/$52.95 Canada
Includes software.

DOS 6 SECRETS™
by Robert D. Ainsbury

ISBN: 1-878058-70-3
$39.95 USA/$52.95 Canada
Includes software.

Paradox 4 Power Programming SECRETS,™ 2nd Edition
by Gregory B. Salcedo & Martin W. Rudy

ISBN: 1-878058-54-1
$44.95 USA/$59.95 Canada
Includes software.

Paradox 5 For Windows® Power Programming SECRETS™
by Gregory B. Salcedo & Martin W. Rudy

ISBN: 1-56884-085-3
$44.95 USA/$59.95 Canada
Includes software.

Hard Disk SECRETS™
by John M. Goodman, Ph.D.

ISBN: 1-878058-64-9
$39.95 USA/$52.95 Canada
Includes software.

WordPerfect® 6 For Windows® Tips & Techniques Revealed
by David A. Holzgang & Roger C. Parker

ISBN: 1-56884-202-3
$39.95 USA/$52.95 Canada
Includes software.

Excel 5 For Windows® Power Programming Techniques
by John Walkenbach

ISBN: 1-56884-303-8
$39.95 USA/$52.95 Canada
Includes software.

 **...SECRETS®**

 INFO WORLD TECHNICAL BOOKS

Windows is a registered trademark of Microsoft Corporation. WordPerfect is a registered trademark of Novell. ----SECRETS, ----GIZMOS, and the IDG Books Worldwide logos are trademarks, and ...SECRETS is a registered trademark under exclusive license to IDG Books Worldwide, Inc., from International Data Group, Inc.

scholastic requests & educational orders please educational Sales, at 1. 800. 434. 2086

FOR MORE INFO OR TO ORDER, PLEASE CALL ▶ 800. 762. 2974

For volume discounts & special orders please ca Tony Real, Special Sales, at 415. 655. 3048

"A lot easier to use than the book Excel gives you!"

Lisa Schmeckpeper, New Berlin, WI, *on PC World Excel 5 For Windows Handbook*

Official Hayes Modem Communications Companion
by Caroline M. Halliday

ISBN: 1-56884-072-1
$29.95 USA/$39.95 Canada
Includes software.

1,001 Komputer Answers from Kim Komando
by Kim Komando

ISBN: 1-56884-460-3
$29.99 USA/$39.99 Canada
Includes software.

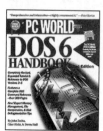

PC World DOS 6 Handbook, 2nd Edition
by John Socha, Clint Hicks, & Devra Hall

ISBN: 1-878058-79-7
$34.95 USA/$44.95 Canada
Includes software.

PC World Word For Windows® 6 Handbook
by Brent Heslop & David Angell

ISBN: 1-56884-054-3
$34.95 USA/$44.95 Canada
Includes software.

PC World Microsoft® Access 2 Bible, 2nd Edition
by Cary N. Prague & Michael R. Irwin

ISBN: 1-56884-086-1
$39.95 USA/$52.95 Canada
Includes software.

PC World Excel 5 For Windows® Handbook, 2nd Edition
by John Walkenbach & Dave Maguiness

ISBN: 1-56884-056-X
$34.95 USA/$44.95 Canada
Includes software.

PC World WordPerfect® 6 Handbook
by Greg Harvey

ISBN: 1-878058-80-0
$34.95 USA/$44.95 Canada
Includes software.

QuarkXPress For Windows® Designer Handbook
by Barbara Assadi & Galen Gruman

ISBN: 1-878058-45-2
$29.95 USA/$39.95 Canada

Official XTree Companion, 3rd Edition
by Beth Slick

ISBN: 1-878058-57-6
$19.95 USA/$26.95 Canada

PC World DOS 6 Command Reference and Problem Solver
by John Socha & Devra Hall

ISBN: 1-56884-055-1
$24.95 USA/$32.95 Canada

Client/Server Strategies™: A Survival Guide for Corporate Reengineers
by David Vaskevitch

ISBN: 1-56884-064-0
$29.95 USA/$39.95 Canada

"PC World Word For Windows 6 Handbook is very easy to follow with lots of 'hands on' examples. The 'Task at a Glance' is very helpful!"

Jacqueline Martens, Tacoma, WA

"Thanks for publishing this book! It's the best money I've spent this year!"

Robert D. Templeton, Ft. Worth, TX, *on MORE Windows 3.1 SECRETS*

or scholastic requests & educational orders please
all Educational Sales, at 1. 800. 434. 2086

FOR MORE INFO OR TO ORDER, PLEASE CALL ▶ 800 762 2974

For volume discounts & special orders please
Tony Real, Special Sales, at 415. 655. 3048

Order Center: **(800) 762-2974** *(8 a.m.–6 p.m., EST, weekdays)*

Quantity	ISBN	Title	Price	Total

Shipping & Handling Charges

	Description	First book	Each additional book	Total
Domestic	Normal	$4.50	$1.50	$
	Two Day Air	$8.50	$2.50	$
	Overnight	$18.00	$3.00	$
International	Surface	$8.00	$8.00	$
	Airmail	$16.00	$16.00	$
	DHL Air	$17.00	$17.00	$

*For large quantities call for shipping & handling charges.
**Prices are subject to change without notice.

Ship to:

Name _____

Company _____

Address _____

City/State/Zip_____

Daytime Phone _____

Payment: ☐ Check to IDG Books Worldwide (US Funds Only)

☐ VISA   ☐ MasterCard   ☐ American Express

Card # _____ Expires _____

Signature _____

Subtotal _____

CA residents add
applicable sales tax _____

IN, MA, and MD
residents add
5% sales tax _____

IL residents add
6.25% sales tax_____

RI residents add
7% sales tax_____

TX residents add
8.25% sales tax_____

Shipping_____

Total _____

Please send this order form to:

IDG Books Worldwide, Inc.
7260 Shadeland Station, Suite 100
Indianapolis, IN 46256

Allow up to 3 weeks for delivery.
Thank you!

IDG BOOKS WORLDWIDE, INC.
END-USER LICENSE AGREEMENT

<u>Read This</u>. You should carefully read these terms and conditions before opening the software packet(s) included with this book ("Book"). This is a license agreement ("Agreement") between you and IDG Books Worldwide, Inc. ("IDGB"). By opening the accompanying software packet(s), you acknowledge that you have read and accept the following terms and conditions. If you do not agree and do not want to be bound by such terms and conditions, promptly return the Book and the unopened software packet(s) to the place you obtained them for a full refund.

1. <u>License Grant</u>. IDGB grants to you (either an individual or entity) a nonexclusive license to use one copy of the enclosed software program(s) (collectively, the "Software") solely for your own personal or business purposes on a single computer (whether a standard computer or a workstation component of a multiuser network). The Software is in use on a computer when it is loaded into temporary memory (i.e., RAM) or installed into permanent memory (e.g., hard disk, CD-ROM or other storage device). IDGB reserves all rights not expressly granted herein.

2. <u>Ownership</u>. IDGB is the owner of all rights, titles, and interests, including copyright, in and to the compilation of the Software recorded on the CD-ROM. Copyright to the individual programs on the CD-ROM is owned by the author or other authorized copyright owner of each program. Ownership of the Software and all proprietary rights relating thereto remain with IDGB and its licensors.

3. <u>Restrictions on Use and Transfer</u>.

    (a) You may only (i) make one copy of the Software for backup or archival purposes, or (ii) transfer the Software to a single hard disk, provided that you keep the original for backup or archival purposes. You may not (i) rent or lease the Software, (ii) copy or reproduce the Software through a LAN or other network system or through any computer subscriber system or bulletin-board system, or (iii) modify, adapt, or create derivative works based on the Software.

    (b) You may not reverse engineer, decompile, or disassemble the Software. You may transfer the Software and user documentation on a permanent basis, provided that the transferee agrees to accept the terms and conditions of this Agreement and you retain no copies. If the Software is an update or has been updated, any transfer must include the most recent update and all prior versions.

4. <u>Restrictions on Use of Individual Programs</u>. You must follow the individual requirements and restrictions detailed for each individual program on the Installation Instructions page of this Book. These limitations are contained in the individual license agreements recorded on the CD-ROM. These restrictions include a requirement that after using the program for the period of time specified in its text, the user must pay a registration fee or discontinue use. By opening the Software packet(s), you will be agreeing to abide by the licenses and restrictions for these individual programs. None of the material on this disc or listed in this Book may ever be distributed, in original or modified form, for commercial purposes.

5. <u>Limited Warranty</u>.

(a) IDGB warrants that the Software and CD-ROM are free from defects in materials and workmanship under normal use for a period of sixty (60) days from the date of purchase of this Book. If IDGB receives notification within the warranty period of defects in materials or workmanship, IDGB will replace the defective CD-ROM.

(b) IDGB AND THE AUTHORS OF THE BOOK DISCLAIM ALL OTHER WARRANTIES, EXPRESS OR IMPLIED, INCLUDING WITHOUT LIMITATION IMPLIED WARRANTIES OF MERCHANTABILITY AND FITNESS FOR A PARTICULAR PURPOSE, WITH RESPECT TO THE SOFTWARE, THE PROGRAMS, THE SOURCE CODE CONTAINED THEREIN, AND/OR THE TECHNIQUES DESCRIBED IN THIS BOOK. IDGB DOES NOT WARRANT THAT THE FUNCTIONS CONTAINED IN THE SOFTWARE WILL MEET YOUR REQUIREMENTS OR THAT THE OPERATION OF THE SOFTWARE WILL BE ERROR FREE.

(c) This limited warranty gives you specific legal rights, and you may have other rights that vary from jurisdiction to jurisdiction.

6. <u>Remedies</u>.

(a) IDGB's entire liability and your exclusive remedy for defects in materials and workmanship shall be limited to replacement of the Software, which is returned to IDGB at the address set forth below with a copy of your receipt. This Limited Warranty is void if failure of the Software has resulted from accident, abuse, or misapplication. Any replacement Software will be warranted for the remainder of the original warranty period or thirty (30) days, whichever is longer.

(b) In no event shall IDGB or the author be liable for any damages whatsoever (including without limitation damages for loss of business profits, business interruption, loss of business information, or any other pecuniary loss) arising out of the use of or inability to use the Book or the Software, even if IDGB has been advised of the possibility of such damages.

(c) Because some jurisdictions do not allow the exclusion or limitation of liability for consequential or incidental damages, the above limitation or exclusion may not apply to you.

7. <u>U.S. Government Restricted Rights</u>. Use, duplication, or disclosure of the Software by the U.S. Government is subject to restrictions stated in paragraph (c) (1) (ii) of the Rights in Technical Data and Computer Software clause of DFARS 252.227-7013, and in subparagraphs (a) through (d) of the Commercial Computer—Restricted Rights clause at FAR 52.227-19, and in similar clauses in the NASA FAR supplement, when applicable.

8. <u>General</u>. This Agreement constitutes the entire understanding of the parties, and revokes and supersedes all prior agreements, oral or written, between them and may not be modified or amended except in a writing signed by both parties hereto which specifically refers to this Agreement. This Agreement shall take precedence over any other documents that may be in conflict herewith. If any one or more provisions contained in this Agreement are held by any court or tribunal to be invalid, illegal or otherwise unenforceable, each and every other provision shall remain in full force and effect.

CD-ROM Installation Instructions

1. Install Internet Explorer from the root of the CD-ROM by running its executable.

2. Install Personal Web Server from the root of the CD-ROM by running its executable.

3. Install ASP from the root of the CD-ROM by running its executable.

That's it! You're done. Don't worry about installing the custom components now; we cover that when you need them in the chapters. Have fun!

IDG BOOKS WORLDWIDE REGISTRATION CARD

Visit our
Web site at
http://www.idgbooks.com

ISBN Number: 0-76458-042-6

Title of this book: ASP: Active Server Pages

My overall rating of this book: ❑ Very good [1] ❑ Good [2] ❑ Satisfactory [3] ❑ Fair [4] ❑ Poor [5]

How I first heard about this book:

❑ Found in bookstore; name: [6]

❑ Advertisement: [8]

❑ Word of mouth; heard about book from friend, co-worker, etc.: [10]

❑ Book review: [7]

❑ Catalog: [9]

❑ Other: [11]

What I liked most about this book:

What I would change, add, delete, etc., in future editions of this book:

Other comments:

Number of computer books I purchase in a year: ❑ 1 [12] ❑ 2-5 [13] ❑ 6-10 [14] ❑ More than 10 [15]

I would characterize my computer skills as: ❑ Beginner [16] ❑ Intermediate [17] ❑ Advanced [18] ❑ Professional [19]

I use ❑ DOS [20] ❑ Windows [21] ❑ OS/2 [22] ❑ Unix [23] ❑ Macintosh [24] ❑ Other: [25]

(please specify)

I would be interested in new books on the following subjects:

(please check all that apply, and use the spaces provided to identify specific software)

❑ Word processing: [26]

❑ Data bases: [28]

❑ File Utilities: [30]

❑ Networking: [32]

❑ Other: [34]

❑ Spreadsheets: [27]

❑ Desktop publishing: [29]

❑ Money management: [31]

❑ Programming languages: [33]

I use a PC at (please check all that apply): ❑ home [35] ❑ work [36] ❑ school [37] ❑ other: [38]

The disks I prefer to use are ❑ 5.25 [39] ❑ 3.5 [40] ❑ other: [41]

I have a CD ROM: ❑ yes [42] ❑ no [43]

I plan to buy or upgrade computer hardware this year: ❑ yes [44] ❑ no [45]

I plan to buy or upgrade computer software this year: ❑ yes [46] ❑ no [47]

Name: _____ Business title: [48] _____ Type of Business: [49]

Address (❑ home [50] ❑ work [51] /Company name: _____)

Street/Suite#

City [52]/State [53]/Zip code [54]: _____ Country [55]

❑ **I liked this book!** You may quote me by name in future
IDG Books Worldwide promotional materials.

My daytime phone number is _____

IDG
BOOKS
WORLDWIDE

THE WORLD OF
COMPUTER
KNOWLEDGE®

☐ YES!

Please keep me informed about IDG Books Worldwide's World of Computer Knowledge. Send me your latest catalog.

BESTSELLING
BOOK SERIES
FROM IDG

TECHNICAL BOOKS

Macworld® Books